Power and Performance in Organizations

Power and Performance in Organizations

An Exploration of Executive Process

Iain L. Mangham

Basil Blackwell

© Iain L. Mangham 1986

First published 1986
Basil Blackwell Ltd
108 Cowley Road, Oxford OX4 1JF, UK

Basil Blackwell Inc.
432 Park Avenue South, Suite 1503,
New York, NY 10016, USA

British Library Cataloguing in Publication Data

Mangham, Iain L.
    Power and performance in organizations.
    1. Organizational behaviour
    I. Title
    658.3   HD58.7

    ISBN 0–631–13083–7

Library of Congress Cataloging in Publication Data

Mangham, I. L.
    Power and performance in organizations.

    Bibliography: p.
    Includes indexes.
    1. Organizational behaviour.   I. Title.
HD 58.7.M37   1986   658.3   85–28684
ISBN 0–631–13083–7

Typeset by Oxford Publishing Services, Oxford
Printed in Great Britain by Page Bros, Norwich

Contents

Preface and Acknowledgements

Most books about the conduct of individuals in organizations seem to me to have been written by people who have read other books about the same thing. Most are parasitic, feeding on concepts and ideas deriving from others; some are cannibalistic, devouring entirely their own species. Some years ago, I became so disenchanted with such texts that I stopped reading them altogether and decided to write my own.[1]

What that means, of course, is that rather than feeding from the common table, I have chosen to eat at other tables less well frequented. I have not eliminated parasitism nor, indeed, cannibalism, but I have selected a series of dishes that may titillate the palate because of their unusual and occasionally exotic flavour.

Enough of the culinary metaphor. The book is designed for use as an ancillary text in final year undergraduate courses and on MBA programmes. It may also be of use to teachers who themselves have but little acquaintance with interactionist perspectives, and one or two of the notions addressed here may well prove to be of interest to researchers. Since it is intended to reach several audiences, it has been constructed so that it may be read in a number of ways.

In particular the notes for each chapter, which constitute about a fifth of the book, have been set off from the text in a fashion which is not particularly common in such works. They are keyed to it only loosely and are also somewhat rambling and expansive, consisting of speculations about particular points, reviews of related work, critiques – whatever took my fancy at the time. The text, therefore, has been written so that whoever reads it, be he or she student, teacher, researcher or the mythical 'general reader', can read it with little or no reference to these notes. Indeed, first time around (What! He expects us to read it twice!) I advise that one reads it in this manner. The case I wish to make is there in the text, as is the supporting material and, for the most part, I avoid asides, references and time-consuming qualifications. On the other hand (or second time around), someone interested in following up certain points, or in challenging aspects of what I have to say, may find it useful to refer to the notes. Certainly, students in search of sources and essay cribs will find this section essential.[2]

Given all of that, it is nonetheless incumbent upon me to point out once more that this is not a textbook in organizational behaviour (a term I dislike in any event). I have chosen to concentrate upon a limited number of concepts deriving from and relating to a limited amount of data, drawn from some fifteen minutes or so of interaction occurring between eight executives, with myself as observer, in a room on an afternoon in August 1983. Those of a quantitative bent will find little to attract them in these pages; those with short spans of attention and a low threshhold for boredom will find the constant recourse to this fifteen minutes somewhat tiresome.

My writing of the book was initially prompted by René Olivieri of Blackwells and subsequently jogged along by Tony Sweeney; without their quiet insistence, enthusiasm and control, I would probably still be at it. Steve Fineman, David Thatcher, David Sims, Bob Cooper, Albert Natchkirk and John Hayes offered constructive critical comments from which I have profited. My final year undergraduate class – Sally, Judy, Heather, Nic, the two Davids, Miles, Notis, Nicky, Marina and Jean-Paul – suffered much of this as it was developed, and remained cheerful throughout. Without them, it would not have been worth the effort. Joan Budge, as always, did a splendid job of interpreting my writing and keeping track of the material. Finally, I am grateful to my colleagues at Friction Free Castings Ltd for their time, energy and support.[3]

Introduction: Chocolate Eggs and Chester Barnard

I have in front of me a chocolate egg, designed in Italy, manufactured in Germany and sold throughout Europe. It is wrapped in foil and secured within an attractive (5 × 2 inch) box proclaiming in several languages the virtue of the product: 'Confiserie recouverte de chocolat au lait contenant une surprise dans une capsule plastique.' When opened, not without difficulty, the packaging is seen to hold the egg (in its protective yet decorative covering) and the egg contains – in this case – a set of miniature plastic tools for the collection of refuse: pan, brush, cart and bin. It also holds a set of instructions for assembling the toys, in a fine print appropriate to the size of the implements. It is worth reflecting for a moment upon this product. Since it is supplied throughout Western Europe in quantity, it implies an organization of some size and, given issues of language and customs barriers, an enterprise of some complexity. The principles that inform it – someone with an idea and the structure and process to translate that idea into a product through the coordination of the efforts of others – are no different to the principles that guide and direct the activities of other larger concerns. What is bizarre is the thought of grown men and women coming together in a multi-national enterprise to sit around a table and deliberate about chocolate eggs. One can imagine what Bob Newhart would have made of it all:

Conference phone New York/Rome:
'Chocolate eggs, Luigi. OK. OK. I'll buy that. What you gonna put in them, Fritz? Toffee? Not toffee. Cream? . . . I like it – cream eggs . . . not cream eggs? . . . jelly beans, Pierre, that's what's gonna be in them! . . . You're gonna put *what* in them? You're gonna put miniature plastic refuse implements in them? You mean . . . uh, huh . . . shovels? Brushes and plastic dustcarts? With wheels that spin? Really . . . well, that's just great, Luigi, just great. Wonderful . . .'

This book is not about chocolate eggs, nor is it at all concerned with a particular product. It is, however, about executives like Luigi, Fritz and Pierre; about how they relate to each other in their attempts to bring off the development, manufacturing and marketing of their product. About, that is, the executive function.

What is taken to be executive work is outlined in Chester Barnard's classic book *The Functions of the Executive*, first published in 1938 and never superseded in its informed description and analysis.[1] Barnard argues that an organization comes into being when certain conditions obtain: (1) there are people able and willing to communicate with each other (2) who are also willing to do something – 'to contribute action' as he puts it – in order (3) to accomplish a common purpose. These elements, he asserts, are necessary and sufficient for organization to occur. The vitality of organizations consists in (a) the willingness of individuals to cooperate, which is dependent upon their belief that the purpose can be determined and achieved, 'a faith that diminishes to vanishing point as it appears that it is not, in fact, in the process of being attained'; and (b) the satisfaction that individuals derive from carrying out the process. When an organization becomes ineffective – is unable to accomplish its specific objectives, be this manufacturing chocolate eggs or putting a man on the moon – willingness disappears and the enterprise disintegrates.

A manager, according to Barnard, operates in two areas simultaneously: he performs a set of functions that relate directly to the technical aspects of his job, such as commissioning a piece of equipment or developing a part for a product. Such activities are, in Barnard's terminology, non-executive. He or she also performs a set of functions relating to the maintenance of the organization as a cooperative activity; such functions, and only such functions, may be taken to be executive: 'Executive work is not that *of* the organization, but the specialized work of *maintaining* the organization in operation.' The specialized work of the Executive is 'maintaining systems of cooperative effort'.

The executive function is not only to maintain cooperation but to achieve it and, presumably, change its nature through persuasion and debate.[2] 'Organization results from the modification of the actions of the individual through control and influence upon . . . purposes, desires and impulses of the moment.' Indeed, 'deliberate, conscious and specialized control' is the 'essence of the executive function.' Cooperation and organization consist of 'concrete syntheses of opposed facts, and of opposed thought and emotions of human beings'. Neither cooperation nor organization just happen, neither is a spontaneous natural phenomenon. The establishment of either is a delicate, a precarious matter, their maintenance an issue of skills and dedication and it is 'precisely the function of the Executive to facilitate the synthesis in concrete action of contradictory forces, to reconcile conflicting forces, instincts, interests, conditions, positions and ideals'.

The Microsituational Perspective

What follows is closely concerned with the executive function. To be precise, it is concerned exclusively with the activities of a small group of managers meeting as an Executive on one afternoon. As will be seen, they are exercised by issues of maintenance, of securing agreement and synthesizing purpose and of innovation, but my aim in presenting them is to seek to describe and understand their behaviour, not to use it as further evidence for or against *The Functions of the Executive*. Barnard provides a frame within which the activity of my group may be set; I am interested in their activity and the various 'readings' of it we can adduce, not in the frame itself. Barnard, as an early example of one who utilizes 'exchange theory' and foreshadows 'negotiated order' ideas, will be mentioned from time to time, as will a considerable number of other writers, but none will be the focus of examination to anything like the same degree as will Paul, George, Derek, Alec, Tony, Hugh, Brian and Eric, who constitute the Executive we shall eavesdrop upon. My interest is not Barnardian, but essentially Brechtian:

> I ought to tell you that I have an insatiable curiosity about people; it's impossible for me to see and hear enough of them. The way they get along with each other, the way they develop friendships and enmities, sell onions, plan military campaigns, get married, make tweed suits, circulate forged banknotes, dig potatoes, observe the heavenly bodies; the way they cheat, favour, teach, exploit, respect, mutilate and support one another; the way they hold meetings. . .[3]

I have argued elsewhere (as have others) that organizations and collectivities do not behave, individuals do, and thus I make no apology for the focus upon a small group of individuals rather than upon the organization, or upon organizations in general.[4]

Microsociology is the detailed analysis of how people 'cheat, favour, teach . . . hold meetings'; the minute by minute concern with what individuals apparently feel, think, say and do as they go about their business. Strictly speaking, there is no such thing as, say, an 'economy', a 'culture' or a 'social class'. Terms such as 'organization', 'group' and 'state' may be capable of legal distinction but remain, for all that, nothing more than collections of individuals acting in particular kinds of settings. Such notions cannot be grounded in any real sense other than by talking about the actual activities of those who constitute the collectivities. It is these individuals who act, not the ideas so beloved of sociologists and philosophers. Terms such as 'group' and 'organization' are simply abstractions from the behaviour of individuals, summaries of scores of pieces of individual behaviour distributed in a particular time and space. Thus Fritz's chocolate factory is an organization, but *what* it is, how it functions, is a product of thousands of pieces of individual behaviour.

Interpersonal Competence

It is this level of analysis which concerns me throughout this book; the realization of the abstract in the particular, the notion of organization arising out of the specific activities of a group of executives. How do they deal with each other in seeking to achieve goals? How do they elicit or disseminate information, secure or resist compliance, support or reward each other? What competences do they display in effecting systems of cooperative effort.

I propose that executives, no less than other human beings, are born psychologists.[5] Indeed, those lacking the skill to handle themselves and others are unlikely to *be* successful executives, however outstanding their technical, non-executive abilities. The good executives – they who would excel in the maintenance of cooperative effort – are better able than their fellows to anticipate and influence the behaviour of those same fellows. Making and selling chocolate eggs is a matter of considerable interest to those of us who would understand more about executive activity. Who persuades whom to do what and how does he or she do it? Who is manipulated, exploited, cajoled, reassured, cared for, put down, humoured, ridiculed, tolerated or ignored?

It is possible to argue that one's success as an executive is dependent upon one's ability to conduct oneself in the complexity of the organization as a subtle, insightful, incisive performer. Successful executives appear to have a natural and/or a highly developed ability to read the actual and potential behaviour of others around them and to construct their own conduct in accordance with that reading. Not that this ability is peculiar to them – we all read behaviour and react – just that the more successful amongst us appear to do social life with a higher degree of skill than the rest of us manage.

Fritz, Luigi, Pierre and their colleagues may have initially shared the technical tasks for the creation of chocolate eggs; a simple division of labour: you do the eggs, you the wrapping, I'll do the boxes. Very quickly, however, a need to coordinate and organize cooperation is recognized and different, higher order skills are demanded: that of understanding, being sensitive to mood and style and bringing the effort of all together with the minimum of friction and trauma; that of rendering the nascent organization effective. He who survives in this role is the person with the most highly developed ability to 'read' his fellows. On a grander scale, those who are successful in the community or on the even more prominent stages of social life, national and international endeavours, may be seen to have a highly developed ability to do psychology on others and on themselves.

And on themselves. Part of the argument of this book is that the ability to do executive work is highly dependent upon one's awareness of one's self. To explain why this should be so, let me take you back for a moment or two to Fritz, Luigi and Pierre. Assume, if you will, that it is early days in the development of their enterprise. Fritz, Luigi and Pierre have (as I shall argue we all have) a marked degree of self interest in any activity undertaken: what's in it for me and how can I maximize my returns (economic, social or whatever)? Fritz, Luigi and Pierre are *calculating* beings, capable of assessing a situation and spotting the opportunities it presents for themselves. They are also capable of recognizing that they need each other if they are to derive individual benefits. No one of them can realize the enterprise alone. Given this, each of them has to have a level of understanding of his fellows, for without it, the enterprise could founder without benefit to any one of them. It is no longer a matter of can Luigi make the eggs, can Fritz manufacture the wrapping, but more, much more a matter of can each of us accommodate each of the others at a level which ensures survival? Each needs a rudimentary skill in reading behaviour. Each does it by reference to his own behaviour. Fritz, no less than Luigi and Pierre, arrives at his knowledge of others by reference to his knowledge of himself. Fritz is able to put himself in Luigi's shoes because he is able to put himself in his own shoes. Uniquely a human being, every human being, has the ability to look in on his own behaviour; to observe it, inspect it, monitor it, speculate about it, rehearse it.

Now, this ability is the key to an understanding of conduct in organizations. Executives, no less than the rest of us, infer what is going on in others from ideas and feelings they have about themselves. Given the ability to reflect upon aspects of our selves, a consciousness of consciousness, we use it to derive guides to our actions with and towards others. Executive skill, from this perspective, is a matter of working effectively and efficiently with others and, equally clearly, a matter of awareness of self and others. Fritz engaged in some solitary enterprise has no cause to develop any skill other than the technical; once dependent upon Luigi and Pierre, his survival becomes linked to his ability to control himself and them. His ability to control their actions (and, to an extent, his own) depends in turn upon his ability to anticipate them. In a real sense, what he knows of the likely actions of his fellows is determined by what he knows about himself. Simultaneously, Luigi and Pierre are seeking to relate Fritz's action to themselves; add a dozen more executives around the table of Chocolate Enterprise Ltd and you have considerable complexity.

The focus of this book throughout will be upon a small group of executives, not only because I have maintained that all social patterns, institutions and organizations are ultimately dependent upon the activity of individuals, but also because, if we are to understand anything about the conduct of people in organizations, it is essential to address the arena where organizing occurs. Coordination and cooperation occurs (or fails to occur) at many levels, but it is a critical feature of the interaction of senior executives. To put it simply: life for senior executives is highly problematic. Each may benefit from preserving the group or team to which they belong and, at the same time, each may benefit from earnestly screwing their fellows.

Some Problems

One difficulty in adopting an approach to conduct in organizations such as that implied above – the study of a small group of people interacting – is that very little is known about how people *do* social or organizational life. Most social scientists, whether sociologists or psychologists, choose not to consider notions such as self, self-awareness, role taking (putting oneself in the shoes of others) and the like. Instead, they focus upon behaviour; what it is that subjects 'do', what is the output; the 'black box' of what goes on in the head of a person is ignored. There are, of course, exceptions to this rule and I will be presenting some of their ideas, but considering that each of us, every day, does social life, it is remarkable that on a formal level we know so little about it. The position taken in these pages is simple: if we are to understand the conduct of people in organizations better, we must address what it is they appear to think about themselves and others, what it is they feel and what it is they say and do – simple to declare, but difficult to deliver.

First, and perhaps most significant, there is the problem of 'voice'; how it is that I, as author of this text, relate to the characters I introduce. Were this a standard textbook, it is likely that I, as author, would not be present in these pages; I certainly would not be taking this opportunity of buttonholing you and explaining my problems to you. As a good scientist, I would seek to cast what I had to say in as neutral a language as possible and to distance myself by several miles from the texts. Were I a novelist, I would have a choice; I could stand off and treat my characters with contempt, disdain or gentle amusement, or I could write a part for myself as hero. My problem is that, given the material with which I have to engage, I can be neither scientist nor novelist. Much of the material I am addressing is of a subjective nature. I cannot know in any objective sense what it is that is going on within the heads of the people with whom I am concerned. I can only give my subjective reading of what it is that I take to be their subjective experience. On the other hand, what follows is decidedly not a work of fiction; I am not the omniscient novelist who shapes and controls the conversations and destinies of each of his characters.[6]

In this book, I tread an uneasy path between imputing thoughts and emotions to my characters in a thoroughly subjective fashion and seeking to explain such imputations in a more scientific and objective manner. As will be seen, such a course is strewn with difficulties, not all of which I am successful in overcoming. Nonetheless, to be both within and without is a normal human attribute; social life consists of periods of intense subjectivity alternating with periods in which we adopt a more objective standpoint on our own thoughts and actions. I am capable of observing myself as if I were someone else, I can and do judge my actions against those of others and against an ideal. Writing about interaction thus is an extension of doing it. The alternation between perspectives, between subjective and objective, may nonetheless prove somewhat dizzying; the issue of 'voice' disturbing.

Familiarity and Complexity

To comprehend some of the other difficulties, I must return to the nature of the executive process which, as I have shown, is a part or an aspect of the process of organization as a whole. For Barnard, the essential aspect, the key element of executive activity is 'the sensing of the organization as a whole and the total situation relevant to it'. It is, as Barnard notes, a matter of art rather than science, aesthetics rather than logic; terms such as 'feel', 'judgement', 'balance' and 'appropriateness' are its currency. Such features are 'recognized rather than described' and known by their effects 'rather than by analysis'. So the core of the executive process (at least as seen by Barnard) consists of a series of activities which are beyond description, let alone analysis. How does one depict 'sensing' and 'feel'?

The assertion that is repeatedly made in *The Functions of the Executive* is that the essence of the executive process is synthesis – the 'art of sensing the whole' and acting in accordance with this 'judgement'. Not that 'judgement' is always sound: some companies and organizations stress one aspect of their activity at the expense of others and lurch from crisis to crisis, a vague sense of the whole only becoming more distinct in the reasons for taking this or that corrective action. Occasionally, however, the art of sensing the whole is present in 'a few men of executive genius, or a few executive organizations, the personnel of which is comprehensively sensitive and well integrated'.

The point of this further recourse to the good Dr Barnard is to emphasize the problems of describing the executive process even as it occurs within a small group. In conducting themselves, in making their decisions, insofar as they exercise 'feel' and 'judgement' in determining what is appropriate for their organization, the social actors with whom I shall be involved do so against a sense of situation which derives from long, intimate and habitual association with it and involves many, many elements which are not spoken about; elements, indeed, which may not be quickly susceptible to verbal expression even by those who appreciate them and operate upon them. It follows that such an enterprise cannot be described, much less understood, by an observer who fails to become 'intimately familiar' with it. The position of researchers and observers, scholars and writers who pay flying visits to organizations, distribute a few questionnaires or conduct a couple of interviews is as ludicrous as the anthropologist who spends a couple of weeks with a particular tribe and seeks to 'reveal all' from this fleeting contact. Such behaviour, of course, is not common in anthropologists; would it were less so in those who purport to comment upon behaviour in organizations.

A related difficulty is that of complexity. To illustrate, I can return to the case of the manufacturer of chocolate eggs. Assuming, for the moment, that I can become relatively familiar with the company and the four or five senior managers who exercise the executive function, what is it that I observe? As good students of Chester Barnard, I observe them 'maintaining an equilibrium of organization activities through the satisfaction of the motives of individuals sufficient to induce these activities' – a neat phrase packaging a lifetime's work and masking the dynamic of interaction. It is likely that each executive not only has different 'motives', but it is equally likely that motives will arise in the process of interaction, that those held at the outset will diminish or grow; that some will be known and disclosed, others known and not disclosed. In other words, any chart of what is going on in any specific encounter can, at best, be little more than a snapshot, a picture postcard. To secure a moving picture, even in black and white, is a very large undertaking indeed.[7]

Language and Metaphors

So, in commenting upon conduct in organizations and in particular upon the executive process, I have the problem of becoming sufficiently intimate and familiar with what is going on to make any sense of it and I have problems which arise because of the dynamic complexity of behaviour in such settings. Even were these to be readily overcome, I would be faced with the issue of my *reading* of the situation I observe. Barnard, for example, who has been my mentor so far, *assumes* a great deal in his accounts of the executive process: he assumes that organizations are 'systems' with 'component systems' and he assumes that the processes which occur are homeostatic – they function so as to bring about 'equilibrium' and 'balance'. Such attributes are not manifest, not intrinsic to the data. They are 'interpretations' put upon activity by Barnard and, as such, entail certain kinds of description and analysis and rule out others.

The language of observation, description and analysis is of fundamental importance. Since humans are talking animals, it follows that their encounters with the world take place within a predominantly linguistic context. As a direct result, their experience of the world is modified by the structure of their language. Language is an organic, self-contained, autonomous system which divides and classifies experience in its own terms and along its own lines. In the course of the process it imposes its own particular 'shape' on the world of those who speak it. The fact that the Vietnamese lived for thousands of years without the pronoun 'I' cannot help but shape their view of the world differently to those of us who may appear to use no other pronoun in our daily interactions. The argument of modern linguists (and linguistic anthropologists) is that language and experience interact and are intimately intertwined. 'A language "creates" reality in its own image. To use language thus essentially involves "getting at" one kind of reality "through" another. The process is fundamentally one of "transference". All language, by nature of its "transferring" relation to "reality" . . . is fundamentally metaphorical.' From this perspective, metaphor is not simply an ornament, an optional extra as it were, rather it is the 'omni-present principle' of all language. A language cannot be 'cleared' of metaphor without using a metaphor in the verb 'to clear'. No use of language can be 'straightforward', that is, free of metaphor, since it will make use of metaphor while making that claim (here, the sense of direct purposeful undeviating movement in a particular direction through space 'transferred' to a way of speaking or writing).[8]

Put this way, language does not simply report things. It creates them. Human beings create reality by imposing concepts onto what the philosopher A. N. Whitehead saw as 'merely the hurrying of material, endlessly, meaninglessly' (itself, of course, a metaphoric statement). On the basis of linguistic evidence it is possible to claim that most if not all of one's ordinary conceptual system is metaphorical in nature. If this is indeed the case then it is possible to argue that metaphors, consciously or unconsciously adopted, structure how I perceive, how I think, and, as a consequence, inform the actions I take.

A couple of other points need to be made. Referring to conduct in organizations as, say, an elaborate dance is much less common than claiming that behaviour is determined by the system (or elements of it); it has become the norm to refer to behaviour in organizations as being system-determined, so much so that the notion is rarely recognized as being a metaphor. It has merged into the background, as in the case of a metaphor like 'the leg of the table'. In this sense, referring to conduct in organizations as ballet is clearly deviant in that it causes the metaphor to be taken as the 'foreground' – it is novel enough, fresh enough, surprising enough to bring about some reflection. In its very deviation the metaphor serves to illustrate how normative, how non-exploratory, how simply reinforcing are most other metaphors. Some if not all 'choices of interpretation' are conditioned by the metaphors habitually called upon. Especially as part of its background, non-deviant function, metaphor implies rather than draws attention to and asks assent for the minutiae of analogies and opposites upon which a particular view of the world depends. The relatively unreflecting acceptance of the view that conduct in organizations is like, say, a system entailing notions such as forces, balances, feedback and so on not only asserts that an organization is like a system, it also asserts that an organization is unlike, say, a performance at Sadler's Wells. Metaphors affirm much more than they challenge; if I am to make informed choices about how I describe organizations, I must cause the metaphors I select to be alienated from their backgrounds, cause them to cease to be taken-for-granted, in order that I may test them for adequacy, clarity, consistency and plausibility.

Reality as a Cliché

Understanding and experiencing one thing in terms of another, the essence of metaphor, is not a matter of simply choosing one domain and effecting comparisons willy nilly. Some perspectives are limited – there is more mileage in comparing one's lover to a summer's day than to a pair of compasses (however Donne may seek to demonstrate to the contrary). Metaphors constitute efforts at exploration and description and, as such, must survive the same sorts of tests as theories (to which they are intimately related) need to survive. Indeed, according to Pepper, survival is one of the tests:

> Since the basic analogy or root metaphor normally (and probably at least in part necessarily) arises out of common sense, a great deal of development and refinement of a set of categories is required if they are to prove adequate for a hypothesis of unlimited scope. Some root metaphors prove more fruitful than others, have greater powers of expansion and adjustment. These survive in comparison with others and generate relatively adequate world theories.

Wallace Stevens once declared that 'reality is a cliché from which we escape by metaphor.' Apart from being one of those sayings you wish you had been smart enough to coin, it alerts us to the fact, partly covered in earlier paragraphs, that many of our everyday descriptions and explanations of events are clichés. Background, non-deviant metaphors have either survived the tests of clarity, adequacy, consistency and plausibility or have escaped subjection to them. Morris and Burgoyne have noted six metaphors which inform the everyday practice of management development: the analogies of building, engineering, agriculture, zoology, medicine and the military. Those enamoured of the first talk of 'laying solid foundations' and of 'keying it (management development) into the established activities of the organization'. The engineers talk of 'stress', 'frictions', 'interfaces' and advocate the slotting in or plugging in of training elements. Their country cousins, the agriculturalists, on the other hand are prone to talk of 'sowing seeds' and 'cultivating' people and even, somewhat more ominously, of the need to 'weed' unsuitable varieties. Zoologists talk of 'breaking-in' young managers and are apt to refer to the organization as a 'jungle'; medicine men and women prefer to talk about 'symptoms', 'organizational health and decay' (bit of dentistry here?) and often have a fine line of chatter concerned with 'diagnosis', and 'taking the temperature of the place'. The military metaphor is widespread with much talk of 'mobilizing resources', 'corporate strategy', 'logistics' and the like; recently I even heard a sales manager urging his 'forces' to 'waste' the opposition.

Most of these metaphors are clear, certainly clearer than Donne's comparisons of lovers' souls to a pair of compasses and much clearer than a great deal of sociological and psychological theorizing. The problem with most of them is that they are not adequate nor, in many cases, can they survive Pepper's test of expansion. After one has noted, for example, that behaviour in organizations follows 'the law of the jungle' and made a few cracks about corporate tigers and office monkeys, there is little more that can be done with that metaphor. Similarly the medical metaphor is limited in its scope. Its most obvious weakness is that it focuses on sickness and disorder rather than health and normal functioning and conjures up the image of the organization as a giant asylum or hospital. It entails altogether unhelpful notions such as wounds, nurses, surgery and enemas. The military metaphor can bear much greater expansion and, possibly because of this as well as the proliferation of related metaphors based upon conflict theories of human behaviour, is frequently preferred. It can even deal with cooperation which it tends to view as 'alliance', though it has problems with non-rational action – emotions – which tend to get in the way of 'achieving one's objectives'.

In testing theories or metaphors, therefore, one needs to look at the analogy in the light of the data with which it seems to accord and that with which it is in less accord. Not only how clear is it and where does it fit the data it adduces, but in which area does it become fuzzy or downright misleading and which data are excluded from consideration by its employment. A related notion is that of consistency; a sound metaphor must have some semblance of internal consistency. It cannot survive by asserting in one place what it denies in another. Thus analogies which take organizational behaviour to be determined by 'forces' and emphasize 'balance' have great difficulty in consistently explaining or even describing change or creativity.

George Psathas adds a couple of other tests with which I am in sympathy, but which may not find such ready acceptance amongst other commentators. The key one is whether the results make sense and are true to the understanding of ordinary actors in the everyday world. If 'second order constructs' (for present purposes my notion of metaphor) 'were translated back into the first order constructs to which they refer, would the observer's report be recognized as a valid and faithful account of "what the activity is really like"?' Is the corporate world indeed a jungle? Or an asylum? In moments of cynicism some may affirm such perspectives, but it is unlikely to be regarded as a valid and faithful account when examined carefully. If, for example, I were to show the following pages to my group of executives, would they be able to discern their activities in a similar fashion?

Psathas' second test is whether the description and accounts of the activities in terms of a particular metaphor or theory would allow others – not directly knowledgeable – to recognize what was going on. 'That is, armed with "only" the knowledge gained from reading the account presented by the observer-scientist, would someone else be able to understand what he was seeing when confronted with the actual life-world reality of the events described?'

So a 'good' metaphor or set of concepts has several attributes: it is clear, consistent, adequate, and capable of expansion. It has also to be plausible both to those whose conduct it seeks to describe and explain and to other interested observers. All science, in the final analysis, rests upon plausibility; if I am unable to persuade others of the viability of my view of the social world it has, by definition, no viability. To be sure, there are rules of persuasion – I have adduced some of them above – but, contrary to the opinion of Aristotle and others, there is no separable language for scientific argument. Logic, rhetoric and poetics each contain – either in the foreground or the background – metaphorical assertions which cannot, given the nature of language, be avoided.

The Do-It-Yourself Palimpsest Book

My approach to describing the actions and interactions of my small group of executives will be through a variety of metaphors, a series of 'readings'. A 'reading' is an interpretation of a particular sequence of events.[9] The unit of description, analysis or criticism is that which we have in front of us – nothing more and nothing less. For example, I will look at a series of interactions and read them as being illustrative of 'exchange'; I will be exclusively concerned in matching this reading with that which I have before me and, for the most part, will ignore events, which do not support this reading. In subsequent chapters, I will offer complementary readings of the interactions, hoping by so doing to enrich that which was initially offered. These readings remain closely tied to the group of individuals introduced in the first chapter. There is no attempt in these pages to deal with macro-level descriptions of conduct; there is little or no reference to, say, structural contingency theory, to Marxist analyses nor to the environment. What I am concerned with here is a series of readings springing from a collection of individuals in a particular situation. These readings will be offered in turn. To play about with metaphor for a moment, what I am about is creating a kind of palimpsest – 'a parchment which has been written upon twice, the original having been rubbed out' (*Shorter Oxford English Dictionary*). My first reading will offer an interpretation which I shall erase and replace by another, but in such a manner that the original reading can still be discerned. Subsequent readings will be offered and, in turn, will be written over the preceding material. Thus a palimpsest is created, a depository of thoughts and ideas, with some elements standing out in a bold hand, some 'readings' more recent than others, but the whole still somewhat inchoate and impermanent. I make no apology for this; given our present knowledge of what executives say, feel and do, I am in no position to offer more than a draft, a rough outline of what I take to be happening.

A couple of things follow from this stance. The most trivial is that this introduction does not contain an outline of the chapters nor, as some will have noticed, are chapter headings readily comprehended. 'Some Consequences of Taking Eric Seriously' gives little guidance as to its contents. It was chosen not only because I like catchy titles, but because I wish to produce a text which is akin to a detective story, one in which the clues to the resolution of the problem (that of securing an understanding of the behaviour of a group of executives) are released chapter by chapter and few, if any, can be anticipated. For those disposed to cheat, the solution is buried in the middle pages, not the last ones.

Less trivially, as mentioned in the Preface, I am in this text. What follows is my selection of a series of exchanges from a long afternoon's meeting and my account of what may be taken to be going on in these particular extracts. To complicate things further, some chapters consist of my accounts of other people's accounts of what may be going on. Sometimes these are accounts of social scientists' accounts, occasionally I introduce the accounts of some of the actors directly involved. Whatever their pedigree, they remain accounts: bits and pieces, words, actions and phrases pieced together to produce, it is hoped, a recognizable state of affairs. In continuing to assert myself throughout the text, I am attempting to signal the irredeemably subjective/objective nature of all accounts of human behaviour.

This book is about the activities of half a dozen managers as they talk, think, feel and act in one brief afternoon. The managers exist – this is not fiction – but their names, descriptions and company identification have been changed. Their exchanges are real. I am with them gathering data to be used later to effect some changes. It is about our behaviour as presented in a number of scenarios which are subjected to a number of 'readings', accounts or interpretations throughout the subsequent chapters. Taken as a whole, however, the readings constitute an attempt to give as full an interpretation of 'what is actually going on' as is possible; in that sense they are interpretations of the meaning of events, they deal with what I take to be 'real' rather than simply the 'apparent' and they are 'close' (they constantly refer back to the scenarios). May I suggest, therefore, that the scenarios, which follow, are read through at least twice before proceeding to the next chapter? May I also suggest that you essay some preliminary 'readings' of the material for yourself and note down your views to add spice and a degree of competitiveness to that which I have to say? You are invited to create your own palimpsest.

1   Scenes from Commercial Life

Afternoon: A Boardroom in the suburbs of London, late in August in
the year 1983. Through a window, broken up by the slats of an
expensive form of vertical Venetian blind, a panorama of chimneys,
rooftops and, ant-like in the distance, a sense of urban bustle. The
interior of the room is like any of a dozen such rooms – standard
executive plush: large, polished, rosewood table with a number of
matching chairs (comfortable yet somehow austere and business-like),
thick carpeting, heavy drapes in simulated velvet covering one end of
the rectangular space. The other walls are panelled in veneered
rosewood, reflecting both the light from the window and from the
spotlights which hang from the grid which, like some piece of stage
apparatus, is suspended from the ceiling. On the table: glasses, water
jugs, well cut ash trays. Writing blocks at each position; pencils neatly
lined up, an expensive looking projector, propped up on a number of
books. Above the head of the table, in front of the curtained wall, a
large white suspended projection screen frowns down upon the
assembly. There is a coffee stand, against the wall opposite the
window, with three glass containers bubbling away; there are a number
of cups upon it and a selection of plates and biscuits. There are two
doors, each flush with the panelling, one almost in line with the
projection machine (which leads to the toilet) and the other at the far
end of the same wall. Midway along the wall facing the screen is a small
table which has upon it, in some disarray, a number of overhead
projector slides and a green telephone of a strikingly modern design.

Nine people are in the room, seated in various attitudes around the
table. I am sitting at the extreme left of the table, back to the window,
attempting to be of no consequence as I scribble my notes. It is a
meeting of executive directors called to review results before the formal
Board meeting (at which others – outsiders – will be present). At the
invitation of Paul, the Managing Director, George Nisbet, the Finance
Director prepares to go through the accounts. He is a man of about

fifty, of middling stature and undistinguished bearing, with a short neck and somewhat hunched shoulders, roundish head covered with greying hair, eyes hidden behind heavy spectacles, weak, almost spatulate nose but a full mouth, giving him the appearance of a somewhat belligerent baby. Dark suit, crumpled shirt, nondescript tie; dandruff on his collar. He speaks forcefully and rapidly, referring both to the charts he clicks into relief upon the screen and to his notes. He avoids eye contact with his colleagues throughout his presentation and appears both embarrassed and blaming in what he has to say. He relates at some length what he terms 'the sorry saga' of 'our failure' to 'manage the business effectively'. His fellow directors, for the most part, listen, look at the projected charts, graphs and diagrams and attempt to follow what he has to say in the papers he hands out to them. None betrays any emotion or signals anything other than a minimal level of interest save Paul, who becomes increasingly and manifestly agitated . . .

George: . . . so we have failed again. For the third year we are going forward with a massive loss. I've got to say that I am ashamed. Ashamed to be associated with such figures. It seems that we, as a team, are unable or unwilling, I don't know which it is, to make the decisions that will turn this operation around. I said the same thing this time last year and we all put our hands on our hearts and swore that it would be better – and, it isn't. It's worse! We go from bad to worse . . . we don't seem to be able to come to grips with the real issues, we . . .

Paul: George, it's not worse. In a number of respects it is much better. Turn back to those charts on productivity, for example, have you got them? Look. The graph has turned up this year . . .

George: Only because we have got rid of hundreds of people; we are actually producing and selling much less than we forecast . . .

Paul: But we are producing more per employee – the trend is in the right direction and, and [*raises his voice as George seeks to interrupt*] and put up the sales graph . . . see there again the trend is upwards . . .

George: Only because we can't go lower. It's not significant, there is some movement but . . .

As George goes on to explain why things are actually as bad as he says they are, Paul becomes increasingly annoyed. He is a man in his mid-forties, lean, athletic and almost completely bald. He has an assertive chin and bright, observant, blue eyes. He has discarded his jacket and rolled the sleeves of his crisp blue shirt to a position midway up his forearms. His tie is conservative and expensive as is his suit, his watch and his pen which he taps in irritation against his writing block, determinedly seeking to interrupt his Finance Director.

George: . . . and it's no use pointing to graphs and figures which show some upturn and claiming that as a success. That's a ridiculous way of looking at things. Christ, last month when we had a preliminary look at the figures, some of you were reporting losses of two and three million against forecast losses of four and five million and expecting a round of applause. A bloody standing ovation!

Paul: Look, George, as I am tired of telling you, against the circumstances, in the situation we find ourselves in, these figures are acceptable. The trends are in the right direction – all of the graphs point upwards. Unlike last year when things promised to be worse . . .

George: And have been.

Paul: Alright. And have been. This year we are ending the year on an up turn.

George: And a thumping great loss!

Paul: I don't like the stance you are taking, George. I don't like it one little bit. I trust you are not going into next week's full Board meeting with this sort of approach . . .

George: Of course not! I know what's expected of me there! It's here and now that worries me. I find these figures totally depressing and completely unacceptable; I am surprised that no one else does. We all ought to resign! I mean, we are responsible for this mess – a loss for the third year. Seven million quid! And nobody seems to care!

The rest of the executive directors seem unperturbed by this outburst. Some smile to themselves, others gaze fixedly out of the window. One, Derek Morgan, the Personnel Director, rises and crosses to the coffee table . . .

Derek: Anyone for coffee?

A number respond affirmatively. He pours several cups. Alec Barrat (responsible for a number of the factories) and Tony Gent (in charge of another territory) look at each other and shake their heads in a kindly, excessively tolerant fashion signalling that, like a raging child or an incontinent lunatic, George ought to be humoured. They have, apparently, seen it all before.

Paul: Yes, white for me. Thanks. Well, let's move on . . .

Some time later in the afternoon. A presentation is being made by the secretary to a small subcommittee of the executive directors who have been considering matters of strategy. This group, consisting of Paul, Alec Barrat, Hugh Richards (in charge of new product development) and the Secretary (Brian Jones of the planning department, not of director status but working directly to Paul, the Managing Director) has been established to determine the 'robust' decisions necessary to return the company to profitability and to recommend these decisions to the full meeting. A highly professional presentation is being run through with a large number of multi-coloured charts and several overhead slides positively bulging with figures. Most of the directors appear to be mesmerized by the numbers and images which flit across the screen. Few comments are made, most questions are parried with 'Well, if you don't mind we'll come to that in a minute.' Eric Wragg, in charge of the 'after market' (up until now the profitable end of the business, charged with parts and servicing as opposed to the supply of original equipment – the major and, presently, unprofitable part), refuses to be deterred. He is a man of large frame and stern, even dour, presence, with thick, bushy eyebrows, strong nose, a determinate mouth and a shock of barely disciplined black hair. He gives off a broad air of importance, an expectation of deference, his entire demeanour leads one to regard him as the kind of person who 'will not suffer fools gladly'. He makes his points in firm, clear tones, not without a trace, a hint, of a Midlands accent, and emphasizes each with a jabbing motion, clutching his folded spectacles in his large fist.

Eric: . . . so I don't want to wait until later. These flicker briefly and then die, but I have a nasty feeling that some of them will be resurrected at some point and it will be said that we agreed with them. What I want to know is whether or not those figures up there include the after market or not?

Brian: Which figures are you concerned about, Eric?

Eric: The ones on the far right.

Brian: These?

Eric: Yes.

Brian: Well, not directly, no. But the after market has been taken account of in our overall calculations.

Eric: I don't understand that. Either it's in those figures or it is not.

Alec:	Look, you don't have to worry about it, Eric. We have taken your market into account.
Eric:	Where? I can't see it. Either it's in or it is not. It makes a big difference to us as a whole. I know no one but me is interested in the non glamorous end of the business, but we get our bread and butter from it, you know. It can't simply be ignored.
Hugh:	It's not being ignored, Eric. It's in there.
Eric:	Well, I can't see it and he [*indicating Brian*] cannot point to it.
Alec:	We took it into account when you came to talk to us about it. You gave us the projections then and we have incorporated them.
Eric:	OK. So it's in there. How much of those figures is original equipment and how much after market? Tell me that. If those people up there constitute our strategic customers it's got to be on OE [original equipment] only. There's no way that they are strategic in terms of the after market.
Hugh:	We are not going to get anywhere with this. I think that we should move on.
Alec:	So do I. We've been round this time and time again. Next slide.

Brian looks to Paul as do both Hugh and Alec. He looks up the table at Eric who holds his gaze for a moment, then shrugs his shoulders, allows a thin smile to appear briefly and places his spectacles on the table. Paul nods to Brian who punches up the next chart. Alec half turns to Hugh.

Alec:	[*Whispering loudly*]: I don't know why we bother to spend so much time deciding things, some clown always knows better.

Later still. The directors are now considering the forecasts for next year which, apparently, have been passed to the Head Office in Manchester. Before each director a bulky, green-backed document has been placed, every page of which is crammed with figures. George Nisbet is once more holding forth; this time with much less aggression. Indeed he appears to be keen to skip through the text as quickly as possible, making reassuring noises to his colleagues, that what they have in front of them conforms 'very broadly to what we agreed at our last meeting'. Paul is at the green telephone – the 'hot-line' – conducting a whispered conversation with one of his superiors in Manchester. Eric is doodling upon his pad, Derek Morgan is staring fixedly out of the window and most of the others present flip through the pages with the air of men who would much rather be somewhere else. Alec Barrat, however, is clearly paying attention; indeed he has done some rapid calculations on his pad and is now reaching into his briefcase for some papers which he scans hurriedly. He is one of the younger directors – in his late thirties/early forties – shorter than average height, slightly overweight with a tense, taut bearing as though his skin were having a struggle to contain his energy. He is prodigiously fluent of speech, restless, excitable (with slightly protuberant eyes and a tendency for his emotions to be evident in his face, particularly around his mouth which, on occasions, twists rapidly into a sneer of contempt for his fellows), possibly prone to stress. A sensitive, earnest, intelligent man, quick off the mark and seen to be inclined to quarrel.

Alec:	Hang on a minute, George. There's something wrong with these figures, isn't there?
George:	I shouldn't think so.
Alec:	Page Twenty Three. Column . . . [*counts along*] One, two, three . . . seven. Forecast figures Eighty Four–Eighty Five. [*There is a scurrying of pages as most search for the relevant passage. Derek is now paying close attention, as are Eric, Hugh, and Paul who has rejoined the group.*]
George:	Yes. [*A non statement, cold, uninviting.*]
Derek:	What's the problem, Alec?
Alec:	Well, my copy says eleven million. Margin of eleven million.
Derek:	So does mine. So what? Doesn't it tally or something? Mistake in the adding up?
Alec:	[*Ignoring the questions*] How did you arrive at that figure, George?
George:	The sum of columns four and six, less the numbers in five.
Alec:	I can see that. I don't want the technical answer – I can do that sum for myself. It's the eleven million I'm bothered about. That wasn't the figure we agreed last time.
George:	I know.
Alec:	[*Consults his papers*] We agreed seventeen million.
George:	Yes. [*He begins to shuffle his papers, looks toward Paul. There is a silence; it is clear that he is not going to volunteer anything further.*]
Alec:	And that's what went to Manchester some [*consults his papers once more*] six weeks ago.
George:	Yes.
Alec:	What are these figures then?
George:	Revised ones.

Alec: I can see that. Revised by whom?
George: [*Looks toward Paul who continues to avoid eye contact*] By me.
Hugh: What is the status of these figures? Does Manchester have these or the earlier ones?
George: They have these now.

There is an embarrassed silence. George gazes down at his papers. Everyone waits for someone else to break the silence, to say the unsayable.

Alec: But these are not agreed figures.
George: [*Looking towards Paul – again no response*] They are.
Derek: What Alec is really saying, but is too polite to say, that it is up to this group to decide what figures go forward. It's our decision and we certainly didn't agree these.
Alec: We must look a right load of idiots up in Manchester; from seventeen million down to eleven in six weeks including a three week shutdown! A barrow load of monkeys could come up with figures like that!
Eric: Got us in one! A load of monkeys.
George: The figures were revised by me and agreed with Paul. I had another look at what was being forecast and decided what had been sent up was not achievable. In fact, I didn't think eleven million was – more like four . . . [*laughter and head shaking around the table*] Paul would not have that, so we sent eleven million in.
Alec: And we are supposed to be committed to that, are we?
Paul: Look, there is no point in getting excited about it. The figures don't mean anything; they will change again – they always do. We seem to be making a great fuss about nothing . . .
Derek: About who decides. That's what.
George: Look, it was holiday time – you were all away. Someone had to make a decision – Christ, surely we don't have to agree everything all of the time? All of us together?

A number of separate conversations break out. The telephone whistles and Paul crosses to it, turning half towards the wall to whisper confidentially into it. Derek Morgan rises and heading towards the toilet says to no one in particular:

Derek: What a way to run a ship!

Towards six o'clock. The meeting has been on the go for four hours. It has now reached Any Other Business. Paul is riffling through a sheaf of papers he has in front of him. A number of the directors seem anxious to leave; cases are packed and clicked noisily shut, watches are consulted, jackets are struggled into.

Paul: One more thing. The Chairman has written a long letter explaining the change in logo.

Hugh: The change in what?

Paul: Logo. He has written setting out what is now to go on the top of our letters, the new colours for the envelopes, the revised packaging layouts . . .

George: Good God! Talk about fiddling while Rome burns!

All are now giving full attention to Paul. On the edge of their chairs affecting almost identical expressions of incredulity at what they are hearing. A number of excited, humorous comments are passed around the table. Paul raises his voice and cuts through:

Paul: In future, all subsidiaries of the main company including ourselves are to have the name and logo of the parent . . .

Alec: Whom God preserve!

Paul: . . . company placed immediately before the name of the subsidiary. Thus we shall become Twinings Friction Free Castings Ltd.

George: We are losing millions and that's what the main Board is spending its time doing.

Eric: What about our subsidiaries?

Paul: What about them?

Eric: What do they become – Twinings Friction Free Castings (LSD Camshafts) Ltd? What a bloody mouthful.

Paul: [*Consulting the letter*] It doesn't say anything about that here.

Hugh: It's probably illegal anyway.

Paul: What is?

Hugh: Changing names like that.

Eric: Certainly is – our name, our logo and our colours are registered trademarks. Cost thousands to change that.

Paul: Will it?

George: Hundreds of thousands.

Derek: What's the letter about? Asking our opinion or what?

Alec: Manchester asking our opinion? You've got to be joking!

Paul: Are you sure it will cost money to put this into effect?

Hugh: Some one up there must have taken that into account . . .
Paul: It says nothing about it here. Nothing about who is to meet the cost of changing. Lots of examples, look all these beautiful mock-ups of what the new paper and the new packaging will look like. [*He passes out the material to willing hands.*]
Eric: Just like Christmas, isn't it?
Paul: It could well be that some one has goofed. [*Delight at this possibility is registered on most faces.*] Eric, can you take this and get someone to come up with a report on its implications – what it will cost, how much hassle it will involve us in and the like.

The meeting breaks up in rare good humour. Someone unplugs the projector, another switches the coffee machine off. Paul catches Alec's arm and steers him into a corner engaging him in deep conversation. Most drift slowly towards the door. Expressions such as 'Bloody idiots', 'Don't know what to do with their time' and 'Fiddling while Rome burns' seem to hang on the air long after the room is vacated. I collect my belongings and, not quite knowing how to take my leave, fade away.

2   Some Consequences of Taking Eric Seriously

'I don't know why we bother to spend so much time deciding things, some clown always knows better.'

It will be recalled that Eric's persistent questioning led to increasing irritation on the part of Alec and Hugh, culminating in the loud stage whisper reproduced above. They tried reassuring him, they tried humouring him, they even tried ignoring him before they concluded that he was beyond redemption and fit only for castigation. No one, with the possible exception of Brian, took his questions seriously; no one appeared to consider that Eric may well have been simply seeking to understand better that which had been proposed to him. Whatever other motives were attributed to Eric, no one appeared to act upon the attribution of genuine inquiry to his actions.

In this chapter, I will focus upon the struggle to understand, epitomized by Eric, which I take to be characteristic of much of human conduct. What I will be stressing in the following pages is the idea of the social actor as an interpreting, meaning-seeking being; a definer and a constructor.[1] Conduct, I shall assert, is constructed. I will offer a perspective which takes Eric's hesitations and doubts seriously – a perspective which depicts both him and his colleagues as struggling to come to terms with each other and with the circumstances in which they are all involved.

The school of thought from which the framework derives is known variously as cognitive theory, social action theory or social constructionist depending upon which text one reads. I will begin by presenting some of the key ideas which are taken directly from a related sociological/social psychological approach usually referred to as symbolic interactionism.

The basic ideas of the symbolic interactionist perspective can be traced through Herbert Blumer to the seminal work of George Herbert Mead at the University of Chicago. Mead was a teacher rather than a writer, and his ideas were assembled into a book, *Mind, Self and Society*, by his students. Blumer is not only the major disciple, he is also the clearest exponent of interactionism and what follows relies very heavily upon his work.[2]

Basic Premises

As interpreted by Blumer, interactionism consists of three basic premises. First, that human beings act toward things on the basis of the meanings that the things have for them; secondly, that those meanings are the products of social interaction; and thirdly, that such meanings are handled in and modified through an interpretative process used by individuals in dealing with the 'things' he or she encounters. Taking each of these three premises in turn, I will consider the implications of each for the understanding and analysis of conduct in organizations.

> Human beings act toward things on the basis of the meanings that the things have for them

Blumer terms this a 'simple proposition', but for all that, it does raise a number of questions. To appreciate the point of view of the interactionists, it has to be recognized that terms such as 'meaning' and 'things' are used in a very broad sense. The meaning of a thing includes more, much more, than a simple dictionary definition. It includes all the complex images and attitudes that the thing elicits for a particular person at a particular time. The word processor used to produce this book, for example, is a thing which 'means' – for me – a great deal more than a device for the electronic registration and reproduction of words, phrases and sentences. It engenders in me a mixture of feelings; apprehension, pleasure, a sense of being progressive, but also a sense of being less clearly in control than when I use pencil and paper, and so on. Things, or objects as Blumer occasionally calls them, include everything that can have meaning for a person; the term is not limited to inanimate objects such as word processors. Physical things are only one category of object that people designate and toward which they act. Language – the use of symbols – makes it possible to designate things which are not physically or materially present. I can and do act towards notions of, say, 'Justice' or 'Peace' without needing to see or touch anything material.

From this perspective, humans are primarily talking animals. As the title of the school of thought indicates, it is language that marks the human off from other creatures. The claim is not that other animals cannot communicate; clearly they can and they do, but, importantly, their communication does not depend upon nor utilize *language* – a set of arbitrary and changeable symbols. No other creatures have the natural and normal capacity to create, manipulate, and employ symbols to direct their own conduct and to influence the behaviour of others. Apes have indeed been taught to use symbols and there is even evidence that two chimpanzees, each taught language, can use it to talk to each other but, to date, we have no evidence of large-scale, creative use of language by these or any other creatures. With vocabularies of some 200 words, the higher apes, while substantially ahead of, say, three-spined sticklebacks, are a long way behind my executives, however restricted their code may appear to be. For humans, language is clearly the predominant form of conceptual organization in a manner that is not natural to other animals. As has been noted elsewhere, the symbol 'transformed our anthropoid ancestors into men and made them human'. Furthermore, it has been argued that no one is truly human until they have attained the ability to grasp and use symbols.[3]

Like the character in the Molière play who discovered that he had been speaking prose all his life, many of us may be surprised to find that we have been manipulating symbols for most of our lives. In order to understand the distinctiveness of symbolic conduct, I must distinguish between natural signs and symbols. The former are cues and stimuli that are associated with particular events. Animals, including ourselves, respond to signs – sounds, smells, and visual stimuli – that elicit particular kinds of behaviour. My dog responds as predictably to the sound of the doorbell (she barks) as I do to the sound of a siren on a vehicle (I move over). Signs constitute the basis for a conversation of gestures and are the most fundamental of all forms of communication. They are, however, more rudimentary than symbols.

Consider another piece of conduct. It is a dark night, rain lashing the ground, little or no moon, when I dimly perceive the figure of an armed man creeping towards me:

'Halt. Who goes there?' [*I cock my weapon*].

'Don't shoot! Don't shoot!'

'Password?'

'Kiss-me-quick.'

'Step forward and be recognized, friend.'

Mead defined symbols in terms of meaning. A system of symbols, or a language, 'is the means whereby individuals can indicate to one another what their responses to objects will be, and hence what the meanings of objects are'. 'Kiss-me-quick' in the dance hall when spoken between consenting adults (of whatever sex) has a very different result to 'Kiss-me-quick' when elicited in the circumstances outlined above. In other words, humans have a capacity over and above the conversation of gestures; the human is a cognitive creature who functions in a context of more or less shared meanings which are communicated, exchanged, modified and enlarged in interaction through language.[4]

An important feature of symbols is their utility in the absence of objects or even events to which they refer. The idea of a password, for example, illustrates this point neatly enough. In an arbitrary fashion, a group of humans can designate any combination of words and can cause them to take on a particular meaning. The ability to furnish the appropriate phrase when challenged is taken to indicate friendly intent, and no further signs nor any actual demonstrations of friendliness are required.

The use of symbols makes it possible for humans not only to short-circuit (and to elaborate) stimuli, it also allows them to designate one another. And themselves. Having and using a name for others and for the self makes it possible for the individual member of a group to see himself or herself and to anticipate actions and reactions symbolically. Put in terms I will develop more fully later, the capability we each have to manipulate symbols allows us to interpret and rehearse conduct in the theatres inside our skulls before committing ourselves (and others) to action. By developing this capacity for imaginative participation, human beings are able consciously to control their conduct. In becoming a 'thing' to myself (an object, an actor – being able to attach a name to myself and anticipate my own actions), I become part of my own environment. Put another way, since I can and do anticipate what 'you' may do in a particular context, it follows that my potential conduct is also likely to be taken account of by you – thus, in order to achieve my purposes, I must take into account your likely views of me and my possible actions. This knowledge – the imagined perspectives on me held by others – enables me to shape and control my actions. Instead of a trial-and-error, suck-it-and-see approach to interaction in which I have to learn from raw experience, I can anticipate what I may do and test it out against my view of your likely responses and, in the light of this appraisal, either proceed or modify my acts, and so on. I thus live in a simulated, hypothetical environment, one that can be (but need not necessarily be) consciously manipulated on the rehearsal stage of the mind.

Blumer and a number of others argue that if conduct is to be understood, it must be known how the particular actor 'defines the situation', for it is from these definitions that conduct emerges. Eric may well be struggling to understand what it is that Alec and Hugh have included in their figures; in any event, he conducts himself in the light of *his* understanding, not upon any 'objective' or 'true' state of affairs. The key data, therefore, for those of an interactionist persuasion, are the constructions individuals put upon the circumstances with which they take themselves to be confronted; a feature of social life neatly summarized by W. I. Thomas (1923): 'If people define things as real, they are real in their consequences.' To understand what is occurring in any social situation, therefore, I must have access to the definitions put upon it (and being revised throughout it) by those directly involved. Alec and Hugh *think* that they know how Eric sees the situation – one from in which he has been excluded and is therefore intent upon 'making trouble' – so their conduct reflects this definition. Eric, on the other hand, claims to be genuinely concerned about the figures and acts upon his definition. The consequences we have observed; the dynamics we are beginning to understand.[5]

Meanings are the products of social interaction in human society.

Blumer identifies two ways of accounting for the origin of meaning – one is to regard meaning as being intrinsic to the thing itself, a natural quality of its objective facticity, and the other which regards meaning as brought to the thing by the individual for whom that thing has meaning. While the latter is closer to the interactionist position than the former, both are unsatisfactory. Meanings arise from and through interaction.

The meanings of particular events, situations, things, people and experiences arise out of the observed behaviour of significant others towards them. The meaning of the office or role of managing director, for example, is given by the way people behave towards that role or function: reverentially, subserviently, or whatever.[6]

Symbolic interactionism holds that meanings are social products, the creations of people as they define and interact. In this sense, as Silverman points out, men come to 'know' the social world through the accumulation of a shared stock of knowledge, and the 'correctness' of this knowledge is continuously tested, challenged, reaffirmed in and through interaction. Clearly it is not a matter of 'simply' taking on the meaning that others hold. Of course I often do that, challenging everything would be terribly exhausting, but I also modify and reject meanings that others hold and seek to impose. The important point for the interactionist is the assertion that my conduct occurs within some sort of framework where I can take the point of view of others into account. Blumer's second premise declares that reality is socially constructed and implies therefore that it is socially sustained and socially changed. The same processes of definition, communication and interaction lie at the heart of changing order as lie at the centre of maintaining it.[7]

> Meanings are handled in, and modified through, an interpretative process used by the person in dealing with the things he encounters.

In his third premise Blumer seeks to emphasize that, given the points made above with regard to meaning being essentially a social product, it would nonetheless be a mistake to assume that an individual's use of meaning is but an application of the meaning so derived. Rather, the use of meaning by a particular individual depends upon an active process of interpretation.

To return to Eric and his persistent questioning. Faced with the graphs and charts punched up by Brian, he does not simply respond. He seeks to attribute meaning to the charts and to the event. It seems to him that it is a session in which those not present at the deliberations of the sub-group may ask questions, may seek clarification and may even challenge some of the conclusions arrived at elsewhere. This is not a definition that either Hugh or Alec share; for them, the large group is required to do no more than listen to the conclusions before ratifying them with the 'minimum of fuss'. Blumer's first premise is thus amply demonstrated in action, humans conduct themselves on the basis of the attribution of meaning to 'things' (events, actions, interactions, attitudes, situations). Furthermore, as Eric persists in his questions, both he and his antagonists begin to discover revised meanings arising out of the interaction. Both sets of actors start with different definitions of the nature and purpose of the presentation of the sub-group's deliberations to the large group as we have seen; both revise their interpretations as a direct consequence of the interaction. Alec and Hugh see it increasingly as a confrontation as, in the end, does Eric. The meaning of the event arises out of the way the actors behave towards each other – Blumer's second premise. Passing the same interaction through a somewhat finer mesh, we can illustrate his third premise. Blumer posits two steps in the interpretative process. In the first, one makes indications to oneself as to which of the manifold things in this situation are relevant. The setting (the Boardroom) and the props (slide projectors, writing materials) enable Eric and the others to reduce the variety somewhat – it's unlikely to be an office party – but the possibilities are still fairly wide. As I have indicated,

Eric selects and acts upon the idea that this particular session is what it is announced to be – an opportunity to develop his understanding of the deliberations of the strategy group. Alec and Hugh choose and act upon another interpretation. Both initial tendencies to apply pre-formed meanings to this particular situation are quickly revised.

Self-Awareness

Thus interpretation may be regarded as a formative process in which meanings are selected, checked and employed primarily through an iterative process of self-interaction. Blumer is very clear about the process:

> Action is built up in coping with the world instead of being released from a pre-existing psychological structure by factors playing on that structure. By making indications to himself and by interpreting what he indicates, the individual has to forge or piece together a line of action.

As seen from the symbolic interactionist perspective, the human being assumes a much more active and reflective role than is the case elsewhere. Interactionist man or woman first identifies what is to be taken into account, makes an assessment of the factors so taken into account and decides to act in order to further such purposes or ends which, in the light of their assessment, appear to be worth pursuing.

From this perspective, individuals may be seen as uniquely self-aware beings who define, designate, evaluate, plan and organize their actions through a process of internal conversation. Actions are not contingent upon the 'objective world' but are an influence upon it: 'The process of self-interaction puts the human being over against his world through a defining process instead of merely responding to it and forces him to construct his action instead of merely releasing it.' 'Joint action', such as characterizes organizations, can be defined as a series of moves 'made in the light of one's thoughts about the other's thoughts about oneself' which are in some fashion fitted together. Each participant necessarily occupies a different position, has a different biography and ascribes meaning in line with his or her own interpretative scheme and in acting conveys to other participants what they take to be appropriate reciprocal actions.

It follows that the basic 'thing' to be identified in any particular situation is the person himself. For Paul, George and each of the others, what needs to be determined above all else in each interaction episode is: 'Who am I?'. In seeking to influence the direction of events, each must know what it is he wants out of the encounter for himself and for the others present. Each person, in answer to the 'Who am I?', is a role identity, a part, as it were, that the individual devises for himself as an occupant of the particular position; these role identities provide plans of action for the self as performer and evaluative standards for the self as audience. For example, George's role identity for giving effect to his role as Finance Director is 'to lay it on the line', and he judges his own performance against this criterion. Other Finance Directors, even in similar circumstances, may have adopted a more neutral, 'simply reporting' role identity.

Exchange and Mart

I can come now to an apparent digression, but one which is necessary if I am to advance the case I am making in any way adequately. Why is it that George behaves the way that he does? Why does Paul persist in what he undertakes? Why is Eric such a nuisance to his colleagues? What does he get out of being so obtuse?

Interactionists consider that, for the most part, why people do what they do is the result of judgement; cognitive but not always conscious deliberation about alternative courses of action. George chooses to do what he does because the payoff to him from doing what he does is greater than the payoff available from any other course of action. Interaction between actors is a function of what each person gets out of the relationship: no pay off, no relationships. All interaction is a matter of investment and profit. A sequence such as any one of these we have presented may be analysed in terms of the performance of selected behaviours. What Paul and his fellow actors do is but a small part of their repertoire and is enacted, since it has been rewarded in the past. Even George, it would be argued, derives some strange benefit in bringing the wrath of Paul down upon his head.

The essence of exchange theory lies in the notion of profit. The outcome, the payoff, the profit is the reward any social actor secures minus the costs. 'The open secret of human exchange is to give the other man behaviour that is more valuable to him than it is costly to you and to get from him behaviour that is more valuable to you than it is costly to him.'[8] The key argument of the proponents of this framework is that when relationships cease to be profitable, they will be abandoned. Presumably, although I have never seen it so depicted, one could construct a kind of stock market chart of relationships: wife and self down six points on the week, self and boss up two, self and bank manager approaching liquidation. Thibaut and Kelley, who are serious and sophisticated advocates of the exchange framework, suggest using a matrix as a way of representing and studying interactions and profits (see figure 1).

The behaviours in the repertoire of *A* (say, Paul in our sketches) are listed across the top of the table and the behaviours in *B's* repertoire (say, George) are listed down the left side of the table. If Paul (as *A*) enacts behaviour *a*, and George enacts *b*, then the payoff or profit would be 6 to Paul and 2 for George. To illustrate, let us take the case of Paul proposing to take on the Headquarters staff with regard to the change in logo. Such an action may be very rewarding to Paul – it consolidates his 'team' in opposition to 'them', it gives him the opportunity to demonstrate 'leadership', and it costs him nothing (Eric is to do the work). George, whilst not exactly indifferent to the issue, derives little reward from it. On the other hand, where he initiates the interaction (as, say, in the first scene) he may derive four units of reward. George's 'Cassandra bit', however unrewarding to his colleagues, may score highly with his own view of himself ('I told them how it was' – brave, fearless executive). It is clearly not rewarding to Paul who seeks, therefore, to shift the pattern more to his own

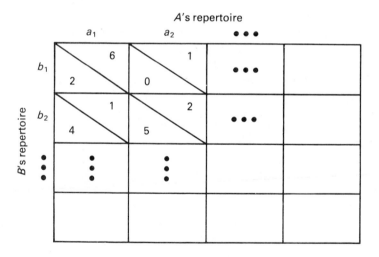

Figure 1 Matrix of possible outcomes scaled according to overall goodness of outcomes (taken from J. W. Thibaut and H. H. Kelley (1959) The Social Psychology of Groups, New York: John Wiley and Sons and reproduced here with the permission of the authors).

advantage. And so on. It is possible to play a large number of variations upon this matrix and to depict shifts in relationships through the course of a particular interaction.

A couple of other points need to be made. Thibaut and Kelley note the importance of what they term 'comparison levels'. There are two. The first is composed of all other relationships a person has experienced and the payoffs received in them. The mean or average payoff can be taken as the zero point; if the current relationship gives more than zero, it will probably be regarded as satisfactory. If, say, Paul's previous encounters as a leader have been ones in which (for whatever reason) those he purported to lead largely ignored him, then he is likely to be pleased with his current ones as depicted in these scenes from commercial life. Whatever else his subordinates do to him, they do not ignore him. However, the comparison may be made with other leaders as well as with his own past experiences. Paul may observe that his superior or, for that matter, his predecessor succeeded in extracting larger amounts of deference, loyalty and obedience out of the team than he can and, on that account, may feel relatively ineffective. The current relationship would thus be rendered less satisfactory than if he had not had the opportunity to make such a comparison.

The second comparison is the comparison level of alternatives. Paul can contrast the payoff of the present relationship with, say, George in and as a member of the team with the possible payoff of other relationships, say, with George on a one-to-one basis as a subordinate. If Paul finds the team relationship more valuable than the one-to-one, then he is dependent upon it, if not, not. Thibaut and Kelley argue that he will activate and repeat these relationships in the settings in which he can maximize his rewards.

The two comparison levels produce, therefore, four kinds of relationships depending upon the general comparison level and that which holds for alternatives. In the first case – perhaps rarely realized in social and organizational life – the current relationship is better than any pertaining up till now (or better than the mean) and better than the comparison level for alternatives. The relationship within Paul's team would be stable and satisfying if all concerned with it were dependent upon it and none had alternatives which he found more rewarding. If, on the other hand, the payoff for all concerned was better than the general level of comparison but not as good as the alternative, it would be satisfactory but unstable. Paul, for example, may be doing better as a leader of the team than he has done in the past, but he may know, and his subordinates may be aware, that under his predecessor (or under another one of them) things were or could be even better. Higher payoffs can be achieved elsewhere (other things permitting). The third circumstance is one in which those involved are aware that what obtains is lower than their general comparison level but higher than the alternatives – 'better the devil we know' kind of attitude. Paul may be worse than we, as subordinates, have experienced (the subordinates may be less responsible or whatever Paul takes as reward), but there is nothing around better. Thus relatively stable but unsatisfying relationships ensue. Finally, there is the circumstance in which both the general comparison level and the level for alternatives is low. All concerned – Paul, George, Hugh, Alec and the others – have experienced better relations and can see better alternatives (working one-to-one, for example). Here may be seen an unsatisfactory set of relations which is about to end.

The scheme, although relatively simple to outline, is a rather complex one to use for analysis. Not only is each actor likely to vary in terms of his perception of rewards and costs, each is also likely to have a different general comparison level and a different comparison level for alternatives. Eric's view of what is a rewarding leader–subordinate relationship may well vary not only from that of Paul but also from that of Hugh, who differs from Alec and so on. To complicate the issue further, comparison levels change over time. As a person experiences what he takes to be satisfactory relationships, the comparison level rises; as he experiences poor relationships, the level drops. So, within a group, a whole set of comparisons vary over time and across actors. If the idea is added that relationships also go through certain stages, and are influenced by power, norms, status and the like is, a thoroughly confusing picture emerges.

In concluding this important digression from the main thrust of this chapter, it is important to remember that any act produces costs and benefits for other persons as well as for the performer. In the circumstances that I am seeking to understand, the performers are interdependent. How George behaves has implications for Paul and vice versa. They *exchange* behaviour to achieve that which cannot be realized independently.

Defining and Role Taking

Given that this may well be the case, how do individuals initiate and sustain interaction? McCall and Simmons provide a set of ideas which may bring us closer to an understanding of the process. The first stage in any encounter, they suggest, is to try to judge others in terms of their significance for our own emerging plans of action; thus Hugh and Alec have to monitor Eric if they are to achieve their ends. This appraisal is not once and for all (although first impressions may be very important), it may be at one level or another a constant process. An individual aligns his action to the actions or potential actions of others by assessing what it is he thinks they are doing or are likely to do – he seeks to give meaning and identity to them and their acts. He does this by a process of 'imaginative participation'[9] – the process of being able to grasp the direction of each other's acts without which human beings would not be able to enter into and maintain group life. Weber expresses the concept as the ability '. . . to put oneself imaginatively in the place of the actor and thus sympathetically to participate in his experience' and Shibutani declares that imaginative participation or 'role taking' consists of 'anticipating what another human being is likely to do [which] requires getting 'inside' him – to his objective experiences, his particular definition of the situation, and his conception of his own place within it'. Imaginative participation or role taking which interactionists hold to be a fundamental human attribute may be defined as the ability to put oneself in the place of others through the use of imagination, to see things with their eyes and, on the basis of these imaginings (for that is what they are), to predict how they will react. Hugh anticipates that Eric will continue to 'make trouble' whatever clarification is offered; thus he frames his conversation and his interaction with that predominant assumption.

G. H. Mead, who was much exercised by the notion of role taking, pointed out that 'taking the role of the other' can mean imaginatively participating in the life of a specific person in a specific interaction or incorporating into one's own actions what one takes to be the view of a wider grouping – the 'generalized other'. Hugh and Alec's dealings with Eric, therefore, are not only informed by that which they imagine to be the likely responses of the latter to their blandishments, but also, in part, by views they have formed about the likely reactions of others to their manner of dealing with him. They feel free to ignore his questions and even to pass open comment upon his actions, since they believe – not erroneously as it turns out – that Eric will receive no support from his colleagues. Whatever the perceptions, the context appears to be one in which both Alec and Hugh feel free to treat a colleague as an 'awkward guy'. One can imagine other contexts in which such comments were either more frank (open, not whispered) or not allowable in any form.

So, summarizing so far, I have depicted a process in which two or more individuals come together to accomplish some joint act. The beginnings of such an endeavour consist of one party offering a definition of what he takes to be the appropriate conduct for the prosecution of the encounter. Eric decides to ask some questions. Brian is clearly willing to answer, Alec less so. He, by a process of self-interaction, clearly comes to the conclusion that Eric is not merely seeking information (given the challenging tone of Eric's first intervention, this may hardly seem surprising). Putting himself imaginatively into Eric's shoes, he does not like what he sees developing, particularly for his own part in the interaction. He does not wish to be placed in the role of one being interrogated. He may well feel that such a process, once embarked upon, threatens all kinds of valued self-identities (as a member of the strategic group, he is privy to information which, whilst restricted, confers power on insiders) and he may, therefore, mentally rehearse courses of action which deny Eric the purpose he attributes to him. Thus the cognitive process of self-interaction and role taking (which may continue throughout the interaction) have 'to do with judging the identities that the various interactions . . . are likely to claim in the situation'.

These processes are allied to two others which McCall and Simmons consider as the more active or expressive processes: 'the presentation of self' and 'altercasting'.[10]

Laying Claim to an Identity

In *The Presentation of Self in Everyday Life*, Erving Goffman sets out to describe and understand the ways in which an individual lays claim to a particular identity in an encounter. Interaction, for Goffman, is frequently 'strategic', consequently a great deal of effort goes into controlling the impression one gives in order to direct the action along lines conducive to one's own ideas (planned or emergent). Goffman makes a distinction between two classes of expression; those that are 'given' and those that are 'given off':

> The first involves verbal symbols or their substitutes which he uses admittedly and solely to convey the information that he and others are known to attach to these symbols. This is a communication in the traditional and narrow sense. The second involves a wide range of action that others can treat as symptomatic of the actor, the expectation being that the action was performed for reasons other than the information conveyed in this way.

Thus individuals, by carefully controlling their expressive behaviours can convey to other individuals - by impressions given and given off – an image of who it is they wish to be taken for in a particular encounter. In so doing they attempt to constrain those others to accept their claims.[11] Eric knows what he is about when he asks his questions and his choice of mild aggression rather than soft request is an attempt to set the interaction off along lines he favours: the colleague asserting his right to know. Of course, should the impression that Eric gives off be less than congruent with the impression that he attempts to give – let us say he questions in a tremulous tone, with a markedly nervous twitch – it may be that his attempts to constrain will be even less successful. Alec and Hugh may respond to the weakness they impute to Eric rather than to the authority which the latter seeks to impose upon the interaction. As McCall and Simmons point out, one's conduct must be of a piece if one's claim to leverage in a particular encounter or interaction is to be sustained.

The obverse of self presentation is the notion of altercasting. Hall describes the process:

> In interaction the participants project identities for themselves and for each other. Not only do they present a particular image of self but they also cast the alter in the position that they would like him to assume.

Eric's assumption of a questioning stance conveys to others that they should assume the roles of information suppliers. A claim to dominance in an interaction simultaneously and necessarily casts others into submissive postures; a claim to weakness is equally an attempt to cast others into the position of strength. In other words, identities may be seen as reciprocal; what Eric does constrains his colleagues and their responses, theoretically at least, in turn constrain Eric. However, it is important to note that neither presentation of self nor altercasting automatically bring into line the roles and identities that individuals party to an encounter wish to enact. The processes outlined above do not structure encounters on a once for all basis; whatever Eric offers or asserts may be accepted or challenged by his colleagues. In many encounters competing definitions emerge and, should all concerned wish to continue the interaction, such definitions must be taken into account. According to McCall and Simmons, it is usual to note a degree of negotiation in encounters:

> Typically the two parties will negotiate some sort of compromise, each acceding somewhat to the other's demands, though seldom in equal degree . . . this compromise definition of the role and character of each is not executed in a single step but is the eventual result of a complex process of negotiation or bargaining.

It is important to stress once more the emergent quality of much interaction. Basic exchange theory looks to organizations as arenas for the expression of internal states or purposes. Interactionism, of course, also assumes that human beings are purposeful creatures, actively seeking to define and sustain their objectives, but adds the important qualification that the result of people coming together is a negotiation, a compromise; joint actions have an emergent quality 'that may not have existed before the parties came together'. The fitting together of individual lines of action provides the basic feature of joint action which, in and of itself, is more than happenstance. It can be seen as a cognitive process of combining separate, partial and sometimes conflicting definitions and competing claims to identity into a meaningful if temporary relation. Temporary since the emergent quality of such 'working agreements' makes their attainment problematic and their course potentially unstable. There are essentially two stages to the attainment of a negotiated agreement. First, the negotiation of social identities – who is being who in the encounter: 'Me Tarzan, you Jane'. Second, the negotiation of interactive roles – agreement on the specifics of the interaction – what is to be done and by whom. The working agreement is thus a delicate balance of identities and tasks; should anyone object to the identity imputed to him, the subsequent joint action may well be of a different character or it may totally break down.[12]

Today We Negotiate

To return to my colleagues waiting in the Boardroom. How do they arrive at a working agreement? I shall focus in particular on the third extract, the one in which George presents the figures that he has sent up to Manchester. In non-routine interactions such as this, the first problem is one of definition. Most of the actors seem at a loss as to how to proceed. The identities, roles and goals which each is accustomed to using no longer seem appropriate; individualistic approaches to such meetings where, by and large, the best course of action has been to 'defend your own patch' or somewhat more aggressively to 'kick over the milk bottles on someone else's step before they kick over yours' do not seem the most appropriate response to the developing situation. It could well be that for a time, at least, each is unclear as to how to proceed. As Alec continues to probe, however, it becomes clear to one or two that he may well need support. Eric, for example, may know this but may well be unable to think of himself as a 'supporter' of Alec, even less so given their previous interactions. Even were he to conceive of such an identity, it may be that he could not play it with conviction. In any event, he may not be able to define the goal. Is the developing purpose to 'screw George?' If so at least that sort of line is familiar. Or is it, as Derek seems to imagine, to assert the authority of the group? And if so what is Paul's reaction likely to be? What does his silence, his avoidance of support for George mean? Is he punishing him for the previous encounter or is something else afoot?

To most of my executives, this is a relatively new situation and their hesitations, their inability to define identities and roles for themselves and others are products of inexperience and unfamiliarity. Those concerned must cast around in an attempt to define what is going on and what is to be their part in it. Given the lack of definition, there are a number of options open to the actors. The most frequently observed is withdrawal. Hugh and Eric appear to prefer this course of action, saying little and sitting back from the table. Alec prefers to edge forward, seeking to find what kind of circumstance he is facing: 'Well, my copy says eleven million. Margin of eleven million.' Derek, at this stage unclear as to what is going on but, perhaps, sensing something odd, something untoward in George's manner of response, seeks to understand Alec's point. Alec, either intent upon his own line or unwilling (perhaps unable) to develop a different kind of relationship with Derek, simply continues: 'How did you arrive at that figure, George?'; he does not want a literal answer but gets one, either because George fails to understand his intent or, more likely given the hostility in his tone, he perceives the intent and chooses to ignore it. Alec edges forward, George's tone and manner acting as a goad. 'I can see that . . .'. If, as appears to be the case, George wishes to shut off the inquiry, his self-presentation is unfortunate since it is such as to further it. He clearly has not got his act together. Alec tentatively but clearly takes the next step: 'We agreed seventeen million.' The intent of his statement is 'Explain yourself, George. Explain yourself.' George simply says 'Yes'. Alec's challenge is ambiguous enough for him not to have to respond. If he wants an answer, he must be much more direct, which he gradually becomes: 'Revised by whom?'. George once more looks towards Paul who continues to ignore him. Such behaviour is likely to have entered into Alec's definition of the situation, hence he proceeds with caution. Something is up, but who is involved? Is this me against George or me against George and Paul? If the latter, the consequences are likely to be different. But Paul is not supporting him. Why not? Because he knows nothing about the circumstance? Hugh, who has sat back for a while, thinks he has discovered what the interaction is about and has hit upon an identity and role for himself. He is less concerned about his relationship with

Paul than is Alec, and has fewer problems with Alec than does Derek; he can therefore support him and essay a direct question: 'Does Manchester have these [figures] or the earlier ones?' The answer stops everyone in his tracks. Each reflects upon its meaning. The situation has now changed from one of exploring to one of considering the implications of what has now been revealed. Again, for most, withdrawal appears to be the best course of action. Alec, however, proceeds. Again, by indirection seeking to find direction out: 'But these are not the agreed figures.' George denies the premise and Derek, seeking to support Alec, directly confronts the issue: 'It's our decision and we certainly didn't agree these.' The pattern of interaction is rapidly developing into one of group versus George (and, possibly, Paul). However, Alec does not build upon Derek's dramatic outlining of the issue. Either he does not perceive it or he does not welcome Derek's support – it is not within his repertoire to handle support from that source. In any event, George's goading promotes an angry outburst which temporarily deflects Derek's purpose and leads to Eric's quite inappropriate attempt at joking: 'Got us in one! A load of monkeys.' No one laughs, Eric withdraws once more. George is stung into a response by the tone of both Alec's and Eric's comments which he appears to read as dismissive and contemptuous. In responding, he associates Paul with his actions, thus overtly confirming his earlier signals. It is now too late for Alec to withdraw and he proceeds until interrupted by Paul who, responding to the obvious acrimony, seeks to downplay the event: 'Look, there is no point in getting heated about it . . .'. The interaction splutters to a halt, finally sealed off by Derek's exit line: 'What a way to run a ship!'. Although all concerned collude in the termination of this particular scene, the issue of who decides does not appear to be resolved. It is of course actually resolved since, by not pursuing the issue further, Alec, Hugh and Derek leave the decision where it was before they raised the matter – in the hands of George and Paul.

Although the episode seems to peter out, it nonetheless furnishes me with one example of what may be termed 'negotiating order'. It has the hallmarks of a negotiation: there are divergent definitions of the situation, there is also the possibility of compromise (although it may not appear so); those involved operate tentatively and provisionally, particularly Alec, and until quite late in the event there is the possibility that no imposed solution will be forthcoming (Paul remains silent, enigmatic). Looked at in these terms, Alec defines the situation, explores his definition, observes and considers reactions to this exploration, moves ahead in the light of his view of likely reactions and repeats the cycle. George observes Alec's intent and decides whether or not to offer concessions. As I have shown, he offers none but has to reconsider as the encounter develops and is eventually driven to justifying himself and his actions. A compromise is offered: look, lads, it was a matter of holidays, no one to turn to and so forth. This is not offered in a manner likely to win friends and influence people but, significantly, George does feel the need to justify his actions – a step which may be satisfactory to Alec and Hugh, possibly even to Derek. The person they see as usually dogmatic and inflexible has been forced to give and, even more worthwhile, we who pushed him into this do not need to accept his compromise. We have the moral victory.

This perspective implies that Alec and his colleagues 'win' and George loses; they allow the encounter to conclude in the manner that is due, with Derek having the triumphant exit line. It is possible, however, to see the conclusion in quite another light. The rewards to Alec of pursuing George are such that, at each stage save the last, it is worth the chase. The costs that he has to bear are those of George's hostility, until Paul is drawn in, his composure temporarily and successfully disturbed by George's stonewalling, when the circumstances change. The costs of annoying Paul are likely to be much higher, the rewards much less tangible. Paul's power to punish is such as to make even the most subtle of warnings an implicit threat: 'We seem to be making a great fuss over nothing . . .'. Paul is the key actor in most of the interactions, becoming more so with every word he fails to utter. Once he has spoken, given his command over both rewards and punishment, his definition becomes one that must be and is taken into consideration.[13]

Routine Performances

Not all behaviour in organizations has this quality of negotiation and calculation. A great deal of observable interaction has a quality of repetitiveness of a stickleback kind which gives the lie to the points made above. Much of what is seen is routine, even ritual, in character. People, particularly those who have had a long association with each other, share common and pre-established meanings of what is expected of them and they perform more often than not without reflection and deliberation in line with those expectations.

In the first extract that I presented, George may be seen to be 'doing his Cassandra bit' and Paul is responding. The others say little and appear to be uninvolved with the proceedings although they, collectively, are being castigated by George. To an outsider, this appears to be a highly dramatic event, one in which the conspiracy of silence around poor operating results is broken. The response culminating in 'Anyone for coffee?' is surprising. Not so to the participants, however. For them, it seems the situation is routine, something with which they are familiar. They can and do readily name the interaction: 'George-doing-his-Cassandra-bit'. They appear to know the rough shape of the interaction: George will 'sound off', Paul will become 'irritated', George will continue, will be interrupted and 'corrected', will modify his stance somewhat and – barring accidents – the 'outburst' will be contained. The roles, including that of the spectators (whose role in this interaction is to sit and stare impassively), appear to be well known and well rehearsed. The pattern of activities that will occur is broadly known and it strongly resembles those that have taken place on similar occasions. 'We have seen it all before.' In such circumstances, those concerned, Paul, George and the others, can and do perform with relatively little effort; once triggered, the routine script is run off almost automatically.

Routine and problematic interactions are *basically* the same. Similar principles apply to both; the former is simply an example of where the issues associated with the latter have been successfully resolved. Once upon a time, far away and long ago, George's outbursts gave the others problems – they no longer do so. Some time in the not too distant future, the members of the group will resolve into a routine the issues of who controls the presentation of figures or – to be more accurate – it will agree a routine script for handling situations where the issue of control is raised. In the next few paragraphs, we will deal with routine, non-problematic interactions, 'situational scripts' as Schank terms them. In so doing we are, of course, describing and analysing for the sake of understanding; it is a manifest nonsense to talk of the routine patterns in such a conscious manner. Routine interaction has the features we describe; by definition, those who participate in it are not aware of these features as and when they interact. They simply perform.[14]

Knowing and Doing

How do people know what conduct is appropriate to a particular situation? How do I know that as I stand before the judge awaiting sentence for reckless driving, wife beating or massive fraud, he will not whip out a banjo and render a couple of choruses of 'Jubilee Rag'? To be clear, I do not *know* that such a serenade will not occur, but given my experience of similar situations (direct or vicarious), I can take it to be unlikely. Each of us has a general knowledge of how others are likely to interact with us and specific knowledge which enables us to participate appropriately in particular encounters. I perform according to situational scripts. Not that each line and each gesture is necessarily spelled out for me, although in some circumstances they may well be. In court, for example, those of us who are not habitual offenders and have missed out on the major television series (*Perry Mason, Crown Court* and the like) may well need direction. At funerals, although I may well be aware of what is expected of me in a general sense – sober behaviour – I may welcome the specific guidance given to me by the funeral director. In the sense that I am using script here, however, it refers to 'an appropriate sequence of events in a particular context'. Scripts are used to handle relatively stylized everyday situations: there are scripts for eating breakfast, travelling to work, greeting colleagues at work, regular meetings at work; scripts for going to a football match, going to a concert, a restaurant, a visit to the doctor's and so on. I make use of them, you make use of them, frequently without reflection, nearly always without conscious effort.

Scripts refer to circumstances in which the situation is specified, those concerned have a number of reciprocal roles to play and each has a reasonably clear understanding of what is supposed to happen. There is, of course, great social economy in all of this since, once the appropriate script has been identified, no one involved needs to invest much energy in determining how to respond.

Let me return to my executives and look in some detail at the general course of routine interaction. All involved have long experience of meeting in groups, most of them with considerable experience of dealing with each other in this setting. This accumulated knowledge provides each of them with identities and roles and clues as to the 'meaning' to be attributed to events and activities. Thus on the basis of the cues available – the figures that George flashes up, his general demeanour, the words he says and the manner in which he says them – many of those present adopt a shared definition of the situation.

Given a 'correct' interpretation of the event and of George's intent – the role he wishes to adopt in this interaction – there are a limited number of roles open to the others present. Falling about with hysterical laughter as he makes his points is unlikely to fit in with anyone's definition of an appropriate response. Supporting George's analysis is clearly a course of action open to others, as is attacking it (the option Paul chooses) and signalling a kind of bored resignation to it (the option taken by everyone else). Theoretically, at least, those concerned do not behave – do not signal boredom – without considering the impact of that conduct upon George (always assuming that he 'reads' their conduct correctly). Conduct is not random and is rarely arbitrary, it is constructed in the light of one's repertoire and the likely response of others to it.

Experience has taught the actors (other than Paul) that refusing to go along with George's strictures, refusing to feel 'shame' and 'guilt' and signalling that refusal through an unwillingness to interact overtly at all, has consequences that – to them – are rewarding. George does not hit anyone, does not storm out (consequences which may have costs which the 'bored' are unwilling to bear), rather he becomes more irritated and burns out rather like a firework. The tangible silence ('You can almost cut the atmosphere when George starts') also has the benefit of provoking Paul. From George's initial definitions – this is a circumstance in which 'I can read the riot act' – we have others' definitions of the situation (including, of course, their view of what George intends), their plans and reprisals which lead to further definitions and redefinitions, possible revision of plans and further actions.

By following this line we are, of course, claiming that in order for those concerned to be able to understand what is going on in a given situation, they must have been in that situation (or one very similar to it) before. All understanding of routine interaction is, by definition, based upon experience. The actions of others make sense only insofar as they are to be expected; once they cease to conform to expectations, the interaction is rendered problematic. Should George break into dance or, equally bizarre given his usual performance, should he begin to praise the collective achievement of the team, rapid redefinitions would need to occur and different performances may well be elaborated and offered.

Labels and Cues

There remain one or two issues to be teased out of the general outline of routine interaction that I have presented. Defining a situation, as I have shown, involves categorizing it, applying a label to it. Once those concerned have labelled George's comments as his 'Cassandra bit', then they know a lot about its meaning, how to deal with it, how it is likely to end ('Not in a bang, but a splutter'). Having labelled a script, I know who is going to assume what roles, what is likely to be the outcome and who is and is not likely to benefit from the interaction ('It doesn't do much for me, but, presumably, it makes George feel better').

Social actors use a variety of cues to categorize situations. Clearly physical aspects help to categorize encounters (that which in theatrical parlance may be termed 'the setting'). The scripts I have been examining occur within a Boardroom which was described in some detail. Such a setting helps to categorize interactions; people within these hallowed walls are likely to be meeting for business rather than social, religious or recreational purposes. The 'props' that are available reinforce these preliminary cues; had the projector been replaced by a Christmas tree and the screen/charts by streamers and balloons, quite another preliminary categorization would have been in order.

Those in the setting help the categorization. Ladies and gentlemen dressed in overalls equipped with mops and buckets signal a different kind of event in the Boardroom to the one I have been considering. Another group of actors – the Main Board directors – as may be seen from the transcripts, cue those same social actors into different kinds of conduct, different scripts. Appearance may also serve to cue others into the appropriate script. George, it will be recalled, avoided eye contact with his colleagues and appeared both embarrassed and blaming in what he had to say. No doubt George's general demeanour is one factor which enables his colleagues to label the encounter.

As is, of course, what he says and does. George is quite explicit about what he takes the encounter to be: one in which he should beat his breast, rend his garments and cause his colleagues to feel shame and disappointment in their performance as a team. Unfortunately for him, such statements by him and such conduct on his part lead them to define the situation in a different manner – one with which, presumably, they are much more comfortable. Unable to cause them to experience the feelings he wishes upon them (and feels himself), he persists until, checked by Paul and unsupported by his colleagues, he runs down.

Once the script headings, as it were, have served to categorize an event for those involved in it, the rest of it is run off with the minimum of reflection. Here we go, George's Cassandra bit, heads down, say nothing, do not convey approval or disapproval, wait for Paul to come in, pretty soon it will all be over. Time for coffee.

The theory with which we are concerned, of course, suggests that many situations do not promote an examination of beliefs, attitudes and behaviour. It is probable that a great deal of human behaviour is mindless, scripted, routine and non-problematic. It is clear that most of us, much of the time, do not pay attention to what we are doing. We do not actively create relationships *de novo* every time we interact with people we know, nor do we agonize over what piece of behaviour is appropriate in circumstances with which we take ourselves to be familiar. Usually the course of joint action will be outlined in advance and we simply fall in with it. Paul, as an astute Managing Director, knows what to expect of his team and they of him; between them they evolve a characteristic way of behaving. A prerequisite for understanding what occurs in meetings such as those we have been concerned with is to understand the historical context within which the observed interactions take place.

The routine nature of much interaction has led many authors to conclude that structure determines behaviour. Interactionists, however, notwithstanding the obviously routine character of much human behaviour, would deny the primacy of structural characteristics. Knowing something about Paul and his colleagues is important in understanding their actions but in no sense do the rules and norms of behaviour they establish *determine* their actions. Rather patterns of recurrent action determine what is considered to be a rule. Organization is the product of interaction, not the determinant of it; at least, not in a straightforward manner.

As we have seen, novel situations, problematic for the participants in terms of how they are to deal with them, continuously arise as they seek to align their own plans and strategies with those of others seeking to do the same.

Summary

Recapping briefly on the argument to date, the interactionist perspective suggests that the joint or collective action of group or organization, even of society itself, must be viewed as an interlinking of the separate acts of the participants. Failure to recognize the base of any such social action in the individual definitions of the situation and actions of the participants leads the analyst or observer to overlook the fact that any instance of joint action must of necessity undergo a process of formation even though it may appear a well-established and repetitive or routine activity. This formation results from the constituent processes of interpretation, definition and the assignment of meaning to the situation and to the acts of other participants that were discussed at the beginning of this chapter. Social order, thus conceived, is a complex 'balance' of working agreements on the basis of which the participants can proceed to deal with the task in hand or the situation which confronts them. Moreover, any instance of joint action has a limited life – one cannot necessarily assume that agreements reached during one phase of a particular interaction will necessarily be carried over into the next. As I have shown, such agreements are continually worked upon, reconfirmed or rejected during the course of the interaction. Paul and his colleagues may initially agree on definitions, rules of conduct and identities, but these definitions are not fixed for all time or even for the course of the particular interaction; conflicting points of view may emerge at any stage in the proceedings and change the entire basis of the interaction.

In making the process of definition and negotiation central to a model of human interaction, it is possible to cover the full range of human association – cooperation as well as conflict, harmony as well as disagreement. The questions such a perspective poses are those concerned with how it is people align their actions to one another, how it is that association occurs, is maintained and is transformed. Other approaches have stressed that order derives from a sharing of norms and values. Interactionists do not accord primacy to such features. For them the alignment of actions may or may not be the result of the sharing of common values. Paul and his colleagues *may* share values but they may also associate on the basis of compromise, out of duress, out of self interest, out of necessity or whatever. To paraphrase Blumer, from this perspective, organization is nothing more (or less) than the formation of *workable* relations.

3   Rubbing Out and Writing In

It is now time for a spot of alienation, a moment or two of reflection, an opportunity to test theory upon ourselves by becoming somewhat more conscious of what is happening and has been happening in these pages. Might I suggest that you return to the introductory chapter and read the final few pages once more? Concentrate in particular on the section sub-headed 'Language and Metaphor'. What metaphors have been advanced in the last chapter? What concepts have Blumer, Thibaut and Kelley, Goffman and the rest imposed upon the 'hurrying of material, endlessly, meaninglessly'? Have these concepts and the root metaphors which guide them 'foregrounded' things? Are they adequate, clear, consistent, fruitful, plausible? Would George, Paul, Derek, Eric, Brian, Alec and Hugh recognize any of what has been offered as a useful guide to them and to their organization?

The structure that is emerging from these pages is clearly one that holds that it is likely to be worthwhile to treat interaction *as if* it were exchange and negotiation and *as if* it were performance. In offering such views, all kinds of things are assumed or taken-for-granted. For example, it is assumed in theories such as the ones I have outlined that human beings operate in an environment that relies heavily upon language and that they are unique in their ability to use it. It is assumed that humans need other humans and that, by and large, they are rational and purposive creatures. It is also assumed, as it has been for centuries, that humans seek rewards and avoid costs. It is assumed (and was explicitly so done in the Introduction) that humans are capable of becoming conscious, not only of what they are doing but of their very consciousness. Finally, it is assumed by both exchange/negotiated order theorists and performance-oriented speculators that persons are active as well as re-active.

A long list of assumptions each leading to discussion capable of filling a volume; for the moment they are but spectres at the feast, dimly discerned, somewhat unsettling, but not a matter of primary concern.

To return to the foreground: social and organizational life *as if* it were *exchange, negotiation* and *performance*. Have these concepts fore-grounded anything? Caused some degree of re-thinking? All three appear to me to pass this test well, though none is new or particularly shocking. They do, however, offer a degree of disturbance. The notion that most of what you or I do is in the service of some form of self-interest is not quite palatable. Notice, for example, how reluctant I am to write '*all* that you and I do is in the service of self'. Desperate for some acknowledgement of *my* altruism, some reward for my magnifi-cent self-denying self? I might not always seek immediate gratification, but, dislike the notion as I do, I have to allow that much of the time (there I go again!) I am seeking some gratification in the medium or long term. The idea of 'performance' is also mildly disturbing. Me as actor. Putting on a display for others, hamming it up, making a scene, flaunting myself in public. Me as a strolling player, an itinerant Thespian with a limited repertoire in search of a setting in which to perform. The metaphors are interesting, they succeed in drawing attention to aspects of behaviour, they are bothersome but, as a matter of fact, they are also non-deviant. Each entails notions that are the common currency of behaviour in organizations: ideas of costs and reward, of bargaining and compromise, of presentation, display, putting on a good show and so on, all notions to which members of organizations have frequent recourse. The quality of common sense, of taken-for-grantedness, simply asserts the hidden power of the analo-gies. Each, while mildly disturbing if pursued at length, is a near cliché.

Are they adequate, clear, consistent and capable of expansion? Again a matter of heated debate, but in my view, each is adequate (each describes minimally, if not fully, some aspect of behaviour) and each is clear and consistent. Of course, if any of them were to be totally convincing, there would be little point in committing all of this to paper. As I will hope to demonstrate in a moment, neither exchange theory nor the interactionist perspective can stand alone. Both, however, are *relatively* clear, concise and capable of expansion, particularly the notion of conduct as performance.

What About the Natives?

What about the natives? Would they recognize the ideas as pertaining to their world? As it happens, I do have the views of the natives, at least on some of the issues. Although they were not always asked to give their perspectives on the particular interaction to which I have been referring, such was the timing of interviews and conversations with them that many of them did comment. Furthermore, in talking generally about their concerns, they provided extensive data about their view of conduct in organizations and about the dynamics of groups with which they were involved. Their views were presented in not such as sophisticated a form as would be embraced by social scientists, but certainly in a manner which reflected how they attempted to make sense of the interpersonal world. Staying with the note of alienation sounded at the beginning of this chapter, I have to remind you that what follows, of course, is not simply an account; it is my account of their accounts. A filter of filters.

A number of them did indeed see their world as one of exchange: 'You scratch my back and I'll scratch yours.' A view expressed forcefully to me on more than one occasion:

> Look, Iain, although this is not a particularly political company to work in, at least not as political as some I have been in, it doesn't mean that you don't have to watch yourself. Hardly a meeting goes by where one or other of us is not offended by something someone has said about his patch. You try to keep things in balance, try not to transgress, because to do so is to invite retaliation, but it is very difficult. I suppose you could say a lot of the time we collude to avoid trouble. I don't challenge Hugh and he – for the most part – doesn't challenge me. At least, not directly. That way we all avoid trouble.

Derek was more explicit still in commenting upon his support for Alec in his interaction with George about the altered figures. Hitherto, as he readily acknowledged, he had been known as someone who could be relied upon to 'make trouble' for Alec; the two were seen to have a difficult and even contentious relationship. Suddenly, here Derek was strongly supporting Alec: 'What Alec is really saying, but is too polite to say, is that it is up to this group to decide what figures go forward. It's our decision and we certainly didn't agree these.' His explanation was explicit and would bring tears of joy to all red-blooded exchange theorists:

> Derek and I do not normally see eye to eye, but on this issue we were in total agreement. I think the *group* is the decision making body, not Paul and Hugh, Paul and Eric, Paul and whoever. Not everyone agrees with me on that. Many of them prefer the old one-to-one decision making. Alec probably does but on this issue he was clearly against it and it was in my interest to support him on it. Let's hope he remembers when it comes up again.

Some of the exchanges were seen as motivated by the working out of psychological needs. George's 'outburst' about the results which, it will be recalled, was greeted by *most* in silence but was seen by some as a need for him to 'do his thing, his Cassandra bit'.

> George's always doing that sort of thing. I can't remember a meeting going by without him sounding off like that. He needs to do it, just as Paul needs to respond in the way he does. As predictable as bacon and eggs, Laurel and Hardy . . .

Some support, then, for the basic idea of exchange; no one of my executives would be likely to reject as nonsensical a model of conduct which stresses – as that of social exchange stresses – the working out of self interests in interaction. A fair amount of sympathy for the view that much of what occurs in this particular organization is comprehensible in terms of economic motives and processes.[1]

It is highly likely that members of the group would also recognize and find plausible much of the interactionist perspective, although educated as most of them are within a strong positivist tradition, they would find the emphasis upon interpretation and subjective views of 'reality' difficult to accommodate. For most of them, I suspect, there is a 'truth' to be arrived at and colleagues do not simply have different definitions: rather, they are 'wrong'. Nonetheless, they would be able – for the most part – to tolerate the idea that the nature of interaction is essentially processual and would certainly accept that their interpersonal world was, at times, highly problematic and uncertain. They would regret it and hold that it should not be so, but it is likely that they would recognize such a description.

Equally, many of them would accept, some with regret, that management is a performing art:

> You have to hand it to Alec. He comes across as clear and articulate, rational and forceful. He makes it very difficult for anyone to take him on.

Concepts such as 'presentation of self' and 'altercasting' could well have considerable mileage in such a context. Indeed, the relatively slight attention given to performance so far would be a matter of disappointment to them. Their world is one in which the ability to articulate one's concerns and to frame one's behaviour so as to realize plans and purposes is at a premium.

It is likely, therefore, that much of the material contained in the previous forty or fifty pages would be plausible. The format might be somewhat overwhelming, but the message, on the whole, palatable. It is, however, unlikely that they would take to the idea of scripts; they may recognize the substance of what is being said – that much of their behaviour is run off without reflection – but they would object to what they would see as the essentially frivolous nature of the metaphor employed. Life, for many of them, is too serious to be regarded as a 'mere play', an entertainment or a passing show.[2] Concepts such as 'negotiation' and 'negotiated order' would find a much readier acceptance.

It is probable that a number of them would be very disturbed by the fluid nature of the self implied in the discussion of interactionism. Blumer and Goffman, particularly the latter, tend to talk of selves and situations rather than about self in situations. The social actors I am concerned with appear to have a marked sense of self and personalities; they make frequent reference to what they take to be persistent characteristics of themselves and others and offer such attributions as explanations. They would be profoundly disturbed by a framework which denied the notion of an actor behind the parts, a player beyond the roles. The fluidity of the self posited by most interactionists would not accord with their perceptions and would, no doubt, be experienced by them as simply disabling. A world in which one could not act as if attributions were stable would be rendered even more absurd. Nor would they be entirely happy with the treatment of power, or rather the lack of attention to it. They would recognize that power is frequently present as a key element in their definitions and, consequently, in their actions. Interactionists and exchange theorists (at least, those I have paraphrased so far) would be seen to be less than convincing about the element that many practitioners take to be the currency of organizational barter.

Finally, one or two of the more astute of them would notice the absence of any discussion of feelings and emotions. On the one hand, they may well deny that emotion *should* have any place in a theory of organizational conduct – rational behaviour is desirable – but would nonetheless recognize that feelings, emotions and passions are powerful influences upon conduct. A set of ideas which accorded no place for them would not be totally plausible.

What Do the Experts Think?

The natives are not the only ones to note the failings of the perspectives I have examined. Interactionism in particular has been faulted on a number of additional counts.[3] Some commentators have pointed out, for example, that the perspective does less than justice to language. It is language more than anything else which, theoretically, links the work of interactionists from different schools. An adequate account of language, therefore, should underpin any of the variants. Given this, it is curious that so little attention has been devoted to it by interactionists since Mead. In most texts the point is made that language is important and that human actors are unique in that they use a complex set of symbols to align their activities. There is usually little or no discussion about basic principles. What discussion there is is often restricted to the nature of language and/or speculative theories about its development from primitive 'calls'. It is arguable that language is an institution, a set of rules that must be followed if communication is to occur; how such an institution comes about and what constraints it places upon individual definitions and therefore upon their freedom to manoeuvre is something that deserves more discussion by interactionists than it currently receives.

A related criticism concerns the lack of conceptual clarity found in interactionist texts. They abound in ill-defined terms and ambiguities; it has about it a degree of 'fuzziness' that many find unacceptable. Notions such as 'impulse', 'meaning', 'mind', the 'I', 'self' are all 'somewhat vague and fuzzy, necessitating an intuitive grasp of their meaning'. For a paradigm which lays so much stress upon meaning, interactionism appears to have arrived at relatively little consensus with regard to its own key terms.

A further and, in many respects, more substantial criticism of symbolic interactionism has been that it fails to deal with what are termed 'structural variables'. Interactionists are seen to have an astructural or microscopic bias; one that by definition tends to be 'non-economic, ahistorical, and with reference to power politics, apolitical'. Symbolic interactionists have acknowledged 'society' as important, so important that they have paid little or no attention to it. This has resulted, in part at least, from the bias imparted to the perspective by Mead who, rather than beginning with order and working back to individual conduct, operated in precisely the other direction, trying to show how social order emerges from interaction. It is undoubtedly true that interactionists have made a poor fist of relating micro to macro concerns, a point elaborated by Gouldner in his trenchant criticism of Goffman:

> Goffman's rejection of hierarchy often expresses itself as an *avoidance* of social stratification and of the importance of power differences, even for concerns that are central to him; thus it entails an accommodation to existent power arrangements.

The criticism is one frequently voiced: to ignore the notion of structure is to imply that life consists of adjustment to the status quo. *The Presentation of Self*, from this perspective, becomes nothing more than a companion volume to *The Prince*, instructing the masses how to cope with the 'overpowering social structures that they feel must be taken as given'.[4] Not that Goffman himself is anywhere explicit about his commitment to such a view; as with a number of issues, he chooses not to address the point. Nonetheless, it is easy to see the world he describes as one in which social actors struggle to manipulate, deceive, bamboozle (choose what word you will) each other in an attempt to survive. What many interactionists fail to consider is the possibility that some social actors are in a position to 'produce reality' in that they can command resources which strongly influence the definitions held by other actors. Symbolic interactionism purports to describe a society in which all men and women are equal; a characteristic which, when coupled with the terminology of exchange and of performance, imparts an exotic, other-worldly air to the perspective.

Goffman's predilection to ascribe priority to existing structures (without fully discussing how such a predilection comes about) results in a lack of attention to notions such as change: 'While the organization has the power to transform selves, it is apparently unaffected by those persons who constitute its human fabric.' It is to be noted that Goffman's lack of attention to structure and power is of a very different order to the lack of attention found elsewhere in interactionist writings. Goffman, as we have seen, considers stratification, class and differential power to be givens and concerns himself with the 'secondary adjustments' necessary for survival under such circumstances. His actors perform within the confines of a tight, immutable script. Other interactionists simply ignore social structure; for them there is no script. All is open to negotiation. Goffman writes as if there were no changing things; others as if all were flux. Both groups, however, fail to deal adequately with power, politics, stratification and class, and the impact of these features of social/organizational life upon conduct.

Self and Selves

The concern of the natives with self and selves is also manifest in the critical response to both exchange theory and interactionism. Mead, who influenced both Blumer and Goffman, suggested that the 'self must be accounted for in terms of social process'. Doing is being. Echoed by Burke and others, such a view ascribes primacy to action and situation over the individual. The self arises out of interaction; selves are the resultant, not the determinant of conduct. Mead, like Goffman, however, was prepared to hedge his bets a little. He notes an inherent duality to self: the 'I' and the 'me'. The former is the spontaneous, impulsive aspect of the self – the part related to biological urges. Since it is impulsive, this aspect of the self, argues Mead, requires an inhibiting agent. Enter the 'me'. The 'me' is the sum of a history of social responses to expressions of the 'I'. The *social* 'me' gives direction to the instinctive *biological* 'I'.

Goffman's terms for these two processes (it is important to recognize that they are aspects of consciousness, even though we are prone to speak of them as structures or things) travel under a variety of names. The 'I' he severally refers to as 'self as performer', 'self as player', 'our all-too-human selves', and notes that as a process it can be glimpsed within encounters. So the actor can 'forget himself' and 'blurt out a relatively unperformed exclamation', or even 'create a scene' by behaving out of character, i.e. impulsively. There is, argues Goffman

> a crucial discrepancy between our all-too-human selves and our socialized selves. As human beings we are presumably creatures of variable impulse with moods and characters put on for an audience, however, we must not be subject to ups and downs . . .

The 'me' aspect of self Goffman refers to as 'character', 'face', 'the virtual self in context', the 'official self', the 'situated self', and not infrequently, simply 'the self'. The control aspect is obvious in the numerous references Goffman makes to the actor's manifestation of 'self control', attempts to 'cover up on the spur of the moment for inappropriate behaviour' and his efforts to 'suppress his spontaneous feelings'. The important point is that Goffman, like Mead, defines the individual as having a multiplicity of selves, each a response to a different situation. On the other hand, Goffman recognizes that conformity is not automatic; interaction is a precarious achievement, threatened by the impulsive 'I'.[5]

The 'all-too-human self', such as it is, appears to inhabit the interstices – the chinks and crevices – which may be glimpsed occasionally between performed selves which, for the most part, are regarded as *the* determinants of being. The notion of actor *qua* actor is not developed in Goffman; his logic leads him in a different direction. We are only what we do. Occasionally, however, he appears to find this position less than satisfactory and tantalizingly offers something else. Indeed in one passage he writes that 'it is . . . against something that the self can emerge', and defines the human as 'a stance-taking entity, a something that takes up a position somewhere between identification with an organization and opposition to it'.

All very unsatisfactory and something which a more developed model of conduct must address. Is the 'self', as Goffman implies, nothing more than playing at being a self? Am I nothing more than the masks I wear? Nothing more than a repertoire of roles? Such a social science declares that there are roles and that these dramatic roles can make selves. Or is there something else, an actor who shapes the roles? A protean self which undertakes roles without losing its deep structure, its core and its centre? Is there more to the self than Mead's the 'I'?[6]

The Dramaturgical Metaphor

A related criticism, applying particularly to Goffman, is that he and others of his ilk do not do justice to the metaphor they so proudly proclaim: self or selves as performer and performances. It is odd that he should have become the champion of the dramaturgical school when one considers that he makes little use of the analogy and that little is ill-informed. In Goffman's theatrical frame, social actors perform, for the most part, within well-understood, well-rehearsed scripts which they have little or no part in creating. His image of the theatre is that found in textbook and more often than not referred to as 'classical' or 'traditional'. Given the overall conservative cast of his thought, perhaps it is not surprising to find him so ready to adopt this view of theatre; a place for a hierarchy of characters, relating in a predetermined manner to each other through a conversation of well-articulated, well-understood gestures and (although not discussed extensively) emotions. Goffman's ideas, almost without exception, relate to the polished performance of a play – the unacknowledged culmination of several days, if not weeks, of improvisation and rehearsal. He seeks to illuminate everyday social life by reference to fully crafted theatrical performances which occur only on and beyond opening nights. If, as he argues, social life is put together like a play is put together, some attention on his part to how a play *is* put together may well have produced even more interesting reflections than he was able to offer.

Goffman's view of the theatre is a restricted one; not only does it leave out the long rehearsal period (hinted at in his mention of 'backstage areas', but never fully explored), it also fails to address that aspect of the theatre which has almost as long a pedigree as that of classical drama – improvisation. If one takes as one's model the notion of classical drama, one may reasonably conclude – as Goffman does – that much of conduct, both within organizations and without, is determined by the text; the web of expectations and routines established by generations of repetitive performance. Given this use of analogy, one moves, again not surprisingly, to an emphasis upon style and interpretation – Goffman's interest in 'secondary adjustments'. If, on the other hand, one gives some place to improvisation – the theatrical activity by which that which emerges is the result of a complex interplay between actor and actor and actor and audience – one's conclusions about the nature of social conduct are likely to be different. The latter offers the possibility of escape from what Durkheim once termed the 'coerciveness of social life'; the former, Goffmanesque position constrains and constricts.[7]

A Matter of Emotion

Interactionists, with one or two honourable exceptions, do not deal adequately with emotion.[8] Mead was not much interested in the emotional element in behaviour and was adamant that the self should be regarded as cognitive. Throughout his work, the emphasis remains on the rational rather than the emotional or non rational. He was followed down this line by Blumer who did, however, note in an early paper that much of our expressive behaviour was emotional and – presumably – functional, since it served to dramatize our claims to be treated in a particular manner. The 'affective nature' of interaction, however, was not something that he followed up, leaving what comments there are to be found scattered around several texts. Goffman does devote several pages to an analysis of embarrassment, treating the emotion as a result or consequence of inconsistent performance rather than a cause of it but, to the best of my knowledge, he makes little or no attempt to deal with any other emotions.

There are a number of reasons for this apparent neglect. First, and perhaps most importantly for those of an interactionist persuasion, given as we are to essentially phenomenological and self-report methods, affective reactions can be exceedingly difficult to put into words. Like generations of novelists, poets and playwrights, we can point to and label passions such as love, jealousy, hatred, pride and the like, but for the most part we have great difficulty in putting into words adequate descriptions of the often subtle and complex phenomena that these labels mark. Emotion is conceptually and linguistically difficult to articulate. The more so since the models that we do have (both at a common-sense level and that popularized by psychoanalysts such as Freud) are essentially hydraulic ones which depict the passions as located somewhere deep inside us. Occasionally feelings well up, burst forth or erupt and, overwhelmed by them, we have difficulty in regaining control, effecting an adequate piece of psychological plumbing, as it were, let alone pausing to relish and identify each and every element of the experience. The hydraulic metaphor tends also to imply that, like burst pipes, emotions are things that happen to us; we, as individuals, have no part in them as agents, but are simply victims. We 'fall' in love, are 'seized' with a fit of anger, are 'stricken' by grief, 'haunted' by guilt and generally 'carried away' by one form of passion or another. For most interactionists emotions, with their obvious and measurable physiological attributes and their apparent location beyond the reach of the mind (other than in psychoanalysis, a strange school, even less reputable than their own), are best left out of account. Like the compiler of Webster's dictionary, they evidently take passion to be 'the state of being subjected to or acted upon by what is external and foreign to one's true nature'.

The Rational Bias

A related criticism and a powerful one is that both exchange theorists and symbolic interactionists have it wrong, since they place such a heavy emphasis upon cognition as a guide to behaviour. Exchange theory, as I have shown, implies that social actors calculate possible returns; indeed, without the premise that actors do adopt a cognitive stance towards the circumstances with which they are confronted, the theory becomes worthless. Interactionists similarly lay stress upon 'the definition of the situation' and upon the ability to simulate and 'mentally rehearse' both one's own potential actions and those of others. Full rationality would require that each actor would need to consider all empirically possible alternatives and the consequences of each before they did anything at all. Such a course of action is not possible. Instead, people consider (when they consider at all) only a limited subset of all possible alternatives; each of us chooses on the basis of less than complete knowledge.

But even the level of choice is questionable. As I have indicated, much of social interaction is not accomplished in this fashion, much of it appears to be run off without deliberation, without reflection. The basis of social order is ultimately tacit, not capable of verbalization, and as such beyond the comprehension of any individual. The best that words can do is to bestow meaning retrospectively. What I have been doing in the last chapter and part of this one is to impute meanings to my performers. Each of them is in a position, should they so desire, to do something similar. Normally, however, neither I nor they would verbalize what it is we are about and certainly not as we are about it, because to do so fundamentally alters the event. Try talking your way through your next interaction with someone, talking, that is, as a process of becoming aware of and making choices about the process of encounter itself rather than about its content. It will not only be regarded as somewhat bizarre (depending, of course, on the company you keep), it will prove to be impossible since, for example, the *activity* of talking itself results in talking but is itself not capable of being verbalized. Many elements of communication operate at a tacit, non-verbal level.

Beginning Again – Nearly

Those, then, are some of the strictures that have been applied to interactionism in general and the dramaturgical school in particular. A more developed approach ought, it is claimed, to be at once less vague and ambiguous in its terminology, less astructural in its bias, more able to accommodate notions of language and talk, power and politics, emotions and the self and be more comprehensive in its use of its root metaphor.

I can make no pretence to offer such an approach. The best I can do is offer in the next two or three chapters notes towards the construction of such an approach. Some, such as those concerned with power, emotion and the self are extensive, others such as those concerned with language and the astructural bias of interactionist thought are somewhat thinner. The terminology used remains vague and ambiguous not only because of its essentially provisional nature ('notes towards . . .') but also because I subscribe strongly to Blumer's ideas on the development of theory. Like him, I accept that the main task of concepts is to *sensitize* us to the social world. A sensitizing concept gives general guidance: 'Whereas definitive concepts provide prescriptions of what to see, sensitizing concepts merely suggest directions along which to look . . . They rest on a general sense of what is relevant.' Sensitizing concepts offer *creative* and *imaginative* ideas about what to look for.[9]

Such qualitative approaches are consistent with that which interactionists take to be the nature of social reality. Social life is not static, not a series of discrete activities capable of being reduced to a question of simple responses to simple measuring devices. There are, of course, circumstances in which behaviour is readily observable and capable of being measured: who speaks, how many times they interrupt, who takes turns with whom and so on. Much of our observation of interpersonal relations – of encounters such as those in the Boardroom – however, involves us in judgements and evaluations. As an observer I have to form a judgement as to the intentions of particular social actors (just as those more directly involved have to make inferences) – an act of imaginative role taking. Such activities are an essential part of being human and cannot be written off as unimportant because they do not accord with the canons of scientific procedure. All science develops through the use of constructive or creative imagination. Social science has no other route, the development of our understanding 'has to be done in a slow and tedious manner . . . developing a rich and intimate familiarity with the kind of conduct that is being studied and employing whatever relevant *imagination* the observer may fortunately possess'. In what has gone before and in what follows, the concepts, such as they are, are imprecise and no attempt will be made to give them neat, standardized definitions nor will any experimental or quantitative procedures be called upon to demonstrate their validity or reliability. The ideas that I am seeking to outline should become less precise as they are filled out or *grounded* by reference to the behaviour of our heroes but, throughout, it should be remembered that my purpose is illumination rather than verification – a purpose which renders much of that which is taken to be proper scientific procedure at best premature.

4   Today We Improvise

One of the elements of both interactionist and exchange theory with which I was and still am unhappy is the heavy reliance upon words and phrases deriving from economics and the practice of negotiation. Throughout these pages, I have adopted the view that an individual offers a definition of the situation, proposes a course of action which is evaluated by others present who decide whether or not they wish to go along with the line suggested. On the basis of this conclusion about what they take to be the first individual's intentions, they frame their responses. If they aim to reject the suggested course of action, they proffer a counter-proposal which, in turn, may be accepted or rejected and a series of exchanges will occur until a working agreement is arrived at or the interaction is abandoned.

Clearly the framework is useful for describing the course of interaction; equally clearly it is appropriate for describing and explaining the actual process of specific interactions. Some interactions *are* negotiations. The individuals are aware that offers are being made and that counter-offers are expected, they are also aware that a compromise is possible. As I have indicated earlier, the metaphor is likely to be useful when considering novel rather than routine situations.

The metaphor of performance, which has an equally long pedigree, is likely to be of more value in addressing the habitual and the expressive. In a sense, the performances that Paul and George enact between them are not negotiations. They are expressions of what each takes himself and the other to be, rather than simply instrumental attempts to resolve particular problems. What they do together is of symbolic importance more than anything else. To conceive of performance in this manner is to conceive of it as does Turner, who holds that performances are the way that individuals reveal reality to themselves and others. The Paul/George interchange and that of Eric/Alec may be seen from this perspective to have an expressive, almost ritual character with each duo doing nothing more nor less than enacting their divergent perspectives for no other purpose than to confirm their reality. Like Hallowe'en, or Christmas celebrations, or May Day parades, their importance lies in the assertion of the ritual rather than in it achieving any particular end.

Conceiving of what is going on between executives as a matter of performance highlighting the dramaturgical nature of interaction allows a number of entailed notions to be addressed. First, I have chosen to depict a number of *scenes*. George and Paul have been through their particular routine at other times and in other settings; the performance they give in the Boardroom on this particular afternoon has both retrospective and prospective features. What they each do is seen by themselves and their audience in the light of what they have enacted in the past. A departure from the ritual would no doubt be remarked upon; either or both of the actors would have to adjust and the audience would certainly feel the need to comment. If, for example, George were not to adopt his hectoring, shame-attributing stance and were to announce instead that, having looked at the figures, he had no comment to make one way or the other, the departure would be such as to create a novel situation. All others party to the interaction would need to render the departure meaningful. Given previous enactments in what are taken to be similar circumstances, George *not* doing-his-Cassandra-bit renders all else problematic. His failure to be simply expressive has implications for all present; the ritual has been violated.

The scene has also to be understood prospectively. The performance George and Paul engage in is related to a later scene scheduled for the same room, but with different actors: the members of the Board. Paul's specific injunction, his urge to cut off George's expressive flow, is directly related to this prospective scene. George, who has no intention of performing in this manner later, believes that the present cast should be given the full benefit of his self and other abasement. Like scenes from a play, specific performances are historically embedded in a larger sequence of events. All concerned make sense of present performances in the light of past ones and in anticipation of future ones. Like a play, behaviour in organizations involves a multiplicity of actions and meanings which constitute the context for a particular scene or interchange.

Another important consequence of adopting a dramaturgical perspective on conduct is that it enables me to talk about improvisation and scripted performances. I introduced the idea of scripts in chapter 2 and wish to re-emphasize that script does not imply that each word of the interaction is predetermined. George and Paul put on a similar performance time after time without necessarily using the same phrases and expressions. The general shape of the performance is known and followed; the specifics may be varied from time to time. Each actor present is able to identify the scene – one in which George abuses us all and Paul becomes angry – and perform broadly along the well-rehearsed lines that have evolved for such scenes.[1]

It is possible to extend the analogy and conceive of what goes on in organizations as a series of performances by a Commedia dell' Arte troupe. The essential fact about the Commedia is that it consists of a constellation of characters who remain the same regardless of the plot they find themselves embroiled in. Like Morecambe and Wise, Stan Laurel and Oliver Hardy, the Marx Brothers and Margaret Dumont, wherever they find themselves, whatever the situation, George, Paul, Alec and Eric remain the same. Paul is perceived by his colleagues to be part autocratic part affection-seeking, Eric churlish and irascible, Alec intelligent and aloof, driven by suppressed aggression, and so on. Each has at his command a stock of ways of projecting and protecting those aspects of them selves and each has bits of 'business' he can draw upon to reinforce his character. Eric jabs his spectacles, Hugh takes time filling his pipe and focuses a great deal of his energy on lighting it, Alec nervously pops mints into his mouth, Paul draws his pen on the table, George is forever pushing his spectacles up. Each in his own way has the ability to supply a line, provide a joke or develop a point *within* character; they are thus able to improvise within a variety of situations. Like any good troupe, their genius lies in their apparent spontaneity. Only the players who are also the audience know the line has been used before, the joke is an old one, the point is laboured and, on occasions, even they are surprised.[2]

What is occurring in the Boardroom is not a tightly scripted, thoroughly rehearsed, minutely directed naturalistic piece of theatre. Rather it is more of an improvisation around a *scenario*. A scenario, or *canovaccio* (canvas), is a schematic description of the performance: it provides the broad theme around which a Commedia improvisation will occur. The theme for Eric's improvisation with Alec and Hugh, for example, may be seen as a kind of David and Goliath, one in which Eric takes on the world as poor, downtrodden David (Parts and Service) and although destined (in this version) to lose, will draw blood from Goliath (the Main Business). Against this canvas, the social actors improvise their sallies, operating not out of a negotiated or exchange framework but out of a kind of theatrical intuition which enables each of them to know how to support or feed, whether by words or action, the others involved in the drama. They must be sure of not straying too far from the main subject, their asides and impromptus must not be too obscure and too divorced from the theme, and each must be able to pick up the cues and return to the theme so that chaos and confusion does not ensue. Each actor, however, has scope for invention and a freedom which allows all concerned the thrill of participation. Social actors with a degree of investment in their roles such as George, Alec, Paul and Eric give splendid ensemble performances. They cue, prompt, support and feed each other against canvasses they have no difficulty in recognizing and display a degree of spontaneous delight in so doing.

Improvisation in the sense that I wish to claim for it is the freedom to depart from the text (the expected words and phrases), the freedom to change the emphasis in certain scenes and to vary the 'business'. It is a difficult notion to grasp, the kind of attempt at a sensitizing concept I foreshadowed earlier, so it may be worth expending a further paragraph or two on it. I will begin by quoting from a seventeenth-century book, say something about actors and then attempt to address the nature of improvisation in social life. First the quote from one Andrea Perrucci, 'Dell' Arte rappresentation premeditata e all' improviso':

> The players stand round in a circle so that all may hear the explanation of the choragus (a kind of actor-manager), nor do they rely on knowing their parts by heart or on having many times previously played in the same comedy, since they must all be in accord with new variations introduced by different choragi in the development of the plot, and also because the names and places may be different . . .
>
> When they have heard all the the characters who have to make exits and entrances and deciding on the ending up of scenes, they can agree with their colleagues about some fresh lazzo (joke or jest) or some new piece of stage business; and can also be sure of not straying too far from the main subject . . . Therefore all the impromptus and additions must adhere to the theme of the comedy so that it will not be too long drawn out. Thus the actors will be able to pick up their cues and return to the plot without forgetting what the comedy is all about, and this will enable those who wander too far from the subject to find their places again, so that the whole affair does not become a confused chaos.

It will be seen from this that I am pushing for a definition of improvisation beyond the commonplace, one that holds that it is an activity which requires no preparation and obeys no rules. Actors on the stage improvise as part of their training and, on occasions, they perform 'improvisations' as did the Commedia dell' Arte. To do so they must know what they are doing; they must know the general framework on which to base their improvisation. They must have some idea of who is supposed to be who, what is to be outlined in the various scenes and how it is all to be resolved. Given this, they can and they do develop their own lines and weave their performances into the performance as a whole.

It is likely that in watching an improvisation organized by Mike Leigh, for example, one could pick up a theme introduced by one or more characters, observe other characters developing and elaborating that theme whilst others echo or accompany it. As any one actor improvises, he or she draws upon his or her knowledge of themes like this and relates it to variations introduced by others; it may even be a theme they have enacted previously. It is likely that performers will take turns elaborating the theme, perhaps they may even do it in pairs or trios before the group resolves it with some form of recapitulation. In performing as he or she does, the particular actor takes into account not only the theme but also the features of their fellow performers and the audience, adjusting actions in the light of this knowledge.

I do not need to labour the analogy. A similar structure may be observed in social life. When George and Alec come together in the Boardroom they have a sense of why it is they have come together, and the specific and the possible range of topics they might talk about. Social actors no less than stage actors have a sense of the thematic structure that they are involved in and they frequently allow each other to take turns in developing the improvisation. What I do wish to stress is the apparent spontaneity of all this; everything appears to happen out of natural impulse. *Apparent* because, of course, the capacity to improvise alongside a particular group of social actors depends as it does for stage actors upon some knowledge of the theme and the performers. It is extremely difficult to improvise (in the sense outlined here) when thrust into strange circumstances in the company of strangers.

Not that this is an issue for Paul and his fellow Thespians. Most of their interactions are of this nature, improvisations around agreed themes. As social actors who have worked together and who know each other's strengths and limitations, they recognize when they can depart from the text, change the emphasis and vary the 'business'. Each performance is unique but each relates to one (occasionally more) of a limited number of themes. Interaction is run off largely without reflection once the script headings have enabled those involved to recognize what type of performance is required of them. They go into their routines with scarcely a backward look: 'I say, I say, I say, who was that lady I saw you with last night?' 'That was no lady, that was the Prime Minister.'

What then are the themes, the scenarios around which the players improvise? It is possible on looking back at the material in chapter 1 to argue that the scenes are concerned with George's anger, with Eric's sense of exclusion, with the group's sense of being pissed off with George for sending the figures to Manchester and with their sense of elation at finding the headquarters group at fault. Possible but misguided, since such an analysis would be in danger of mistaking the effect for the theme. George's anger is related to a theme but is not the theme itself. What underlies the scenes I have presented and all forms of interpersonal relations (whether based upon exchange models or not) are the twin themes of power and status. All human social interaction is based upon relations of power and status.

Clearly I need to say a little more in justification of that rather bald statement and much of the rest of the chapter will be devoted to supporting it. For the moment, however, I wish to do no more than assert that the idea of a two-dimensional model to describe and explain social life has widespread support. Writers and researchers often find in their studies of interaction and interpersonal relations a dimension that reflects the notion of power (variously termed threat, coercion, domination or control) and a dimension that relates to status (variously termed voluntary compliance, respect, affection, trust and the like). It is possible to assert, therefore, on the basis of a convergence of theory and empirical research that the themes which occupy my performers are the same that occupy all groups involved in complex social activities: those of power and status. There is nothing more or less to observe in my executive group than improvisations around issues of power and status.[3]

Power always has about it an element of coercion. It may be seen as a process by which one individual (or group) extracts compliance from another individual (or group) despite a conflict of interests or intentions, through the control or proposed manipulation of resources/commodities which the other individual (or group) values.

Such a formulation implies that power is a collective transaction. No individual (or group) simply has power as an attribute or capacity. Power is something that occurs between people; it is a relational concept.[4] One individual – the source of control – signals his or her intent, demands support or compliance with it and manipulates or threatens to manipulate valued resources to secure such support or compliance. The other individual – the target of control – interprets the source's intent, assesses the consequence of non-support or non-compliance and constructs what he takes to be appropriate action. The source and the target are interdependent; the source requires a party from whom to extract compliance, and the target requires a source with whom to comply for power to be said to exist.

Let us take the concluding comments of the encounter between Paul and George in the first of my scenes as an illustration.

Paul: I don't like the stance you are taking, George. I don't like it one little bit. I trust you are not going into next week's full Board meeting with this sort of approach . . .

George: Of course not! I know what's expected of me there! . . .

For power to be said to be evident in the relationship, Paul needs George and George needs Paul; the relationship is not simply one of dependency, each needs the other.

Equally clearly, power can be seen to be goal-orientated. Both Paul and George may be said to share a common objective: compliance. Compliance provides Paul with a show of deference and, presumably (my experience is imagined, not realized), provides George with the gratification of having avoided punishment. It is worth noting that the source designates the gratifications that George, as the target, is to receive – both what it is, and how much of it he is to have. Nonetheless it is still possible for George (or any target in any situation) to refuse to play the game; the consequences may be dire, but fundamentally Paul's gratification depends upon George's agreement to provide it for him. Power always and inevitably involves a common objective and is subject to negotiation and adjustment. This is not to say that power is symmetrical, but nor is it entirely asymmetrical either. Paul and George are in a power relationship only so long as George is willing to submit.

It is worth stressing that in a power relationship, as in any other, the source and the targets improvise order; they interpret one another's gestures and align their actions in the light of those interpretations. Consider again the exchanges between Paul and George in the first of the scenes presented earlier. Paul signals to George that he would like him to comply with his views of the circumstances: 'George, it's not worse . . .' George either does not read this signal or chooses to ignore it, with the result that Paul is forced to adjust by communicating his views in a more forceful manner, raising his voice and asserting himself. Again George ignores him and Paul becomes specific: 'Look, George, I am tired of telling you . . .' George continues to treat his boss's strictures as unimportant and forces him into declaring 'I don't like the stance you are taking . . . I trust you are not going into next week's Board meeting with this sort of approach.' When a target resists, the source must seek to overcome it.

It follows from all of this that a further distinctive feature of power is the element of conflict. Paul probably can carry out his wishes (to have his optimistic view of events prevail) despite resistance from George. As Etzioni puts it, power is characterized by the source's 'capacity to overcome part or all of the resistance', to do something in the face of potential or actual opposition. If George readily agrees with Paul, shares his perspective, I cannot and do not talk about power and compliance.

Finally, as implied above, power involves intentions. Paul speaks in the manner that he does with the clear intent of causing George to behave differently and, in the final passage, George signals his intent to meet Paul's demands. Power is only present where there is some implied or actual threat or reward to secure compliance. George may well perceive, as Paul's tone and general demeanour changes towards him, that persisting in his self and other castigation will lead to Paul withholding some benefit from him or even – God forbid – taking him at his word and inviting him to leave.[5]

Profit and Power

It should be clear from the previous few paragraphs that I am holding firmly to the view that such transactions as do occur within power relationships arise from and operate within a framework deriving *ultimately* from exchange theory: that is not to claim that the social actors consciously negotiate within such a framework. I cannot go much further without introducing some ideas deriving from a non-interactionist, Peter Blau, whose major contribution to that which I am concerned with here lies in his exploration of the origin and consequences of power in social relations.[6] He notes that the 'paradox' of social exchange is that it serves not only to establish bonds of friendship between peers (what Simmel terms 'the bond of interaction'), it also creates and maintains differences between persons. Supplying benefits to others may serve as an expression of friendship, but it may also serve as a means of 'establishing superiority over them'. A benefactor creates obligations and implicitly claims superiority to those he obligates.

To illustrate: Derek renders an important service to Alec and in obligating him implicitly gains superior status. If Alec is in a position later to return the benefits, he discharges the obligation and, in so doing, denies Derek's claim to superiority. Derek, for example, supports Alec's claims to discuss the alterations in the budget and, for a time, theoretically, Alec is in debt to him. Although on the same hierarchical level, Derek has a claim upon Alec and is thus morally, even if not hierarchically, in a superior position. If Alec supports Derek in some interaction with others that both recognize as the rough equivalence of the previous service rendered to Alec, then the debt is discharged. If, however, Alec supports Derek in some event that manifestly outweighs the previous obligation, then Alec effectively makes a counterclaim to superiority in the relationship. If, however, Alec fails or is unable to reciprocate with benefits that are as important to Derek as the latter's are to Alec, the former's claim to superiority is validated.

It follows that the ability unilaterally to supply important benefits is a basic source of power. In the final analysis, Paul's ability to control and shape the conduct of his managers is dependent upon the resources at his disposal. The attainment of power, Blau notes, is dependent upon four conditions. First, those to be subjected must not themselves have resources that the benefactor needs, otherwise they are in a position to bargain. Second, there must be no alternative sources of supply; they need the particular benefactor. Third, they must be unable to take by force the benefits they desire. Fourth, they must not undergo a shift in values such that what they previously desired is no longer desirable. If, argues Blau, these 'four conditions are met, they have no choice but to comply with his wishes and to submit to his power in order to obtain the needed benefits'.

To return to our transcripts once more. We can infer both from what is said and what is not said that Paul has a considerable degree of power over the others present. Not that it is absolute, but it does appear sufficient. In the third scene, for example, we see the beginnings of a revolt: 'What Alec is really saying, but is too polite to say, is that it is up to this group to decide what figures go forward.' The implication is that Paul needs the support of the group, more openly stated later: 'About who decides, that's what!'. The revolt, however, peters out, demonstrating all too clearly that Paul does not feel that he needs their support. The members of the group acquiesce, recognizing with varying degrees of consciousness that they are not in a position to bargain. Paul controls access to Manchester, as he controls decisions about promotion, remuneration and, ultimately, the employment, or unemployment, of those present. The position will be changed if, and only if, the other members of the group find means of forcing him out or changing their values such that the rewards he is able to dispose of are no longer relevant to them.

Under such conditions as most of us work in, then, the exchange processes promote differences in power. Someone like Paul, who has at his disposal benefits that others cannot do without, who is *relatively* independent of any services that others may render to him (a point which we will take up later), and in a circumstance where benefits cannot easily be obtained elsewhere nor taken from him by force, can attain and maintain power over others by making satisfaction of their needs (for employment, remuneration, approval and the like) contingent upon their willing compliance with his directives. Under such circumstances, subordinates begin to talk of the 'rights of the boss' and their own 'obligations' to do what he wishes.[7]

Thus it is that relationships that may be seen as beginning as ones of mutual advantage are transformed into power relations. There is a basic difference between power and mutual social exchange, just as there is a basic difference between social and economic exchange. The criterion which creates the distinction is one of control. In economic exchange, the exact conditions of repayment are specified when the transaction occurs. I will pay for my car at monthly intervals until the end of 1986. In mutual social exchange, the nature and timing of the return are decided upon by the person who benefits. I, who have just benefited from a Christmas drink with my neighbour will decide when and in what form (if at all) I will reciprocate – a drink, a dinner, a loan of a lawn mower. In power relations, however, the return is made on the demand of the one to whom it is owed; the creditor calls the tune. Unilateral dependence transforms a relation between peers into a power relation between superior and subordinate.

The exercise of power, of course, need not be overt. Paul does not confront his group with issues of employment and reward. For the most part, they comply willingly with his directives, they 'go along' with him in the direction he wishes to take. That is because they collectively approve of his power (they, in turn, benefit from such an approval in their own dealings with their subordinates). When considering Paul's directives, his subordinates judge them in terms of social norms of fairness. Should they consider his demands unfair, or worse, exploitative or oppressive, they will cease to regard the exercise of his power as legitimate. As Blau so concisely puts it: 'Collective approval of power legitimates that power.' In complex situations, the differentiation of power gives rise to other social processes which, Blau argues, may be conceived of as constituting 'a secondary exchange that becomes superimposed upon the primary one characteristic of interpersonal relations'. More of this in a moment. First, building upon Blau's ideas, more about the sources of power.[8]

Persons and Offices

The sources of power are basically twofold (though other writers may make finer distinctions than will be presented here): positional and personal. Paul's office or structural position provides him with the potential for exercising power: he can hire and fire, he can promote or demote, give or withhold money, he can manipulate important symbolic rewards (titles, access to meetings, parking spaces) and he is clearly party to information that others are not. Other offices, that of George for example, provide him with access to information (he may be aware of financial details denied to his colleagues and even to Paul), but he is not able to hire and fire his peers.

Clearly, office or structural position is an important source of potential power. It is not the only source nor necessarily the most important one. Personal characteristics are also important; in some circumstances more important. Alec, for example, is much more articulate, much more verbally skilled than Eric. He makes the most of his office and whatever knowledge comes his way. He marshals his arguments and argues with a verbal dexterity which is the envy of some of his colleagues; Eric makes his point and doggedly repeats it again and again. Not, in this situation, the way to win friends and influence people. Neither Alec nor Paul, however, could be said to display charismatic power; those extraordinary and quasi-mystical characteristics which Weber held to be the distinguishing features of great leaders. Religious leaders may be said to have it (Jesus Christ, Buddha, St Augustine), national figures (Winston Churchill, Joseph Stalin, Napoleon, de Gaulle, Adolf Hitler), even some captains of industry (Henry Ford, Sir Michael Edwardes). It is, however, a slippery concept and, like leadership itself, difficult to distil into specific attributes and characteristics.[9]

The amount of potential power each actor possesses derives in part from their office and its perceived importance in the organization. The potential for power, therefore, may be said to derive from the division of labour and the importance ascribed to certain offices within that division. Not, please note, that *demonstrated* importance is the critical element; in other times and cultures, priests, soothsayers, sociologists, operational researchers and all manner of persons have been accorded potential power on the *belief* that what they had to say was important to an enterprise.

Potential power is also personal. Paul's position, his location in the structure, provides him with considerable potential power. Others in the group may occupy important offices (George, for example, may have exclusive knowledge in the finance area) but, for much of the time, given the setting within which we are concerned with them, his exercise of potential power is largely a personal one. Neither George nor his peers can coerce one another (except through Paul), and they cannot offer or deny money (though they can and do offer support and blame). Through recourse to personal characteristics, verbal dexterity, charisma, transparent honesty and integrity or whatever, they can only seek to enhance the value of whatever knowledge they may possess.

What is it we are saying about the nature of social relationships? Primarily that the division of labour not only facilitates exchange, but that it also creates a degree of dependence and thus may give one person (or group of persons) potential power over another or others. This point was well understood by the exchange theorists whose work we considered in chapter 2. There it was argued that exchange and dependence were key features of most social relations: that without dependence there would be no reason for exchange, since neither party would need the other to accomplish his or her end. Dependence exists everywhere that one actor's outcomes are contingent upon the responses and actions of another. Potential power, in turn, is a function of perceived dependence. Paul's power (in part) is a function of George's perceived dependence upon him. Insofar as George thinks that he is unable to achieve his ends without the assistance of Paul, the latter is powerful. Dependence, it was further outlined, was determined by comparison levels for alternatives. Paul's power is ultimately a function of how far George and his colleagues, individually and collectively, can achieve desired ends in a setting which excludes Paul and how far they value the particular outcomes they are attempting to achieve with him. If they can achieve their ends elsewhere, his potential power is relatively low (their dependence upon him, that is, is slight); if they are not much exercised by the particular ends, again Paul's influence is a matter of little consequence.

Such a concept, of course, highlights the importance of definitions. What particular actors *construe* as alternatives and dependencies become key aspects of the power–dependence relation. What George *takes* to be his alternatives, what he *takes* to be his degree of dependence, influences his conduct. In pure exchange theory (as in pure economics), actors have complete information on the market; they know the alternatives and the relative costs/benefits. In life, however, actors do not have perfect information, nor, given our individual needs to achieve personal ends, are we likely to supply or be supplied with the necessary information. Paul, for example, may have little or no ability to influence the person to whom he reports in Manchester. It is not in his best interests to divulge this to George or to any of the others. It is likely to be in his interest (or, to be more precise, he is likely to see it as being in his interest) to manage the impression he gives and gives off so as to suggest that he is more influential than he knows himself to be. George and the others are thus deprived of important information and conduct themselves in the light of the definitions they *are* able to form in such circumstances. Again, as we have seen, the management of impressions is a crucial aspect of interaction in the building of working relations. Dependence is a dimension of power; manipulating others' perceptions of it is a central concern of all those who would exercise dominance in social relationships.

Part of Paul's potential power derives from his ultimate control of the resources, not only those which are to be supplied to each of his managers (important though this may be to those around the table), but also to each and every one of them as individuals. As Managing Director, the merit element of each man's pay is in his gift. He controls and provides what may well be an important resource, not only for what can be purchased with the income but also for what it signals. Money in many organizations is a symbol: I am paid a handsome amount so I must be valued. I must be worthwhile, I must be thought to be doing a good job. If I am a person of private means, the purchasing power is a matter of little or no consequence, but the fact that a large or small amount has been awarded to me is a matter of consequence.

Paul's office, of course, is more important than as a source of private income; through him, for it is he who argues the case for the Division at Manchester, each of the others derive the money to operate their departments. Upon him and his skill at milking the company, the survival of all around the table is taken to be dependent. This power, of course, is not absolute; the survival of the enterprise is thought to depend at various phases upon the development of the product, the ability of those concerned to make it in appropriate numbers at an appropriate quality at an appropriate cost, and upon the ability of the sales force to sell it. The point I am making is no more than an illustration. In the setting with which we are concerned, Paul appears to have power since he can exercise discretion over the allocation of money to individuals and to the departments or units for which they are responsible. At other times and on other occasions, it could be that one or other of them is in a position of relative power since he controls a valued resource that Paul (or others) require. It is as well to remember that Paul's potential power depends upon staying in office and to stay in office he must fulfil his obligations to Manchester. To fulfil these obligations, he needs the support of his colleagues; if the output of one of his general managers appears to be critical to Paul remaining in office then, clearly, that manager has power, however temporarily, greater than Paul.

The Managing Director, therefore, is thought to be powerful because he controls whatever funds are available. (The fact that he may choose to plan and allocate through a Budget Committee does not alter the argument; in the last resort, he decides.) In our example, Paul is considered important and powerful because it is he and he alone who deals with the great unknown – Manchester. In the literature concerned with power in organizations, this is referred to under 'strategic contingency theory' as 'coping with uncertainty'. Eschewing the jargon, what this means is that Paul (or any actor/unit) is powerful to the extent that he or his office appears to cope with important uncertainties that no one else is thought to be in a position to deal with. Manchester – the Head Office – has contact with a number of the executives around our table, but on important matters, such as the levels of profit to be achieved, the reduction or expansion of plant, the nature of the product to be manufactured, it deals directly and exclusively with Paul. Manchester is the major unpredictable uncertainty with which this executive group has to deal and Paul is central and not substitutable in those interactions. He is able to declare what is or is not likely to be 'acceptable to Manchester' and he, alone, conveys the attitudes and beliefs of his executives to his superiors and, of equal importance, the attitudes and opinions of his superiors to his own subordinates.

Given the idea of centrality in coping with uncertainty, it can be seen that, in certain circumstances, power may be seen to accrue to other functions and individuals. Assume that, for example, the international currency situation became less stable; given that much of the company's earnings are made overseas, the ability of George, the Finance Director, to cope with the uncertainty could be seen to be of considerable importance to the organization and his potential power enhanced accordingly.

In both examples, those of Paul and of George, power appears to depend ultimately upon knowledge. Paul controls his subordinates by revealing to them the directives coming from Manchester (having, of course, striven long and hard to convince his superiors of the case for Friction Free Castings Ltd). George has the knowledge and expertise to deal with the currency situation. It is important to both of them that they are seen as irreplaceable; it is not in George's interest to reveal the mysteries of international currency dealing, although it may be in everyone else's to seek to discover them.

Control of resources, and both having the ability and being in a position to cope with uncertainty are not the only features associated with perceived power. Paul appears in arenas (Manchester) to which the others have only limited access, and is present at different levels of decision making. He is involved with choices made by his own team and is part of the decision process at Manchester; he can affect the process at levels that his colleagues cannot (although they, of course, may have been involved in the formulation of proposals at levels below to which he has not been party). It follows that he is in a position to influence, if not control, the decision premises and/or the basic objectives at several levels, a power perceived to be not wholly open to his immediate subordinates. He knows, for example, that the 'figures for Manchester are not important', since he has experienced the changes which occur at that level; his colleagues do not have this information but, more importantly, they do not have the opportunity to participate in the discussion at that level. Such changes as are made and the manner in which they are made are beyond their experience.

Tiresome though it may be to labour the point, it is an important one. Decisions are largely the product of the parameters which surround them; given X, Y and Z, what decision is viable? Those who define or who participate in defining X, Y and Z (or any one of the constraints) are potentially more powerful than those who make the decision within the boundaries set for them. George, Derek and others can talk about the business of Friction Free Castings Ltd; Paul and his superiors appear to be able to decide whether or not there should be a Castings business at all and given that, they set the constraints (financial, market, political, social) within which it is to operate.

There is another related area that we need to consider before moving on to aspects of personal power: control of choices presented for decision. Let me remind you of the exchange between Eric and his colleagues.

Eric: . . . so I don't want to wait until later. These flicker briefly and then die, but I have a nasty feeling that some of them will be resurrected at some point and it will be said that we agreed with them. What I want to know is whether or not those figures up there include the after market or not?

Brian: Which figures are you concerned about, Eric?

Eric: The ones on the far right.

Brian: These?

Eric: Yes.

Brian: Well, not directly, no. But the after market has been taken account of in our overall calculations.

Eric: I don't understand that. Either it's in those figures or it is not.

Alec: Look, you don't have to worry about it, Eric. We have taken your market into account.

Eric: Where? I can't see it. Either it's in or it is not. It makes a big difference to us as a whole. I know no one but me is interested in the non-glamorous end of the business, but we get our bread and butter from it, you know. It can't simply be ignored.

Hugh: It's not being ignored, Eric. It's in there.
Eric: Well I can't see it and he [*indicating Brian*] cannot point to it.
Alec: We took it into account when you came to talk to us about it. You gave us the projections then and we have incorporated them.
Eric: OK. So it's in there. How much of those figures is original equipment and how much after market? Tell me that. If those people up there constitute our strategic customers it's got to be on OE [original equipment] only. There's no way that they are strategic in terms of the after market.
Hugh: We are not going to get anywhere with this. I think that we should move on.
Alec: So do I. We've been round this time and time again. Next slide.

It is clear that Eric is here challenging a set of decisions taken by a sub-group from which he has been excluded. The reaction of his colleagues is such as to alert us to the fact that his behaviour threatens a rule that hitherto has been accepted without question: that if someone asserts something to be the case – 'Look, you don't have to worry about it, Eric' – then trust is expected, not confrontation. Leaving that aside, Eric is highlighting the fact that the sub-group has been in a position to determine the choices that are being put before the larger group for decision, thus allowing the latter the illusion of participation. What is presented is the result of analysis and discussion during which some information has been taken into account, some has not, and some choices have been proposed, analysed and accepted (others rejected). What the larger group is asked to confirm, therefore, has been to a large extent predetermined; the 'action' has occurred elsewhere, the decision is up for the rubber-stamp. In challenging this, Eric not only signals his own relative lack of power (he has not been a member of the sub-group), but he also indicates for us the perceived power of the individuals who were members of the sub-group. They and they alone appear to shape the premises upon which the larger group is to make its decision. Paul, Alec and Hugh, having defined the alternatives, have a far greater impact upon the final decision than anyone else in the room. What is more, they resent the challenge to this that Eric represents:

'I don't know why we bother to spend so much time deciding things, some clown always knows better.'

It could be argued that the aspects of power that we have discussed so far are essentially structural. That power arises largely from what may be termed 'system requirements'. This is clearly not the perspective adopted throughout this book, in which we have argued that life in the 'organization' is a process of 'organizing'; that despite my predilection for Brecht, there are no laws for survival, certainly none corresponding to the physical laws with which the systems theorists are so taken. Most things, I have argued and will continue to maintain, are negotiable, little is determined. What is important to Friction Free Castings Ltd is what persuasive actors within that setting *take to be* important. Not what in some objective sense *is* important, but what a particular coalition takes to be important. If, as a number of them do, they define the after market as relatively unimportant, then it is so and Eric, the executive responsible for it, has little influence upon the discussion. If, on some other occasion, he can persuade them that his definition of the situation is one that should prevail, then the balance of power changes – temporarily. The working agreement which accords priority to the after market may be challenged by, say, Derek, the Personnel Director, who may be able to persuade his colleagues that a revision of terms of employment is absolutely critical to the organization (on moral *or* economic grounds – the determination of the ground is also subject to negotiation). The power to determine reality is what the struggle is about; reality is not determined for the actors, they construe it, improvise it and act upon it.[10]

An important qualification to all this must be noted here: conduct *is* the result of improvisation between social actors, but it must be remembered that all such improvisation occurs within a structure within a set of institutions and within a series of frameworks which constitute the medium of exchange. Paul, George and the others are engaged in affirming and reaffirming the patterns which should and do exist between them, but they do so within frameworks which define some responses as sensible and appropriate and others as nonsensical. Such frameworks are normally 'tacit' or 'pre-conscious'.

For example, Paul (and his predecessors) in the job of Managing Director has always offered an explanation of his actions in terms of his authority, his legitimate 'right' to take certain decisions and institute certain actions. The result is that over the years it has become part of the tacit understanding of all concerned that Managing Directors can and even should behave in a certain fashion: 'after all, he is the gaffer' – a matter of common sense, a moral imperative. Once upon a time, far away and long ago, such a definition was created and sustained, now it guides and constrains the interpretations of virtually everyone present. The actors have created (or, at least, not thought of challenging) a social structure which now informs their very interpretations. In this sense, the notion of office interpenetrates that of personal performance.

The very structure of Friction Free Castings Ltd may be seen not as a matter of effectiveness but as an outcome of a struggle for control within the organization. For example, the Strategic Development Group has been set up to exclude some from its deliberations. Occasionally, one person appears to have the power to produce reality for others. More often, however, the interactive or negotiable nature of it is evident. Power cannot be realized in isolation; Paul is powerful to the extent that others perceive him to be so and *consent* to him being so. To appreciate this point fully we need to put it within the framework outlined in the first couple of pages in this chapter. Paul begins an interaction with George (or any interaction with anyone else, for that matter) at a point on the power dimension which both acknowledge (not necessarily consciously). Paul is prone to manage, direct and control George around certain issues – say, the presentation of results. Thus with regard to this particular item on the agenda, the history has been that whatever the challenge, Paul has finally had his way. His power has prevailed. On the other hand, for reasons of style (Paul much prefers to be cooperative, to be participative) and to comply with norms which appear to hold that crude assertion of power is not acceptable, Paul would much prefer it if the outcome of the event was that George deferred to him as a gesture of 'positive and respectful submission'. If, in effect, George accorded greater status to Paul. George, for his part, would probably be happy with either a rise in power or in status; he cannot force anyone to accept his interpretation of the figures nor, apparently, are they willing voluntarily to accord much importance to his views. The pattern of what ensues may be seen as one in which George seeks to increase his power by forcing his conclusions on all present, Paul seeks to deflect him and casts him into giving respect to him, Paul, (by being reasonable) and finally concludes by virtually ordering him to comply.

It is important to note at this point how power shades into status. Paul takes a risk whenever he attempts to assert rather than to persuade; the risk is that George will *not* comply. All power is ultimately based upon an element of consent. It is certainly an extreme thought but were George and the others to refuse to go along with Paul's intentions to the point of risking unemployment, his power would diminish considerably.

Status and Persuasion

Power I have defined as essentially the 'chance of a man or a number of men to realize their own will in a communal action even against the resistance of others' and I have indicated that in the strictest possible sense it is, finally, voluntary. I may weigh up the risks of resistance and decide to comply or I may resist come what may. If the latter, the case of the martyr for a cause, power cannot and does not prevail since the target does not modify his conduct. Nonetheless, leaving aside such exceptional beings, most commentators would agree that power involves compliance with the wishes of those who are perceived to be powerful. Status, on the other hand, involves going along with someone or something because one wants to do it, because one wants to accord respect, affection, agreement or whatever to the other. If in the relations between Paul and George, Paul has high status, this means that he receives more in the way of voluntary compliance from George than George receives from him. Again, as with the power dimension it is possible to plot the amount of voluntary compliance or status each receives or is accorded by those with whom they interact. In my group of executives, Alec is accorded high status by many because of his ability to construct and present an argument, and Eric is held in low esteem because of his tendency to be dogmatic and repetitive (features which may well afford him high status elsewhere).

In groups of peers such as those I am concerned with here, the emphasis is upon the reconciliation of differences, not upon the invocation of force. Paul is, as it happens, temperamentally disposed to be participative and cooperative, but even were he not so, there would be strong pressure to move towards status relations since the costs of power relations (in terms of having to deal with repeated and perhaps sustained resistance) would be too high to sustain. When status becomes the desirable dimension along which exchange will occur, persuasion rather than naked threat and command becomes the preferred currency. Naked force is rare in organizations.

> One generally shuns the coercive label like the plague, takes pains to deny that he is bribing others when he offers them inducements, and represents himself as a persuader – if possible, as someone using 'rational persuasion'. Persuasion is especially valued as an instrument of democracy . . . Officials of government proudly proclaim that ours is indeed a system run by persuasion . . . Inducements and constraints are said to have no place in solidly democratic forms of government; they are the coinage of, the realm of corrupt governments or of totalitarian regimes.

Echoes of Blau's notions of fairness and equity here.[11]

What is meant by *persuasion*? For present purposes I will assert that persuasion is a circumstance where conduct is modified by both verbal and non-verbal symbols which primarily appeals to reason and/or emotion.

Clearly I need to say a little more about that definition if I am to persuade anyone to accept it. First, on the issue of the modification of conduct, it could be argued that what matters is not what people think, what their attitude is, but what they do, what behaviour they express to be taken account of by others. In a sense, despite what he says, what Paul requires ultimately from George in their disagreement over an interpretation of the trading figures is not a change of attitude on the part of George, but a different piece of conduct almost irrespective of conviction: 'I trust you are not going into next week's Board meeting with this sort of approach.' In the final analysis, however much he may like to change George's attitude, what Paul wants by 'next week' and preferably now is a change in George's conduct, what it is he is saying. He wants George's behaviour, his verbal output, to be aligned with his, Paul's definition of the situation. The function of power is to bring about an appropriate alignment of behaviour, not necessarily to convince someone of the rectitude of the modification necessary to bring that about, however desirable from an ideological or philo-sophical position the latter may be.

The function of persuasion, however, *is* to bring about this alignment by means of argument, symbolic manipulation or expert knowledge. In persuasion (which is much nicer than power) the target agrees with the source's point of view because he takes the claims to be appropriate or correct. In power relations, Paul wishes George to change the words he uses; in status relations, he wishes him to change his way of thinking about the issue.[12]

The Importance of Language

Whatever the dimensions of interaction, the importance of language cannot be overestimated. Language is criticially important in the construction, maintenance and changing of realities; change the words and phrases and you may well change the outcomes. Paul attempts to persuade George by both verbal and non-verbal means, by the manipulation of symbols. His posture, his wagging finger, his tone of voice convey the import of his message to George, but it is above all in the words that he uses that he seeks to mould and modify the latter's response. George, for his part, consistently rejects the messages and pursues his own interpretation. A similar process is observable in the second extract when both Hugh and Alec seek to convince Eric that he has nothing to worry about. Language, and in particular the choice of words, is an integral part of persuasion with the associated non-verbal signals serving to reinforce the attempt. Had, for example, either Hugh or Alec accompanied their reassuring noises to Eric with evident signs of non-verbal agitation at the substance of his questions, their attempts at persuasion would have been even less successful than they were. The paradigmatic example of persuasion, of course, is not to be found in such meetings but in advertising, the patter of salesmen (particularly that of insurance brokers and used car vendors) and honeyed words of politicians. Nonetheless, language is the currency of interaction at all levels of encounter and its manipulation is a key feature of persuasion. Regardless of definition, the resources available to negotiate statuses are similar and primarily verbal.

Organizations are created, sustained and changed through talk. There is nothing good or bad in this world or any other but talking makes it so. Organizations, enterprises of great pitch and moment, are constituted by active, wilful individuals talking to each other. For Peter Gronn, talk is the work of administrators; their principal task is to keep talking in order to build the kind of social reality they take to be necessary. It is through words that members of organizations negotiate, it is through words that they appeal, persuade, request, coax, cozen, assign, declare, debate, agree, insult, confer, teach, advise, complain, irritate, anger, correct, socialize, recruit, threaten, promise, praise, ridicule, condemn and dismiss. At the more senior levels of enterprises, executives are expected to be able to listen efficiently, to be able to read quickly and with comprehension, to be able to write and talk persuasively. Poor performance in any aspect of these language skills must disadvantage a person; he who is unable to listen well may fail to understand, fail to receive advice and instruction. He who is unable to talk well is unlikely to succeed in either seeking help whenever appropriate or in influencing others through persuasive communication.[13]

But I digress. I was with Gronn, who claims that control is gained and lost in the corridors of the organization through the medium of talk. To be sure, in our scenario Paul appears at one point to demonstrate his power by saying nothing, but such an illustration merely serves to highlight the normal circumstance. The very fact that he is not saying anything sows doubt and confusion in his subordinates; they hang upon his words, virtually forcing him to define and resolve the circumstance: 'Look, there's no point in getting excited about it. The figures don't mean anything.' Their acceptance of this ruling is in part a function of his position and his authority as the Chief Executive; had George said the same thing, the effect, no doubt, would have been different. Part, however, is a result of Paul's personal skills in listening and talking.

In one of the few pieces of work by a management theorist concerned with language, Pondy argues that the leader's use of language may well be an important factor in 'determining his effectiveness, both in enhancing his credibility and in managing the influence process'. I would take this further and continue the argument advanced so far in this book that the construction of meaning accomplished through the medium of language is *the* central feature of interaction and, thus, of the process of organizing. Pondy appears to be putting forward the case that the effectiveness of a leader lies in his ability to 'make activity meaningful for those in his role set – not to change behaviour but to give others a sense of understanding what they are doing'. Such a formulation appears to beg the question of how it is they got to be doing what they are doing in the first place. His argument appears to accord language a role of explanation, of justification and rationalization. Clearly language is used in this manner; in the scenario I have presented, Paul seeks to assert that the figures mean one thing against George's view of what the figures mean. Words and phrases are seen to be important in rendering an optimistic or a pessimistic interpretation of the data. Language, however, is not limited to 'rendering activity meaningful'. Paul, as we have seen, *is* initially interested in changing George's behaviour and his attitude, his verbal output, and he uses words to bring about this shift.

I am in danger of overstating my case but, nonetheless, will assert once again that those features of the organization which are often taken by the members to be crucial for its survival and are said to be determined for it (by the 'environment', the 'system' or whatever) emerge not from outside but from within, from a process of definition, construction and improvisation such as I have outlined in this chapter. Language can, and in my experience does, fundamentally affect the decisions that are made. Consider for a moment the last of our scenes:

Paul: One more thing. The Chairman has written a long letter explaining the change in logo.
Hugh: The change in what?
Paul: Logo. He has written setting out what is now to go on the top of our letters, the new colours for the envelopes, the revised packaging layouts. . .
George: Good God! Talk about fiddling while Rome burns!

All are now giving full attention to Paul. On the edge of their chairs affecting almost identical expressions of incredulity at what they are hearing. A number of excited, humorous comments are passed around the table. Paul raises his voice and cuts through:

Paul: In future, all subsidiaries of the main company including ourselves are to have the name and logo of the parent. . .

Alec: Whom God preserve!

Paul: . . .company placed immediately before the name of the subsidiary. Thus we shall become Twinings Friction Free Castings Ltd.

George: We are losing millions and that's what the main Board is spending its time doing.

Eric: What about our subsidiaries?

Paul: What about them?

Eric: What do they become – Twinings Friction Free Castings (LSD Camshafts) Ltd? What a bloody mouthful.

Paul: [*Consulting the letter*] It doesn't say anything about that here.

Hugh: It's probably illegal anyway.

Paul: What is?

Hugh: Changing names like that.

Eric: Certainly is – our name, our logo and our colours are registered trademarks. Cost thousands to change that.

Paul: Will it?

George: Hundreds of thousands.

Derek: What's the letter about? Asking our opinion or what?

Alec: Manchester asking our opinion? You've got to be joking!

Paul: Are you sure it will cost money to put this into effect?

Hugh: Some one up there must have taken that into account.

Paul: It says nothing about it here. Nothing about who is to meet the cost of changing. Lots of examples, look all these beautiful mock-ups of what the new paper and the new packaging will look like. [*He passes out the material to willing hands.*]

Eric: Just like Christmas, isn't it?

Paul: It could well be that some one has goofed. [*Delight at this possibility is registered on most faces.*] Eric, can you take this and get someone to come up with a report on its implications – what it will cost, how much hassle it will involve us in and the like.

There is no question of after the event rationalization here: meaning is being created before our ears:

'Good God! Talk about fiddling while Rome burns!'

The accepted, widely shared common definition of the situation: the Chairman and his merry men fritter away time on matters which we 'at the sharp end' regard as – at best – amusing. The scene is set for a small amount of 'taking the piss':

'Whom God preserve!'

Eric, however, is not amused. He cuts through it all with a clear, direct question. 'What about our subsidiaries?' In a very short space of time, the situation has changed from one of mild amusement at the antics of their superiors to a matter of consequence, a decision has been reached: 'Eric, you can take this . . .' and a determination to challenge the proposed change is in the air. Words such as 'illegal', 'registered trademark', 'hundreds of thousands' and 'it will cost money' have evoked quite a different atmosphere to the one which obtained when the subject was introduced, although the possibility of someone senior having 'goofed' remains a delightful prospect to most around the table.

Here we have the group, in this case led by Eric, defining that the reality as defined by the Chairman is not amusing or trivial but a matter likely to be of consequence to them. Not only will the proposal cause confusion and difficulty – 'Twinings Friction Free Castings (LSD Camshafts) Ltd' – it will also 'cost money', and since our heroes take money to be a matter of importance (at least insofar as the spending of it to bring about the proposed change can be used to embarrass their superiors), they decide that simple amusement is not the most appropriate response. In doing so, language is of the utmost import-ance. Had Eric been more equivocal and less direct, the amused definition ('Load of bloody idiots') may have prevailed. Had George not escalated Eric's 'thousands' of pounds to 'hundreds of thousands' (and he, remember, is the Finance Director and perceived to be authoritative in such matters), again the meaning evoked may have been substantially different. This group shares a concern with 'money', particularly money defined as 'cost', which at other times and in other circumstances may well not concern it as much. Given its history and its culture, its shared definitions, then Eric knows and George knows that phrases such as 'thousands' and 'hundreds of thousands' will cut through any amount of joking.

Summary

There are writers on power and politics in organizations who ignore the use of language in organizations. At best, they see it as important in the context of the *exercise* of power. In this formulation, language is useful in developing support for and legitimizing decisions that are reached on the basis of power. Power – from this perspective – appears to derive automatically and unequivocally from 'conditions of resource control and resource interdependence'. Much influenced by the work of Edelman (which is concerned primarily with political institutions), this school of thought sees language not only as serving rationalization, but also as serving to obfuscate and dull the senses of the hearers such that their own best interests would not be accurately assessed.[14]

Clearly this argument, or at least a part of it, is valid. Language is used to focus interests, to mobilize support and to justify actions. It may also be used to obfuscate and confuse. Paul, George, Hugh, Eric, Alec and Derek each attempt to claim precedence for their definitions; as stressed in the earlier discussion, they are 'negotiating' order amongst themselves on almost every occasion they meet. George's pre-emptive bid to have his definitions obtain, 'we ought to be ashamed', is an attempt to have the figures taken to mean what he takes them to mean. Paul's refutation is an attempt to discredit this attribution. Here, as in every organization, there is no shortage of competition.

Language, however, is not limited to the denial of ground to others and the advancement of one's own cause, nor is it simply a matter of internalization, still less so a matter of obfuscation. Reality, I have argued, is socially constructed, whether or not a particular resource (material or otherwise) is valued is, ultimately, a matter of definition and the processes of definition are shot through with language. Whether or not the executives in the Boardroom define, say, the market as critically important and assign power to the marketeers is a function of the development of a shared language and set of meanings. It is not, repeat not, some thing which thrusts itself upon the collective consciousness and, in the manner of the cuckoo, tips everything else out. Consider once more, briefly, the scene concerning the logo. Initial definitions take the letter from the Chairman as one more joke. There is clearly a shared definition to tap into here – Head Office is always good for tension relief, the corporate scapegoat in Manchester. Eric, reinforced by George, suggests that it will cost a great deal of money to effect the change; some humour persists, but the emerging definition 'instruction as problematic' rather than 'instruction as half-witted' begins to emerge, tying in to an already shared definition that 'cost' is something to be avoided. This shared definition itself may be overturned if, for example, someone were to argue that the change may be beneficial to the company's image (elaborating, no doubt, on the importance of image to some value they all shared or could be persuaded to share). The point of all this is, of course, that this is not a matter simply of the *exercise* of power, here power arises *from* the definition. Eric emerges empowered to do something from this discussion, talk has created some action, not simply rationalized it.

Talk has also been the primary medium of exchange. Eric came into the episode concerning the logo with relatively low status and relatively low power. The previous episodes had done little or nothing to enhance his standing – he was treated with a mild degree of contempt in the scene concerned with the after market – 'next slide' – and his attempts at joking in the discussion around the figures despatched to Manchester were not greeted with enthusiasm. He emerges from the logo interaction, however, a number of points up on the status dimension, most if not all others present being happy to fall in with his definition of the situation and his implied suggestions for resolving it. Although Paul issues the instructions for resolving the matter, everyone present is aware that Eric has been a key actor in all that has occurred.

Turning to other actors in other episodes, it can be argued that George loses quite heavily in a number of them. Paul forces him to comply around the profit figures whilst his colleagues ignore him, thus confirming his low standing on the power dimension and possibly reducing still further his status. The discussion around the figures sent to Manchester does even less for his reputation with his colleagues, although it could just be seen as confirming his power when allied with Paul. 'Their' will does after all prevail and 'their' will is, essentially, George's in this particular instance.

Alec moves up a number of points on both power and status dimensions. His challenge and the support it finds perhaps signals that, in other circumstances, he may go further and directly challenge Paul; in any event, he succeeds in getting an explanation despite George's resistance. In the eyes of his colleagues, his determination and skill in presenting the case may well have enhanced his reputation such that they are even more ready to defer voluntarily to him and his views in the future.

Paul emerges from the afternoon's events more or less as he went in. He has not succeeded in gaining along the status dimension. George conforms because he has to and with bad grace; the challenge to the Manchester figures fails not because any one is convinced by his reasoning but because they sense punishment, the exercise of crude power, should they persist. His attempts to exercise participation may, however, be seen to be rewarded in the final episode, though much of the credit for the outcome is likely to be accorded to Eric rather than to Paul.

One final and important point. The analysis of these interactions and my determination to relate incidents to the twin themes of power and status has given the exchanges I have highlighted a character they do not possess when heard and seen in context. I am not claiming that an explicit *negotiation* occurs around these themes; I am claiming that power and status are the fundamental scenarios or canvasses against which my social actors improvise. I am arguing that they behave as they do in a regular and relatively routine fashion. To be sure, there are elements of the novel in what they do (and I return to these later) but for the most part, despite the language of analysis I have used here, they do not reflect and weigh up each action; they simply run off well-rehearsed performances with minimal reflection. In a sense, what we see occurring before us is emblematic; it is a display of the relations which obtain between them, almost a celebration of where they are at interpersonally. They cooperate at one level to keep it so. Uncomfortable though it may be for one or two of them, it is ritually enacted time after time with little or no thought or possibility of radical transformation.

5 Several Characters in Search of Confirmation

This has proved to be one of the more difficult sections to begin. Up until now, I have been engaged in talking about others, with but the most occasional aside about me and my activities. Sitting like a ghost at the feast, I have observed, inferred, imputed, attributed and devised accounts for the doings of all and sundry. Now I am required to address the issue of self which I can probably best do by talking about *my* self, and am immobilized, frozen in my tracks, arrested at my keyboard. I take it that what I am experiencing is akin to that which Paul, George and the others experienced when I first appeared and sat at the table with a tight smile upon my face and a notebook clutched in my hand. For a time they became clumsy and embarrassed, pursuing their collective task with a degree of stiffness and awkwardness that took a number of meetings to dissolve. Like me now, each and every one of them became self-conscious. I thought I understood what they were experiencing.

But only in part. Of all the issues raised in these pages, that of self remains the most elusive, the most difficult to glimpse, let alone to capture and pin down in deathless prose. In getting these few lines of introduction down, I have, in some manner, assumed a distance from my self, sought refuge in my role of author, distracted my consciousness of self sufficiently to allow me to write something, but not for long . . . even as I commit this phrase to paper . . . a sense of some process beyond the writing me . . . watching, evaluating, monitoring.

Given what I had to say in the previous chapter, it is clear that my inhibition is related to my sense of putting my status at risk. I wish you, the reader, to think well of me. In putting on the line my worth as a writer and, anticipating some upset in relations as a consequence of making a poor fist of this chapter, my emotions are engaged. Some important aspect of my self must be under threat. Risky though such an enterprise may well be, I wish in what follows to extend my understanding not only of my self but of the other selves seated around the Boardroom table. What I am interested in is who I am in the Boardroom and who the other people are. What roles are we playing and with what degree of involvement? I am interested in these questions for the light that answers to them may shed on the nature of the executive process. What is it about us that results in this particular set of interactions and that sustains the pattern I have commented upon in the previous chapter?

Unlike a number of interactionists, I hold and will seek to demonstrate that there is something in each of us beyond the roles we assume, an actor, as it were, behind the parts we each play. If, as is assumed in Meadian/Goffmanesque social science, individuals act out roles ascribed to them by society, then I shall argue there must be a centre which allows the individual to learn how to play roles; a centre of cognition which Cicourel terms 'the deep structure'. Simmel appears to posit an actor behind the roles:[1]

> To play a part, not just as hypocrisy or as deceit, but in terms of the involvement of the individual's life in a single expressive form which is entered upon in some pre-existing, predetermined way, is part and parcel of the way in which our everyday life is constituted. Such a role may be appropriate to our individual self, but it is nevertheless something other than this individuality and not an intrinsic part of its innermost and unitary being.

Just as, in the theatre there is an Olivier or a Kean playing Othello – although if the performance 'comes off' they are barely discernible – so, in social encounters, there is a performer behind the parts. Doing is not all there is to being. We appear to have a capacity to act, but we are more than we present, and more, in some cases much more, than the parts we are cast in. We may perform in a relatively unreflecting manner or we may, on occasion, consciously seek to define and structure events to reduce equivocality and to further our own ends and purposes. In no event is our conduct totally determined; in no event is it totally free. We are, at once, both determined and determiners; constrained and free; actors who perform with sincerity and, on occasion, actors who are intensely aware of themselves as performers. The awareness is well caught in this extract from William Cooper's splendid book *Scenes from Metropolitan Life*, as the hero struggles to propose to his lover:[2]

The conversation was satisfactorily started. The remarkable thing was the length of time between the individual remarks. It seemed to be taking hours. But then how can one take an impressive length of time to say 'I am suffering'? I thought of saying it in other languages. 'Que je souffre!' – or would it be more French to say 'Qu'on soufffre!'? Recollecting scenes from Dostoevsky, I thought that if only I knew the language, Russian would be just the ticket for me . . .

'Why do you want to marry me, darling?'

I had a choking sensation. I did not reply . . . Oh dear! I looked at Myrtle. Her round hazel eyes were fixed on me, with a serious, intent, trembling look.

It was the moment everything we had been saying had led to: it was the moment I had come for. She was waiting to hear me say that I could not live without her, waiting determinedly with deep emotion. I could not say it. With unexpected insight, I knew it was not truthfulness that prevented me – I could have lied to her as most men would. It was pride. I would not bend my will an inch to hers, even to get something I wanted.

I muttered something incoherent. I felt I had the rest of my life in my hands. I really was suffering. And I could not help noticing how farcical it was. I managed to say clearly what I had been muttering.

'Life seems utterly useless . . .'

It was as far as I could go. Was it enough? I wondered. Oh, would it do?

There was a long pause. Myrtle put her hand on mine. She sighed. The critical moment had passed . . .

The Received View of Self

I recognize that it would be foolish in a text of this nature to proceed as if each of you were already familiar with an interactionist perspective on the self. I have not presented much of it in these pages and discussion of self, or selves for that matter, is often neglected in other texts purporting to deal with behaviour in organizations. I will offer, therefore, some common assertions which I will seek to refine in later paragraphs (though I cannot promise not to comment as I make them).[3]

It is clear that the watcher, the ghost in the machine (who, incidentally, has been splendidly distracted by the last couple of pages) is not simply a collection of facts about me. Such elements as height, weight, nationality, religion, marital status, occupation and hobbies constitute my public identity. To be sure, they are part of *me* but they are not my self. I am more than this, perhaps much more.

To have a self is to have the capacity to observe, interpret, construct and direct one's own behaviour. *I* can act towards *me* as I can towards any other social object or 'thing' (to use Blumer's phrase). Like Cooper's hero, I can become aware of me performing as I perform; I can evaluate what I am up to, can praise or blame myself, can encourage or despair and can alter course in mid-stream. Each of us has the capacity to edit a performance in real time, to monitor and adjust conduct on line.

The argument put forward by Mead and accepted by a large number of interactionists is that the self is not a 'thing' or an object in the sense of being an entity but is rather a process – a dialectic involving an 'I' and a 'me'. The former is akin to Freud's 'id', the wilful, unpredictable, creative aspect of the self; the latter, the 'me', is the Freudian censor, the inhibitor, that element of the self which represents, as it were, the audience, what others will think of our putative action. The 'I' is impulsive, the 'me' constraining and channelling. The 'me' sets the limits within which the 'I' can perform.

Taking the instance of behaviour given by Cooper, it is possible to read it as a dialectical process involving an 'I' and a 'me'. The hero, for example, has an impulse to frame his suffering in different languages, but refrains; his impulse is checked; on the other hand, his 'me' tells him that 'She was waiting to hear me say that I could not live without her . . .'; he cannot reconcile his 'I' with the demands of the 'me'. What Cooper does (far better than Mead or any other interactionist) is to illustrate the process of carving out a level of action that mediates between what Meadians would describe as one's impulses and the expectations of others as represented by one's internal censor, the 'me'.

It is possible to suggest that the self has essentially the same form as social interaction (a view not widely shared by interactionists). Rather than regarding the 'I' as some kind of biologic urge, it is useful to regard it as that which is essentially idiosyncratic and individual, a kind of Gyntian 'Self':

The Gyntian 'Self' – it's the regiment
Of wishes, appetites and desires; -
The Gyntian 'Self' is the sea of ambitions,
Needs and demands; in fact, whatever

Causes my breast to heave uniquely,
And makes me exist as the 'I', that I am.

Part biologic, but more a matter of ambitions, needs and demands, faced always by the 'me' representing the views of particular and/or generalized others.[4] Thus encounter can be seen as a continual process of both interpersonal and intrapersonal exchange; as a social actor, I not only improvise order with you, I also improvise within my self . It follows that any social actor can conduct parallel conversations (internal and external) and, more important, can be one thing to themselves and another to their partners. I can, for example, recognize that Paul, George, Eric or whoever is an ass, yet maintain towards each and any one of them a front which implies that I hold him in the greatest respect. In this manner, I can (and do) distance myself from any particular encounter or role; the line of action I forge with others is improvized both intra and inter personally.

This view of social interaction is not novel but it has not been extensively developed; most interactionists have rejected the 'I' in favour of the 'me'.[5] The latter is seen as a matter of perspective, the former as biologic or given. I believe that there is considerable advantage in regarding them both as perspectives and in considering what goes on inside one's head as paralleling what goes on in an exchange of perspectives between two social actors. I will develop this view shortly. For the moment, I need to follow the crowd and deal with the 'me'.

Through a Glass Darkly

In Mead's words, 'we are more or less unconsciously seeing ourselves as others see us.' Not that what Paul and George attribute to me is identical with my view of my self but that, given that they are significant actors in my life, what they think will influence my *self-concept* – my notion of who I am and what I am about. To say that I am what other people take me to be is, of course, nonsense. I cannot fully know what Paul and George think about me, I can but infer it from what they say and do. The notion that others are mirrors to the self needs a little explication. Cooley's (1964) view that:

Each to each a looking glass
Reflects the other that doth pass

should alert us to the fact that it is not one's self that appears in the looking glass, it is only one's reflection. It does what you do but, unlike other people, it does not look back at you. It is but an image of you. People as mirrors, on the other hand, not only reflect but also interpret and distort.[6] The self-concept is thus decidedly not an exact reflection but rather an imputed sentiment. In my early dealings with Eric, for example, it appeared to me that he saw me as an 'academic', said in such a way as to imply one of the lower forms of life, someone who had 'never got his hands dirty' and thus of little value to him. In attempting to resist this imputed sentiment and to protect my own view of myself, I presented myself as someone with business experience and a strong practical bias; elements of me that are not valued in a university, and consequently have to be disowned or, at least, not promoted there, but which appeared to be important to Derek, Paul, George and the others.

From this example, it appears that there are a number of aspects of the self-concept: how, that is, I see myself in the Boardroom or at the University, how Eric actually sees me (that which in conversation with me or someone else he would attribute to me) and what I, in the absence of disconfirmation, take his evaluation of me to be. I take it that when he refers disparagingly to the activities of consultants in general that he is actually talking about me in particular, just as I take it that when I am welcomed in what appears to be a warm and friendly manner into the meetings, most of those present value me and my activities. That there is a conflict of perceptions and apparent attributions is a matter of consequence for my idea of me; should Paul share Eric's apparent view of me, then I may have a considerable crisis of identity. My perception of myself as a competent manager and skilled helper has arisen from interaction and is largely sustained through it. Prolonged perceived disparagement of this claim would cause some painful re-evaluation.

Mead identified the 'generalized others' as the 'organized community or social group which gives to the individual his unity of self'. Despite the confusing terminology, what is meant by self in this context is the 'me' aspect of it. The self is the dialectical process involving the 'I' (Mead's biologic impulse, my 'Gyntian' self) and the 'me', the structure of attitudes which are derived from the social milieu of any particular actor.

Whether the attitudes of others towards me have any impact upon my self-concept clearly depends upon how significant they are to me. I reject the idea that I am nothing other than what other people think of me; some of them have got me wrong. When Eric considers me to be 'academic', he has distorted me; this is not to deny that for him I am the man who 'sits in on meetings, says nothing and does nowt'. What is important is what the process of self makes of this attribution and reflection. I am more, much more, than the facts and the attributions. I am not just a creature of other people's real or imagined perception of me. I am responsible for my self concept. I construct my self concept out of the rags and tatters of opinion which surround me. *I* am what *I* take my self to be. Mine, like yours, is a do-it-yourself self.

Some folk are more significant than others in the process of construction. Those whose opinion I care about greatly have a stronger effect upon my self-concept than those to whom I am indifferent. In many aspects of myself I look for confirmation *or* confrontation with those for whom I have respect. If, for example, I were to take Eric to be a highly skilled, very effective writer with a great deal of experience in analysing and bringing about change in organizations, then his views of me would be of considerable importance to me. I do not, so they are not. On the other hand, I am not indifferent to him. I strive to bring about a reappraisal on his part, I attempt to induce him to see me as I see myself. I am not content to ignore his attributions since he has significance for me. I care about what he thinks, not as much as I care about what Paul and Alec think of me, but Eric's views are of consequence.

The Knower and the Known

It is clear that I am talking here about two distinct aspects of the self: the knower and the known. The former is in the strictest sense not an entity; it is the process of continuing interpretation, it is the *constructing* of the parts rather than the parts themselves, the assuming of the roles rather than the roles. This process orientation is difficult to grasp and has been referred to variously as the 'transcendental' or 'insubstantial' self. In essence, the argument for such a process is that neither I nor you can describe what goes on in our minds without reference to some pre-supposition such as a transcendental self. It is this conception of the self that allows us to do what I have done in the previous couple of paragraphs, reject some opinions (or all of them), become conscious of my own deliberations (act self-consciously), render all things significant or irrelevant. The self enables me to conceive of myself as autonomous; the self as watching and organizing provides me with a potential for escape from you and your opinions and, more importantly, from 'me' and my opinions (those aspects of you internalized and accepted as my own). The self is the holding of the ring for the interplay of the 'I' and the 'me'. It is the point of reference from which I interpret and constitute my world. It exists as a process just as one must presuppose a process of acting if one is to understand how stage actors come to assume characters. I am struggling with the analogies here in order to pin down the elusive, the insubstantial, the transcendental. No stage actor is able to say how he puts together a character, his characterization is an amalgam of the previous parts played, the sediments, as it were, of other occasions and opportunities and the views of his fellow actors and those of his director. The process of acting involves a dialectic between that which is in him (or her) as a performer (the 'I') and that which is suggested to him by others (the 'me'). Social life is no different, the self is in part the process of conceiving and rehearsing, checking and selecting.[7]

What is constituted out of this process is a concept of how I see myself being and performing. At one level, I constitute my self as a set of thoughts, plans, choices, evaluations, emotions, which are of a relatively enduring nature, at another level out of this (the primary content of the 'I' from my perspective) in interaction with the 'me', I construct and deploy a particular identity for a particular situation. Lest more confusion arise than is absolutely inevitable in a discussion such as this, let me hasten to add that from my perspective the 'I' is not simply biologic, nor necessarily impulsive; it is my enduring view of my self (of course subject to change over the medium to long term). It is the biographical aspect of myself, the lived experience, the residual from previous dialectical exchanges between the emergent 'I' and the generalized other as represented by the 'me'. Long before the 'I' emerges, I have been *given* an identity, *ascribed* one by other people. My parents, my family, my friends, my teachers, set up the structures of my world long before the process of self-reflection, the dialectic between the 'I' and the 'me' becomes established. I learn how to think of myself in a context of dependency, becoming for all intents and purposes what I am for other people. The struggle for the adolescent and for the adult (rarely, in fact, resolved) is to become one's self, to become one's own man or woman. In the final analysis, I cannot escape seeing myself as others see me, since part of their perspectives (accrued over the years) I have internalized as the 'I' and continue to address in the conversation between it and the 'me'. Given all this, it is hardly surprising that the expressed or imputed opinions that other people hold of me are of concern to me and that they are the key to most of my emotions.

Autonomy and All That

Some react to the notions expressed in the previous paragraphs by declaring unilateral independence and cutting themselves off from others. They constitute themselves as loners and resolutely resist attempts to influence them; becoming, as it were, all 'I' and as little 'me' as possible. Others react by becoming hypersensitive to others, becoming all 'me' and little 'I', chasing every opinion seeking to constitute themselves as others would have them constituted. For the former, the inner-directed, the regard for the self, often referred to as self-esteem, is constructed and defended in relative isolation (given what has been said above, it is impossible to think of oneself without some reference to others). For the latter, the other-directed, self-esteem is almost entirely related to the opinions of others.

There is, of course, a position between the two extremes; one where the self concept is not isolated nor totally swamped by others. Such a self, the autonomous self, is able to maintain distance whenever and wherever it is taken to be appropriate, but is also involved with and responsive to the opinions of others. Such a self, although developed and maintained intersubjectively, will determine whose opinions will matter, which relationships will define and which will not.[8]

I wish to push this a little further before seeking to apply some of it back in the Boardroom I left a number of pages ago. I define my self-concept in terms of my relations (actual or potential) with other people; in a fundamental manner, I constitute myself insecure and/or secure, aggressive and/or defensive, loving, jealous, angry, proud, ashamed or whatever. I constitute myself out of the emotions I hold about people. As I will argue in chapter 6, emotions are related to dealings with other people particularly around issues of power and status. I am my emotions; I constitute who I am out of my judgement that it is appropriate to be kind, nasty, angry, fearful or whatever in this particular circumstance with this particular group of people. In constituting such a self-concept and acting upon it, I risk either confirmation or disconfirmation. Who I am, who I wish to be and who I am allowed to be, is ultimately and irrevocably tied to the nature of my relationships with other people.

Meanwhile, Back at the Ranch

Dealing with other people is a threat to the world as the particular actor defines it. In attempting to share with others his view of the world, George risks disconfirmation of it and, should this perspective be one in which he has a particular investment, disconfirmation of his self-concept. He feels shame about the figures, believes others should also feel shame, and projects that emotion; their response is something that may have consequence for the way he views himself. Each of us, in offering any part of us to others, may be expecting friendship and trust but may receive insult and rejection. It is not surprising, therefore, that few of those seated around the Boardroom table appear to be willing to share much as they interact. One has an overwhelming sense of subjectivity, each protecting his own, rather than of intersubjectivity, sharing and cooperating.

The executive function, if it is to be exercised properly, requires a pooling and sharing of interests and a reconciliation of them. Such a process demands that Paul, George, Eric, Alec and the rest are (a) prepared to say where they stand and (b) prepared to revise their opinions and/or to accept a compromise. They can improvise within a power scenario or within a status one. Paul, the Managing Director, can relate largely as his office or as Paul, the collection of emotions, hopes and ambitions. Of course, the distinction is a false one since each of us relates both in a role and as a person, but the amount we communicate about ourselves and our office/role varies from individual to individual and across time. Paul, as I have indicated, is quite capable of asserting his management role and invoking his power, but prefers in many circumstances to seek consensus, to look for cooperation, even affection from his subordinates (or 'colleagues', as he would refer to them when in this frame of mind). George similarly seeks to assert his power as Finance Director but, unlike Paul, is not looking for affection from his peers, he projects his shame and looks for some return on that investment. Getting none, he is as thwarted as Paul is in his search for consensus and both become angry. Both invest some meaning in their interactions, both risk an aspect of how it is they see themselves, both experience a degree of disconfirmation which may impact upon their self-esteem and both offer another improvisation, that of anger, in defence of their self-esteem.

Eric's approach is different. The discussion concerning the after market serves to reinforce his self-esteem. He invests in the encounter on the basis that no one else other than he is interested in the Service end of the operation: 'I know no one but me is interested in the non-glamorous end of the business. . .', and as the interaction ends with a whimper, not a bang, it serves to support his reading. His own self-concept may well be that of a lone figure kicking against the rest, it is certainly one that he maintains whatever the evidence to the contrary: 'Well, I can't see it and he (indicating Brian) cannot point to it.' He appears to define his colleagues as not worthy of trust and appears to maintain that definition to the end. To be sure, in saying anything at all he risks disconfirmation, but since he is apparently not disposed to hear it, the risk appears to be slight. Saying what he does say in the manner that he says it also is an investment: Eric as the bluff, no-nonsense, manager. It works perfectly, since that is what he is taken for and all ends on a suitably sour note. Eric, having mildly upset one or two others, can retire into the corner feeling warm and secure and, characteristically, disgruntled.

Alec adopts yet another approach. He edges into an investment decision as he talks to George about the figures, taking quite some time to declare his hand but then doing so with a vengeance: 'We must look a right load of idiots up in Manchester. . . . A barrow load of monkeys could come up with figures like that!' The controlled anger, however, in the repeated phrase 'I can see that', and in his manner is picked up by George and by the others around the table. Alec's anger serves to force an explanation and even half an apology from George, 'Look, it was holiday time . . .', and partially justifies it. He rapidly reverts to caution once Paul intervenes and says nothing more, or, at least, nothing that can be heard above the general babble.

Who Am I to Be?

For each of us, there are a number of ways in which we can relate to other people. In my initial encounters with Paul, George and company, I restricted myself to relatively distant or 'objective' relations with them; I was a researcher/consultant/academic and they were executives. In my more insane moments, I occasionally thought of them as 'subjects' with myself cast as 'scientist'. Such casting, of course, is relatively safe, since in defining them as objects and keeping my distance from them, not revealing any important aspect of myself to them (although to some of my peers the identity of 'scientist' would be of significance), I risk little. Increasingly, however, and particularly as that aspect of my activity concerned with observation diminished and my participation in the meetings increased, I had to address the question that each of them were asking of themselves. What kind of interaction is this? How far do I wish or need to be involved? What do I think about this or that issue and is it worth saying any of that? Can I risk exposing myself in this way? Is there a collective view emerging here that is worth more than my individual one?

Our upbringing and experience provide us with a structure of emotions and thoughts with regard to status and power which form the basis for the construction of our interpersonal worlds. Paul is a composite of pride, anger, affection, trust, fear, disdain, admiration, risk and defensiveness, as is George, Alec, Hugh, Derek and as I am. Each of us is or is not to a greater or lesser degree prepared to share aspects of ourselves with others; we can stay aloof or we can risk our investments. As structures, these thoughts and emotions, these constructions override all of the 'facts'; Eric sees what he wants to see in the figures (or, rather, he does not see what he does not want to see in them) and thus maintains his sense of self-esteem and dignity. It is these constructions that lie behind all of the parts we play and that influence each and every interpretation that we make; it is they that give us the degree of self-consistency we each experience and it is they that fuel the encounters we each experience.

What am I to Be?

I need to distinguish who I am from what I am. The answer to the former I have attempted to outline in the past ten or so pages. I am the knower and the known; the acting and the enactment; the performing and the repertoire. What I am in a particular circumstance is a performer of a particular *role*.

The notion of role is a key concept linking the self with others and, by extension, with the organization of which he is a member. As with everything I have been talking about, the difficulties and usages of the concept vary from commentator to commentator; some consider role to be actual behaviour, some a matter of expectations for behaviour deriving from partners, from reference groups or from society in general. One or two consider role to be a set of expectations as to what one should do deriving from one's own views of the situation (other's expectations affect one's behaviour because they influence one's own views).

I need to point out the difference between self and role. The knower and the known – the self – may be invested in a particular role or it may not.[9] I can perform my role as researcher with a fair degree of accomplishment with little or no investment of myself in it. Derek does a more than adequate job as a Personnel Director, but expends little of himself in that role; as an internationally recognized expert on butterflies, however, his investment is relatively large. George's commitment to the role of Finance Director is almost total; waking and sleeping, he orients most of his conduct around this consuming identity. In this case, his role has virtually merged with his self-concept; George apparently prefers to use the same role behaviours in a variety of situations. I have not depicted him in such circumstances, but his tendency to assess every situation – social or professional – in terms of cash, profit and loss, has led to a circumstance where others expect him to do it. It has become the *essence* of George as seen by himself and others, in a way that clearly he finds rewarding. He persists even though others joke about it and attempt to 'send him up' (perhaps *because* they so do).

Most of us most of the time are able to separate our ways of seeing ourselves from the roles we play (though not without difficulty). I have a repertoire of roles: teacher, researcher, writer, father, husband, cyclist, musician, chairman of various committees, member of others, advocate, and so on. As a repertoire, it is relatively enduring, though not necessarily stable; my expectations of myself as father, for example, have been modified in interaction with my children throughout our relationship. Not that my role has been made anew each time we have interacted, but it has been modified. In a similar manner, my role as consultant has been created and modified in interaction with others, notably in my relations with the executive group which figures so prominently in these pages.

None of the foregoing explains what I or any of the others *do* in a particular circumstance. It does not account for role performance nor does it explain why it is that I or George, for example, select a particular role for performance. Social actors seek roles and ways of performing roles according to a hierarchy of prominence;[10] thus I perform a particular role, say that of researcher, with varying degrees of investment depending upon how high the performance of that role stands in my current hierarchy (and how salient I take to be the present circumstances for its performance). To be specific, acting as a committed researcher seeking to sustain the role of social scientist with this group of executives may involve me in recording their interactions on videotape, administering paper and pencil tests to them at selected intervals, suspending their interaction while I check perceptions, even in wiring them up to measure physiological response. The reward to me in doing all of that (assuming for the nonce that it were to be possible) I may deem to be worth the costs. So possessed am I by that particular role that I take it to be appropriate to enact it in the manner I have indicated. In reality, however, in most circumstances I undertake my research on a much lower profile; I observe, I take notes, I participate in discussion whenever appropriate and I save my questions until after the event.

My calculations are not hit and miss; they are influenced by my experience. I have tried various approaches and this particular setting appears to be like that one in which I maximized my profit, so here goes. I may also have observed directly or indirectly (through reports) others enacting the role of researcher and arrived at my definition of that which is likely to be acceptable and appropriate by that route. Not that all of this profit maximization is within my control. How I perform in the Boardroom is influenced by what it is I take to be others' expectations of that role. Paul, George and the others take it that researchers *ought* to be objective, ought to come armed with tape recorders, interaction protocols and the like and, and if I perceive that my profit is related to my conforming to their expectations, it could be that such an enactment may assume a higher place in my prominence hierarchy. Similarly, should a significant other be present, then my selection of a particular role enactment may become a matter of consequence. Given that there is just me and the executives in the room, I may well perform in a different manner to that in which I would perform were another researcher/consultant present from whom I had respect and who controlled some rewards for me. It may be important to me to be held in high esteem by this person so I would tend to pay more attention to what would appear to be appropriate role enactment to him or her than I would to those in the room whose presence I take to be less significant.

It is important to remember, however, that depending upon the nature of myself, other people are more or less important to me. As an autonomous being, I can and do reward myself; not only do I take other people's reactions into account when carving out a role for myself, I take my own into account. If a particular performance as a researcher holds the promise of great reinforcement of a particular way of seeing myself, then I may perform it in that manner even though it is not approved of by a whole host of others. Qualitative researchers are singularly obtuse in persisting with their idiosyncratic emphases despite considerable punishment from journals and peers.

It follows from all of this that in enacting a role I will tend to go for that enactment that has the highest preference rating. In most circumstances, I will maximize my profit and decline to incur heavy costs; if a particular performance will require a great deal of effort from me, will involve me in considerable negotiation of it with others and will take time, I will tend to relegate it in my hierarchy. If, in addition, the performance requires me to take a risk, if it is something which I do not enact frequently, and thus have little experience of, I may eschew it altogether. I do not often present results to large groups, do not often take part in research conferences, I much prefer to disseminate what I have discovered through conversation. My role as researcher (which in itself is not one which accords with what others take to be research) is one with which *I* am familiar and, because I am familiar, one which I tend to repeat.

Performing Executive Roles

In enacting the roles of Finance Director, Managing Director, General Manager, Personnel Director, Planning Manager and Researcher/ Consultant, each of us seated around the Boardroom table is more or less possessed by the particular roles we present.[11] Each of us maintains or fails to maintain a degree of distance from our presentation. George's distance from his presentation of self as Finance Director is minimal, he is possessed by the role, so much so that it virtually merges with his self and is closely related to his self-esteem. Given this, it is to be expected that his emotions are brought into play to buttress and defend his essence. An attack on any aspect of the Finance function is likely to be construed as an attack upon George personally and addressed in this light by him. Paul is also possessed by his manner of enacting the role of Managing Director; he attempts to smooth over all disagreements and seeks what he takes to be consensus to the exclusion of all else. He is unhappy with disagreement and certainly takes no action to explore such disagreements as do arise. Failure to agree, however superficial that agreement, he takes as an affront and, as I have shown in commenting upon his interaction with George, is likely to construe events in emotional terms. George's caustic and repeated dismissals of Paul's view of events promotes irritation and, finally, anger – the latter no doubt partly fuelled by Paul being forced to abandon his consensus-seeking behaviour and adopt a less desirable, more autocratic, stance.

Eric, on the other hand, despite the assurances of his colleagues, is able to maintain his stance of dour scepticism throughout his interactions with them. He plays his role provocatively and appears to take a degree of pleasure in having others repeatedly assure him of something or other whilst signalling throughout that he does not really trust their assurances. If his behaviour is purposive and if that purpose is to irritate others, he succeeds and is aware of his success. There are clearly other ways of playing this particular role, but again from the reaction of his colleagues, it can be taken that Eric characteristically does not explore them; the essence of him (for them) is that of the curmudgeon, the churlish fellow, the person who will remain unconcerned and untrusting, come what may.

Alec likewise is another whose essence appears to be bound up with his role performance. He edges in to confrontations and, having taken some time in laying the groundwork, abandons the scene as soon as he meets opposition, most notably when this opposition comes from Paul. He gives off signs throughout most of his interactions that he is unhappy with the course of events and that he is in a state of controlled, barely suppressed aggression. He is perceived as combative and pugnacious but, having once struck out, as quick to retreat to the safe ground. The enactment which concerns us here, of course, is not a simple one. Alec, like one or two of the others, is seeking to perform the role of group member rather than simply that of General Manager. Neither he nor the others is clear about this enactment; he does not know what he *ought* to do as someone with a collective responsibility, so his habitual caution is somewhat exaggerated in the sequence I have commented upon elsewhere. His retreat may be characteristic of him or it may indicate that he is not possessed by this role and is able to maintain a distance from it.

The others present in the setting provide little by way of evidence one way or the other as to their enactments; Derek appears to be quite 'laid back' about most of that which occurs but I do not present enough information to discern whether or not that is characteristic of him, is *essential* or is one among many ways he may enact his role. I, myself, appear hardly at all and say nothing; such an enactment of my role as researcher is but one way of enacting it. It is within my repertoire to adopt a higher profile and, on occasion, with this group I do so. I am, however, not heavily invested in the role and am but slightly involved in defending any action (or failure to take action) in performing it. My performances as a writer and/or a consultant are roles which I take to be more worthwhile and in which I have a much more substantial investment.

What occurs in the Boardroom of Friction Free Castings Ltd is a series of improvizations around power and status enacted by a number of performers. Who these performers are, how heavily invested they are in their roles, has a considerable influence upon the dramas they enact. Over the months and years they have been together, they have developed a series of routines which maintain their relative positions on the power and status dimensions in more or less the same balance. The roles they enact, the aspects of themselves they invest are such as to make substantial change unlikely. Indeed when innovation is threatened, when the balance is disturbed, they, like the rest of us, invest their performances with a degree of emotion that often further serves to reinforce the status quo. It is to this aspect of performance that we now turn.

6   Once More with Feeling

In this chapter I want to advance the notion that emotion, like any other role, is socially constructed; that emotions are in fact roles, more temporary than most, but roles nonetheless. George being angry is, at root, George enacting anger in a similar manner to which he enacts being a Finance Director. George knows how to perform anger because he knows the socially prescribed set of responses to be followed by a social actor if he is to be taken to be angry, shameful, proud or whatever. In a moment or two I will elaborate this view and argue that emotions are directly related to power and status and constitute responses to judgements that these elements are to the fore in a particular encounter, but for the present I wish to consider the more common approaches to emotion or passion.[1]

The eighteenth-century perspective on the Passions held that only one strong emotion might possess the mind at one time; the mixture of jealousy and pity, love and hate with which (if we are to believe that which appears upon our screens) we are all too familiar were not conceived of by the learned folk of the 1750s. The kind of thinking they indulged themselves in is well summed up in William Collins's 'Ode on the Passions', written in 1747, which persisted as a set piece well into the nineteenth century. The Passions he enumerates were Fear, then Anger with his eyes on fire, then Despair which was 'sad by fits, by starts 'twas wild', and then came Hope; there followed Revenge, who 'threw his blood-stained sword in thunder down', then Pity, who was characterized as 'dejected', followed by Jealousy; next come 'pale' Melancholy, in turn succeeded by Cheerfulness, 'A nymph of healthiest hue'. Finally come Joy, Love and Mirth – six laudable Passions and six evil Passions.

An innocent age indeed, pre-Freud, pre-Jung, but one which shared with our own age the idea that emotions happen to us. In the age of innocence, that of pre-scientific psychological thinking, the poets, dramatists and novelists structured language and thought about the emotions within a framework which suggests that they are 'forces' which humans have to 'suffer' or 'endure'. Freud did us all a great disservice when he took over this kind of language almost lock, stock and barrel. He talks of 'forces', of 'energies' and of 'impulses'; true, he locates them within the human frame, but somewhere deep within it depicting the human psyche as a kind of cauldron of pressures screwed down lest their release overwhelms us. His terminology, not far away from that of the poets and dramatists of whom he was so fond, is that of hydraulics: 'cathexis' means filling, 'catharsis' release. In Freud's view, pressures from the unconscious threaten to enter consciousness in their demand for 'discharge'. Emotions are forces which threaten us, things which happen to us. Whatever happens in my consciousness, whatever happens in yours, from a Freudian point of view is the result of the impulses, instincts and forces which are boiling around beneath in the unconscious or subconscious.

Jung, too, is something of a hydraulic engineer. In his terms, 'Emotions are not "made" or wilfully produced, in and by consciousness . . . They appear suddenly leaping up from an unconscious region.' They are the 'intrusion[s] of our unconscious personality . . . To the primitive mind, a man who is seized by strong emotion is possessed by a devil or a spirit; and our language still expresses the same idea, at least metaphorically. There is much to be said for this point of view.' From this point of view, George's emotion in expressing shame and anger to Paul and the others is beyond his control. It is an 'impulse', a 'force', a 'drive' beyond his conscious agency that erupts and spills over one and all. If challenged, he could and probably would excuse himself by claiming that he did not know 'what possessed' him.

Such theories have little appeal to interactionists such as myself. They minimize the importance of consciousness. If the hydraulic model is accepted, the notion of a conscious agency can be dispensed with; there is no room for it. It is but a small step (and one taken by many a psychologist) to ignore consciousness. One can focus upon the cauldrons, as it were, and upon the consequences of the pressures released or repressed. Interactionists, concerned as they are with meaning and purpose, have little or nothing to contribute to such explorations. No interactionist perspective on emotions could hold that they are beyond control; it could not go along with Freud and Jung (and, it must be accepted, much of common sense) and posit emotions as things 'which produce themselves and have their own life'. Emotions are decidedly not independent of us. What George does, George does; it does not simply happen to him. Emotions are things in the psyche which are produced by the social actor.

Getting Het Up . . .

Before going on to demonstrate that emotional roles are the product of consciousness, that they are expressions of motive and purpose, I must deal with the objection that will have sprung to the lips of many of you. 'Hang on a minute, I *feel* upset when I am angry. Like George, I go red in the face, my pulse races . . .' Anger for you and George is the bodily change. You are, of course, in good company, that of William James:

> . . . bodily changes follow directly the Perception of the exciting fact, and that our feeling of the same changes as they occur *is* the emotion.

Unfortunately for James (and for you, if you are of the same opinion), his thesis was determined to be incorrect; it has been shown that the same visceral and neurological changes accompany very different emotional states and that artificial induction of these changes did not produce the appropriate emotions. Subjects were injected with epinephrine (an adrenal secretion that produces flushing, pulsating, anxiousness) and exposed to different social situations. Far from reporting the same thing, which would be the situation were James to be correct, subjects reported feeling fear in fearful circumstances and anger in offensive circumstances. Sensations produced by body chemistry are not themselves emotions.[2]

They are, however, closely related to them. Being angry and being fearful, though they may be different emotions, do invoke some physical sensation. It does not follow, of course, that the sensations are the emotion. They accompany emotions, but they do not, in and of themselves, constitute them. Emotions are not distinguished by discriminating one set of feelings and sensations from another. To illustrate, consider once more the exchange between Paul and George. George's initial displayed emotion is one of shame: 'I've got to say that I am ashamed. Ashamed to be associated with such figures . . .' The logic of the situation as perceived by him dictates the emotion, not the bodily sensations; he sees himself as responsible (at least in part). Later, he becomes angry in response to challenges from Paul. 'Of course not! I know what's expected of me there!' Again the logic of the situation calls out the response – an unreasonable accusation which I must refute. The physical sensation may be slightly different, but the emotion is clearly not merely the sensations.

Emotions, even in common parlance, are not simply sensations. George's shame and/or anger may be deemed 'reasonable' or 'unreasonable', 'warranted' or 'unwarranted', even 'right' or 'wrong', 'justified' or 'unjustified' *in the circumstances*. No such evaluations are offered in the realm of sensations and feelings; we do not talk of George's pulse rate as being 'unreasonable' or 'wrong', we do not consider his flushing to be 'unjustified'. An emotion, any emotion is more, much more than its physiological manifestation.

The Logic of Emotion

Emotion is a matter of intention. George's 'shame' and George's 'anger' are projections into the world, they are indictments in the one case of himself and others – 'I find the figures totally depressing and completely unacceptable; I am surprised that no one else does' – in the other, of Paul and his unjustified imputations. The anger is his and the control and expression of it his, there is a logic to emotion and a reason behind it. Emotions do not just happen, they are *about* something; that is to say, they have intentionality.

George is not simply ashamed or angry; he is ashamed *about* the figures, he is angry *at* Paul because Paul imputes that he, George, is likely to behave inappropriately at the forthcoming formal Board meeting. True, at times George, like you and me, may experience what is taken to be emotion without there being a particular incident or object which precipitates it; significantly, however, this is termed a 'mood' – he is in a bad mood – and is to be distinguished from more specific emotions. Moods, however, like the more specific emotional enactments, structure our perspectives on the world and influence our lived experience. From the point of view of an interactionist, neither moods nor emotions simply happen. An emotion is a process involving self and others – George is angry with Paul, George is generally depressed with the world; in neither case is the state something which is purely in the mind. Emotions and moods are ways of relating self to others.

In a very real sense, therefore, an emotion is a judgement or set of judgements, something that we do in relating to others. In being angry with Paul, George is saying something about how he sees himself in his world, where it is he stands and what he takes to be an affront. Emotions, from this perspective, are therefore dependent upon opinions and beliefs. A change in George's beliefs or definitions (that, for example, Paul was being humorous rather than offensive) entails a change in his potential emotional enactment (George being angry that Paul should question his integrity). George cannot be angry if he does not believe that he has been offended. George's enactment of anger is the judgement that he has been wronged. His earlier shame is his judgement that he is responsible for the poor performance of the company as reflected in the figures. An emotion, any emotion, is a judgement about self and/or others.

No incident in and of itself is sufficient for emotion. The figures are available to all, the same 'facts' displayed for each member of the executive to peruse. The figures do not call out the same response from each individual. George is ashamed, Paul shows a degree of pride and pleasure, most of the rest appear indifferent. Emotion is not, therefore, a simple reaction; it always involves a degree of evaluation, an interpretation of the significance of what is occurring. George does not simply respond to the figures any more than he simply responds to Paul's comments about the projected Board meeting. At some level and with varying speed he interprets and evaluates both; he structures his response in the light of his interpretations and evaluations.[3]

Attitudes and Emotions

Those of you who have remained sufficiently distanced from the case I am putting will probably have begun to object that my emerging definition of emotion as a construction and a form of potential enactment puts it very close to that which others may term attitude. What I appear to be saying is that emotions are evaluations and judgements, but relatively consistent ones. George will be tuned, as it were, to anger, quick to take offence, whereas Hugh, for example, will be less disposed so to do. If that is what I am saying, then it is not far from prevailing definitions of the concept 'attitude': 'certain regularities of an individual's feelings, thoughts and predispositions to act towards some aspect of his environment'.

I am happy to go along with part of the definition; emotions may have a certain regularity. I am not so happy to accept the subsequent phrase. Emotion is not feeling (although it may be accompanied by feelings and sensations), but nor is it necessarily manifest in action. Nor is it a predisposition to act. I can be angry, can be proud, can even be fearful *without* necessarily showing any outward sign of my emotional state. What is more I can pretend to have an emotion which I do not have; I can simulate expressions of anger, pride and fear. If the idea of pretending is to make sense at all, it must follow that there is a gap between the internal construction of an emotional role and its expression. Manifestly I can have the one without the other. It is worth noting that I can behave in exactly the opposite way to how I would normally be expected to behave, given the particular emotion; I am kind and generous to someone with whom I am angry, humble at my moment of pride and brave before the lions.

There is little or no logical connection between the construction of an emotional role and its enactment (any more than there is between attitude and behaviour). My role as angry person may be expressed (or not expressed), may be denied or proclaimed. If owned, its expression may be appropriate or inappropriate and may come out in many different ways. George chooses to proclaim his shame in front of his colleagues but acknowledges that, although no doubt he will continue to experience the emotion, it is not something that he will display in the more formal setting of the Board meeting. His *intentions* at the two meetings are different. His emotion is clearly something different to his tendencies to act in a particular manner. George's shame is his indictment of himself and his colleagues; his expression of it is also under his own control. The choice to say something or not to say something is part of the structure George imposes on the world. Emotion and subsequent behaviour are constructions not predispositions or invasions from outer or inner space.

Emotions and the Self

I may or may not have an attitude towards the siting of Cruise missiles in the United Kingdom, towards dogs fouling the pavement, towards abortion or towards the wearing of the kilt. I may be more or less invested in all or any of these causes (or, as it happens, none of them), but it is clear that without some heavy investment of my self, none is likely to be a matter of emotion to me. Emotions are the consequence of relatively intense evaluative judgements which are not only important to me, they are *about* me, about my sense of self. Emotional roles are those roles that are particularly important to us, and concern matters in which we, as individuals, have invested conceptions of ourselves. George, both in his role as Finance Director and as a self, cares about the performance of his company; it means more to him than his dog, his neighbours, Christian Aid, perhaps even his family. Judgements about company performance, therefore, are to him matters of consequence, matters of emotion. Figures endow George's life with meaning.

For the others, figures have less meaning. Alec's display of anger towards George about the alteration in the figures may be because he has invested something of himself in the group as a group; his emotions involve people rather than figures and he may well regard George's action as a betrayal of trust, a denial of solidarity. His anger is the construction that he puts upon George's refusal to declare what has been going on; his intense evaluative judgement arises because of his relations to his colleagues *as* colleagues.

The ultimate object of George's emotions, or Paul's, Alec's, mine or yours, is always one's own sense of personal dignity and self-esteem. As Denzin puts it: 'Emotion is self-feeling. Emotions are embodied, situated self-feelings that arise from emotional and cognitive social acts that people direct to self or have directed toward them by others.' Through emotions we make and unmake our selves; the judgement that pride is appropriate raises my self-esteem, that shame is called for constitutes me as someone of lesser value. Paul's anger attacks George's sense of who he is just as his projection of shame on to Paul prompts the latter's defence which becomes, in turn, offensive to George.[4]

A Matter of Judgement

I have claimed throughout most of the preceding paragraphs that emotional roles arise from judgements and particular kinds of judgements at that, what Solomon terms 'constitutional judgements'. The figures do not automatically bring about a sensation of shame; Paul's strictures are not in and of themselves offensive. In the former case, the figures are constituted as being worthy of shame since they are the objects of George's shame, in the latter Paul's comments are constituted as being offensive by George's anger. Once constituted as shameful or worthy of anger, it is so and the sensation and the experience of the emotion is real. For the experience, it matters not a jot whether or not someone else considers the figures 'shameful' or 'offensive', nor does it matter that some time later upon reflection, George may own that his emotions were unwarranted. Shame and offence were constituted by *George's* construction *at the time* and insofar as he expressed them (and/or they were discerned by others), they entered into the subjective worlds of his colleagues.

George, like you or I, has to decide in real time what to make of a particular comment; his choice, his judgement is critical. If he decides that Alec, Hugh or whoever is 'taking the piss' and acknowledges that such behaviour is not to be treated 'seriously', he in so doing constitutes a world (his world) that may well accord with that of his colleagues and he responds in kind to the 'kidding' that is the norm. He may, however, evaluate the comment as extremely offensive and in so doing *makes it so*; the consequences for his world, if not for anyone else's, are profound.

Neither George nor the rest of us create the forms of interpretation or standards of evaluation which we employ. Judgements, like most other things, are learned from parents, teachers, peers, significant others and example. The problem for me in working with Paul and his team is one of discovering what forms of interpretations and standards of evaluation are common. It is, of course, a problem for them as well, since interpretations and standards change; what was acceptable last week, what was regarded as legitimate for 'kidding' and 'joshing', may no longer be so. What aroused Paul's ire today may not provoke him tomorrow, whereas an apparently innocent comment may be constituted by him as massively offensive. There are no fixed standards of interpretation or evaluation for any emotion, every judgement is a statement about how a particular individual sees his world at the time. If you 'come too close', 'touch me upon the raw', I am likely to respond emotionally and dogmatically.

Dogmatically since my emotion as a judgement constitutes my world and shuts it down arbitrarily and firmly. Having declared your remark to be offensive, I am no longer in a position to be 'objective' about it; *from my point of view*, what you have said is offensive and I am incapable of seeing any other interpretation, nor am I keen to listen to explanations of why my emotion is incorrect. It is my judgement. Declaring your words to be offensive makes them so. Given this declaration, I am not disposed to see anything other than offence; I am no longer open to persuasion. Good, bad or indifferent though such a state of affairs may be, it is the kind of world I live in; neither George nor I, nor you for that matter, inhabit a world in which 'objectivity' or 'open-mindedness' prevail all of the time. We are caring, involved, committed souls, a collection of judgements about relations, trust, responsibility and the like which, taken together, are our sense of what we are, our self. The *motive* of passion, therefore, is the protection of one's image of oneself. What then of the *cue*? At least in life in organizations, the cue is to do with power and with status.

In the kind of analysis I attempted earlier, Paul may be perceived to gain power but to lose status, whereas George may lose power and yet enhance his status. For example, Paul's ultimate exchange with George 'I trust you are not going into next week's full Board meeting with this sort of approach . . .' restores his power (which may be perceived to have been slipping away in the previous exchanges) at the cost of his status (lost on having to assert himself – though it must be recognized that in the eyes of some present his status may have risen *because* he exercised power). George, on the other hand, may be seen to have lost a degree of power (such as he had exercised in the course of the interaction to this point), but in refuting Paul's aspersions, may be seen to have risen in status. Since, however, neither Paul nor George in respect to each other can both gain *and* lose power or status at the same time, there are only four possible changes that can actually occur as a consequence of a single interaction episode. Since power and status are matters of perception, what others take to be the outcomes massively complicate the picture. George may lose status in Paul's eyes and, simply because he does so, gain it from his colleagues. For the sake of simplicity of exposition, I will stick to dyadic relations for most of the rest of the chapter.[5]

Outcomes are always due to an agent. Paul *himself* is responsible for an outcome, or George (or some *other*) is responsible. If Paul believes that he is responsible, the emotion that he calls into play may well be different from the one that he calls out if he takes George to be responsible. Leaving aside the complexities introduced by the notion of perception which is lurking behind much of the foregoing, it can be seen that Paul may accept that he is responsible for some or all of the outcomes in terms of perceived changes in power and status, he may assign all responsibility to George (or, for that matter, to some other present or imagined) or he may share responsibility. So, given the exchange outlined above, Paul's desire to invoke some emotional role or other, assuming that he perceives a change in power and status as an outcome, will vary according to whether he attributes it to his own lack of skill, George's bloody-mindedness or the intervention of third parties ('the rest of them just sat on their hands and said nothing!'). Indeed, Paul could experience a mixture of roles: sorry for himself so ill used by George, angry with George for having provoked him, and scornful towards the others for having sat on the sidelines.

Given what has been said earlier about the nature of improvized order, it will not be a surprise to find that this section builds upon these ideas and holds that emotion is as much a product of interaction as it is a particular (if temporary) pattern of relations. Paul becomes involved in the sequences of exchanges with George but neither comes naked to the conference table. They have a history of emotional relations with each other, they know where they stand vis-à-vis power and status. One or other or perhaps both may not like and may be interested in changing it, but for the sake of analysis it is possible to indicate the state of play, as it were, before the kick-off.

Paul, for example, in terms of his power relationship with George, may perceive it as adequate or imbalanced – too much or too little. If he perceives it as adequate, then it is likely that at the onset of the interaction, he will be feeling relaxed and relatively secure; he perceives himself to have nothing to fear from George. If he perceives himself to have too little power in relation to George (he is a maverick, has an independent income and a capacity to highlight difficulties second-to-none), then he, Paul, may experience a degree of anxiety and even a modicum of fear. If, on the other hand, Paul perceives himself to have too much power and further, should he recognize that in the past he has simply forced George to comply, he may feel guilt or even remorse. Guilt is a form of negative self-evaluation that occurs when an individual acknowledges that his behaviour is at variance to a moral standard. Thus Paul may recognize that 'civilized conduct' ideally does not involve forcing one's subordinates to comply; he may recognize that he has violated notions of 'fairness', 'consensus' and the like and may castigate himself for such departures from the moral imperatives of his reference group.[6]

Staying with Paul for the moment, it can be seen that should he feel that he has too little power and that he himself is the agent of that circumstance – he is to blame – he is likely to experience fear and anxiety. He may still experience fear and anxiety if he attributes the cause of his insufficiency of power to George (or some other, real or imagined), but he may turn this into hostility and anger towards George (or the other). Subjugation is one result of having too little power, a degree of resignation even, but it is equally possible that an attempt to take on the source of any anxiety is worth undertaking. Insufficiency of power, when experienced as caused by other rather than self, may lead to strong feelings of revolt and rebellion. Similarly, when others appear to accord me excess power, seem very keen to defer to me as a superman, far from feeling guilt, I may begin to rejoice in my powers and to feel that whatever I do to them is justified and deserved. They are asking for it.

So the emotion related to power present at the onset of an encounter, any encounter, may vary according to perception and to attribution. Those relating to status vary along similar dimensions. If Paul receives an adequate amount of voluntarily given reward and gratification from his colleagues, then he enters the encounter feeling good. Buoyant, happy, relaxed, at one with the world. Should he, however, experience an insufficiency of status, the consequent emotion is likely to be depression. Should he take himself to be the agent of his insufficient status, the resultant depression may be related to feelings of despair and hopelessness. It is likely that a person experiencing themselves as the agent of their own poor standing also experiences themselves as unable to do anything to rectify the situation; I am rejected by the person with whom I must interact and I deserve to be rejected. This may lead to a degree of aggression directed toward the self – very different, of course, to the circumstance in which Paul (or any other self) attributes his relative lack of status to someone else. On such occasions, the self feels itself worthy, but is denied benefits and gratifications by others. Depression may still be experienced but is often marked by anger and hostility directed towards those who are taken to be the agents of status denial.

Excess status, the according of what the actor concerned takes to be too much reward and gratification, calls out feelings of shame. To feel that one has received more than one's due is a ground for shame (at least in our culture in the latter part of the twentieth century).[7] When self is thought to be responsible for the excess, that what is accorded to one is down to false pretences, then the self is likely to feel embarrassment, guilt, a feeling that one has benefited well beyond the appropriate level. Should other rather than self be the perceived agent of excess status, the result may again be a degree of anger and hostility. In the self-as-agent case, Paul, for example, is aware that his displayed level of competence is a front, he is responsible for inducing the status accorded him and is aware that it is out of proportion. The circumstance is different where others regularly accord excessive status to an actor who takes himself to be performing at a much lower level. If Paul is continually told what a splendid chap he is, he experiences pressures to be a splendid chap in every imaginable way, he has to live up to his reputation which may well prove to be a considerable strain, if not an actual impossibility. The discrepancy between what Paul takes himself to be and what others give him credit for evokes embarrass-ment and, perhaps, shame; the fact that someone else persists in this unrealistic assessment may provoke hostility.[8]

So Paul and George, I and whoever I am relating to, you and your partners have, as it were, an emotional balance sheet when they meet and interact. The balance of power and status which holds social actors together and apart influences whatever they do together, our anticipa-tion of particular events also influences each and every interaction. Paul, for example, anticipates that his interaction with George will be difficult or easy as he gets into it (he adjusts his view as it develops) and as a consequence approaches the exchange with a degree of pessimism or optimism. Emotionally he may anticipate the warm glow of enhanced status as George readily falls in line with his views, some reduction in the amount of guilt he experiences in imposing his power upon him. George, on the other hand, may anticipate little change in the power balance whatever the temporary elation in holding forth, but some credit from his colleagues for having had the courage so to do. Both may experience a degree of anxiety about likely out-comes.

That this should be the case is so because the result of interaction, of any interaction, is that power and status have either increased, decreased or remained the same. The possibilities for the balance sheet are mind-boggling. Consider dear old Paul once more and his concern with his status. In relation to George he can be in a position (at the outset) of insufficient status (he receives less than what he takes to be his due from George – I propose to ignore agency for the moment), adequate status (he receives 'enough'), or excessive status (too much). In the course of the ensuing interaction, this balance is likely to be in flux and at any point may be further depicted along nine possible outcomes. Paul may be said to have gained, continued or lost from the position he began with; thus if he considered himself to be in a position of insufficient status, he may have moved towards the adequate level, or stayed the same or experienced even less status accorded to himself. If adequate at the onset, may have remained so, may have moved towards the insufficient pole or towards the excessive. If excessive, become even more so, stayed the same or moved towards adequacy. What emotions are called out, therefore, depends in part where Paul starts from, what he anticipates and what is the particular outcome. It also depends, as I have indicated, on who one takes to be responsible for the status (self or other) and to whom one directs one's emotion (self, immediate other or third party). A complex moving picture which, even had I time and skill enough to depict, would exhaust the space available. What should be clear is that since the currency of interaction is power and status, and since emotions appear to be related directly to these aspects of relations, interactions are frequently matters of consequence: the stuff of joy, exhilaration, anguish, anger and despair. Success in interaction is defined as creating and maintaining relations of status and power with others that promote happiness and security. Failure is the opposite of this and experienced as debilitating. The process of improvisation is not academic chess in the head, theatre of the mind, but something much more visceral and bound up with one's own sense of self; of worth, value and self-esteem.

Improvising Feelings

At the risk of labouring the point, I wish to return once again to the exchanges which occur between Paul and George.

Paul: Look, George, as I am tired of telling you, against the circumstances, in the situation we find ourselves in, these figures are acceptable. The trends are in the right direction – all of the graphs point upwards. Unlike last year when things promised to be worse . . .

George: And have been.

Paul: Alright. And have been. This year we are ending the year on an up turn.

George: And a thumping great loss!

Paul: I don't like the stance you are taking, George. I don't like it

one little bit. I trust you are not going into next week's full
Board meeting with this sort of approach . . .

George: Of course not! I know what's expected of me there! It's here
and now that worries me. I find these figures totally
depressing and completely unacceptable; I am surprised that
no one else does. We all ought to resign! I mean, we are
responsible for this mess – a loss for the third year. Seven
million quid! And nobody seems to care!

Picking up the extract with Paul's statement and assuming for the
sake of this exposition that George is able to perceive that his boss is
being critical of him, the sequence may be said to run off somewhat in
this fashion. George hears the statement 'Look, George, as I'm tired of
telling you . . .' and picks up the tone of controlled anger in Paul's
voice. It is conceivable that within the theatre of his head, as it were, he
is able to rehearse what is going on, taking his own role and that of Paul
towards him: I am being reasonable and assertive pointing out that we
should all feel bad, and Paul appears to be becoming annoyed; were I
in his shoes would I (as Paul) consider what I (as George) am saying to
be irritating? No. No point in getting heated about this, continue on
same tack:

'And have been . . .'

Paul, in turn, receives this piece of information and plays that out in
his head and defines it as more of the same. George is persisting with
his line, can't he see that my view is correct, we have a legitimate claim
to feel good which he appears to dispute; I have a right to be irritated. I
am becoming agitated, keep calm, simply refute:

'Alright. And have been. This year we are ending the year
on an up turn.'

George's stream of consciousness: My God, he is simply persisting
with the same line. Can't he accept my authority as Finance Director? I
have cause to be angry, can't the man see the point:

'And a thumping great loss!'

That does it. The man is obtuse, he is openly defying me and stating
that I am wrong:

'I don't like the stance you are taking, George. I don't like it
one little bit . . .'

What kind of person does he take me for. Doesn't like my attitude. Nothing wrong with *my* attitude, what needs sorting out is his and those of the rest of them sitting like dummies around here. How dare he assert that I would be stupid enough to make these remarks anywhere else:

> 'Of course not! I know what's expected of me there! . . .'

It is worth noting that George is attempting to induce a sense of shame in all (he returns to it at the conclusion of this speech) and Paul is trying to inculcate pride. Temporarily they both settle for anger.

The exchange is constantly monitored against the self, '*I* think this and *I* think that.' It appears to have the following trajectory: (1) Paul *judges* George to be behaving in an inappropriate manner and in so doing (as I have illustrated much earlier) *constitutes* the offence; (2) George picks up the hostility, (3) checks it against his own views and judgements (which, remember, have constituted the figures as an occasion for shame) and determines to continue his line which (4) he does, in turn (5) causing Paul to pick up that he, George, is not backing down and to constitute this as further grounds for offence. This judgement is no doubt now accompanied by some physical sensation. Paul senses a tenseness in his body, a flushing and pulsating which agitates him. He, wishing no doubt to appear emotionally mature, regulates the expression of his anger (6) which George chooses to ignore (7) and replies in line with his judgement 'And a thumping great loss', construed (8) by Paul as even more offensive, and so on . . .

In summary, the emotion that is experienced in a particular situation is, as with all other forms of conduct, constructed and improvised. The definition of the situation is the key process: by interpreting what is going on through the process of role taking, identities are defined for self and others and performances are constructed in line with these attributions. George looks at the situation, sees himself as a director 'responsible' for the proper conduct of the company affairs, casts his peers into similar 'responsibility' and determines that, having 'failed' in their duties, he and they *should* feel 'shame' and 'guilt'. Having chosen the definition and the emotion rule, he follows it and, no doubt, experiences the appropriate feelings.

Emotion rules, like interpersonal rules, are learned.[9] Throughout life, instructions are received ('Don't cry, it's not that bad! ') and learning is derived from observation. From this supermarket of emotion rules, social actors choose and seek to apply, always guided, of course, by their desires to maximize reward. If a particular emotion is regarded as pleasurable, then actors will seek to promote it; if experienced as unrewarding, people will seek to avoid it. As I have argued before, we each attempt to structure our interactions in ways which we feel rewarding (even if, occasionally, such rewards are not too obvious; some actors, for example, will cause the termination of a relationship simply to confirm 'I told you so'). Emotions are structured in a similar fashion, avoiding or promoting them in line with ends and purposes. Not simply short term goals and purposes: although I may dislike 'anger', I may act in a way which will produce that state in order to arrive at the pleasurable state of having won my point, maintained or enhanced my power and status. George, Alec, and the others risk boredom, anxiety and an element of fear to maintain or disturb power and status relations in order to arrive at the feelings of elation associated with success.

The Regulation of Emotion

It is worth noting at this point that the emotional market-place is as subject to regulation as the cognitive one. One can be accused of 'lacking feeling', one can be castigated for causing embarrassment to others in becoming 'over emotional', and one can be accorded status for displaying 'emotional maturity'.

Averill, whose views are very similar to those of the interactionists, though he does not claim allegiance to the school, offers some broad classes of rules that may well apply to emotions in general. There are three types of rule – constitutive, regulative and heuristic. For the sake of illustration, I intend to begin by applying the scheme to a non-emotional example – a Board meeting. Some rules to do with legal composition of the Board, to do with frequency of meetings and to do with duties constitute the activity as a Board meeting. Without the formal constitution, without the panoply of minutes and the adherence to Roberts Rules of Order, there is not a Board meeting. There may well be another kind of meeting, but its validity as a *Board* meeting would be open to challenge. Other rules are regulative. For example, in the Board meeting, Paul may determine and have everyone agree that no item may be debated longer than forty five minutes or, more trivially perhaps, that no one should smoke. Such rules do not determine whether or not the event we are witnessing is a Board meeting, they simply influence the way it proceeds. Averill's third category is somewhat more slippery. Heuristic rules determine strategy. Effective Boardroom performers recognize situations in which one course of action is preferable to another, they have a grasp of what is appropriate. Paul and, as it turns out, George both have a grasp of what is and what is not going to be appropriate at the Board meeting. Not that George doing his Cassandra bit would invalidate the Board meeting as a Board meeting, nor can Paul or any one else put forward a regulation that outlaws such behaviour (that would challenge the constitution of a Board meeting); what both can do, however, is recognize behaviour which will result in a 'successful' Board meeting rather than another. They can and do behave strategically.

Now it can be argued that similar types of rule apply to the emotions. To illustrate, let me return to the sequence of exchanges between Paul and George. The latter claims, in effect, that the performance of the company is such that each and every one around the table ought to be ashamed. Paul contests this view and asserts that the performance is reason for pride (not exultation, but certainly a modest degree of self-congratulation is in order). The rest do not appear to care either way. It appears that the performance of the company is not a matter that they feel involves them to the extent that they feel either shame or pride. They appear indifferent. Whether or not they are, or should be, is not a matter which concerns me at the moment, the apparent indifference furnishes us with a clue to a constitutional rule of pride and shame. To be proud or ashamed of something, the existence of which is not seen to be connected with the self, violates one of the constitutive rules of these particular emotions. Put more clearly than the actual example affords one the opportunity to do, there is no reason for any one in the room to feel proud or ashamed of the River Avon, which I can see from my window. It has no connection with any of the selves in the Boardroom and is nothing that they or I have any responsibility for; the constitutive rules of pride and shame indicate that connection and responsibility, an involvement of self, are necessary to those emotions. Obviously it can be argued that all in the room should be proud or ashamed. They are, after all, managers of the company and as such can be expected to invest some aspect of themselves in its activities. Such, however, is not the point at issue. Paul and George feel 'pride' and 'shame' respectively and, given the involvement of aspects of themselves, such feelings are appropriate. There are, of course, also rules of how 'shame' and 'pride' should be displayed – regulative rules. Gnashing of teeth, rending of garments, cutting one's flesh with thorns and sharp stones may be deemed excessive even for George and dispensing champagne somewhat over the top for Paul.

Regulative rules not only refer to the way a particular emotion is organized and expressed, they may also indicate the appropriate expressive and psychological responses. A death of a close friend or loved member of the family is the occasion for a degree of sadness, weeping is not only permissible, it is to be expected. In such an event, there are clear rules for emotional conduct (which, interestingly, vary from culture to culture); there appear to be rules for, say, length and depth of emotional experience. A quick burst of tears followed by laughter is unlikely to be considered 'sincere', whereas should either Paul or George continue their angry exchanges for longer than a few minutes, it would be regarded as excessive.

Beyond the constitutive and the regulative, there do appear to be heuristics for the expression and feeling of emotion; were this not to be the case, professional actors would find little employment, as Hamlet bears witness. Social actors such as Eric on occasion get it completely wrong: 'Got us in one! A load of monkeys!' No one responds, no one finds the statement amusing. Laughter is not deemed to be appropriate. Alec's cold, almost taut, controlled probing in the same extract is a distinctive and distinguished performance. A skilled display of intensifying feeling culminating (if subsequently undercut by Eric's echo of the phrase) in 'A barrow load of monkeys could come up with figures like that'.

The argument of Averill, Heiss and others is that Paul, George and the others 'know' what to feel in a situation which arises, since they 'know' the appropriate 'emotion rules'. The definition of the situation provides them with a basis for choosing the rule. Defining an event as a funeral cues the appropriate emotion, defining it as a party cues quite different sensations. Actors tend, therefore, to experience the emotions they 'should' have, those that are expected of them and that, given effective socialization, they expect of themselves. Not that all necessarily either define the situation in a similar fashion or experience the same emotions. George defines the figures as evidence of poor stewardship and experiences 'shame' and, perhaps, a degree of 'guilt'. Paul defines the circumstances as a 'turnaround' and urges George that 'pride' and 'pleasure' are more appropriate states to summon. In a very real sense, George is being attacked for feeling the 'wrong' thing, a circumstance which is not uncommon. The fact that 'emotion rules' are applied often without much thought should not lead us to believe that such rules do not exist. Paul implements the rule for the situation as he defines it, George experiences emotion in line with his definition; both sets of feeling are linked to particular definitions. Sharing the definition would no doubt lead to similar emotions, different in degree, perhaps, but similar in kind.

It is clear that other people are as important to a discussion of emotion as they are to any other aspect of interaction. George presumably feels 'shame' because of what he takes to be the attitude of his peers and superiors to his performance: 'We ought to be sacked.' No doubt having indulged in rudimentary role taking – what do these results mean, what will Paul and my colleagues think about it, so how shall I conduct myself – George is surprised to have got it 'wrong'. Or is he? It could be that in a somewhat complex manner he 'enjoys' being out of step and having the 'right' feeling (shame) since, in terms of a wider or more specialized community (the business world, say, or finance directors), his definition is the one that would prevail, not Paul's. Whatever the 'truth' of this particular encounter, the dynamics remain the same: in order to know what emotion is appropriate, the actor must define who he or she is to be. In many circumstances, social actors not only know who they are to be, they also know what emotions are appropriate. They have the script and know the characterization expected of them, thus they have little need to improvize. In other circumstances, however, there is an element of the problematic in the encounter. For the First Player on whom Hamlet comments in the well-known passage on the hypocrisy of actors,[10] the expectation is clear and the appropriate emotion to be displayed readily at hand. Less so for Hamlet himself, who seeks to induce passion appropriate to his own circumstance:

> Yet I,
> A dull and muddy-mettl'd rascal, peak,
> Like John-a-dreams, impregnant of my cause,
> And can say nothing . . .

Hamlet could be a victim of 'emotion rule strain' just as, arguably, George suffers from it. Both find it difficult or impossible to act consistently with the emotion rules that each believes to apply to the situation. To be accurate, George expresses 'shame' and 'guilt' which *he* defines as appropriate to the circumstances, the strain for him is the lack of consensus about the proper rule to be followed. For Hamlet, it is more a case of conflict of emotions; love for mother conflicting with the anger induced in him by the knowledge of her marriage to the person responsible for his father's murder.

Interactionists propose that we can also suffer from 'emotion overload' – rules cannot be obeyed because the actor does not have the energy to follow them. In moments of crisis or, for that matter, of exhilaration, the energy expended in a particular direction is such that it blocks out other emotions. Alec, for example, concentrates his anger around the manipulation of the figures, he is aggrieved by George's action in altering them, but somewhat cautious in his expression of concern since he is not fully aware of Paul's role in the recalculation. So obsessed is he with these emotions – anger and fear – that he cannot cope with Derek's sudden and unexpected support. He has nothing left with which to show pleasure in this unlooked for and unusual alliance.

It should be clear by now that I am putting forward the view that emotions, like other forms of behaviour, are more or less institutionalized ways of interpreting and responding to particular classes of situations, notably those involving elements of power and status. Following James Averill, I would claim that emotions may be conceived of as cognitive scripts that influence how a particular actor defines a particular situation, how that actor responds and how he or she monitors that response. I do not hold that such scripts are innate or genetic; they are the internal representations of social norms and rules such as those I have elaborated in the preceding paragraphs.[11]

A Matter of Judgement

Nonetheless, most of the foregoing may have been read as special pleading, a desperate attempt to drag emotions, feelings and passions into an interactionist framework. Using oneself as an instrument (putting oneself into what one takes to be the shoes of the writer by putting oneself in one's own shoes), you may well have concluded that emotions are neither defined nor negotiated; they simply occur apparently without prompting and occasionally to your surprise. True, an emotion is something we *do*. It does appear to be of the order of reaction; called out by a signal, a reaction to a stimulus. Just so. Social actors *do* emotions, they enact them, at times they seem to be possessed by them. None of which gainsays anything that I have argued in the previous paragraphs. A little repetition may be in order.

Emotions (like some other apparently more cognitive ways of responding and interacting) may be seen as 'judgements'. Power and status are important dimensions (some would say *the* most important) of how it is social actors position themselves in social space and thus come to regard themselves. Judgements of this kind occur, as I have claimed, under conditions where power and status relations are threatened or are upset; since such relations are critical, related to notions of self-esteem, it follows that emotion is directly related to self-feeling. An emotion is a basic judgement about our selves, about where we stand in relation to our intentions and those of others, about the realization or failure to realize our values and ideals. Paul's anger is a judgement that he has been wronged by George; George's initial shame *is* his judgement that he, as Finance Director, has performed badly. It is the invocation of a pattern of response – which Averill terms a 'transitory social role' – which is taken to be appropriate to the circumstances. Sadness, guilt, anger, pride or whatever are judgements, evaluative ones, about situation, self and others.

The figures that George presents do not bring about emotional reactions; both George's and Paul's emotions are judgements about the impact of them. The figures – or any other stimuli – are never sufficient for emotion. Emotions always, everywhere and inevitably involve personal evaluations of specific incidents. A change in definition (for example such as Paul seeks to induce George to make) entails a change in emotion. Emotions are related to interpretations, not simply reactions to 'facts', still less the eruption of feelings from within. True, George's 'shame' and 'guilt' may well be accompanied by perceptible differences in heart-rate, in breathing and excretion of sweat, but if persuaded 'pride' is a more appropriate judgement, 'shame' will disappear instantly leaving only the feelings – the physiological activities which are no longer 'shame' but simply feelings. The emotion is the judgement, not the physiological state.

If, as is being claimed, emotions are judgements, why should it be seen that they 'happen' to us? Actors remember making judgements about other things – careful, rational, thought-through, well-argued decisions; not so with emotions. They appear to be beyond control and resistant to what are taken to be the normal processes of decision making. It is, of course, arguable that emotions are no different to the constructs discussed in an earlier chapter; very few judgements are, in fact, reflective and deliberate. Custom, practice, experience and conditioning have rendered much of our lives unproblematic and unreflective. My constructs, my habitual definitions about what is or is not 'funny', what is or is not 'fair', what is or is not 'honest', lead me to make decisions and to conduct myself in a particular manner without recourse to extensive or even minimal processes of rational deliberation. I make hundreds of such decisions in a day without thinking about them; I make an equal number of emotional judgements equally without reflection. Occasionally I operate strategically: should I let fly at so-and-so, should I expose myself to attack by owning to my ignorance? However, for much of the time my conduct and my emotions are run-off without reflection and without deliberation.

I may well reflect upon my actions and my emotions after the event. My actions are justified or not by recourse to revised definitions. I was wise not to raise that issue because subsequently George did and he had his head bitten off. Thus wisdom was my guide, not lack of courage. I reflect upon my emotions and disown them. I remember feeling 'hot and bothered', 'agitated', and take it that my feelings have been 'aroused' by some one or some event. Once 'aroused', they are 'beyond my control'. I may take it that the arousal is involuntary, but it is my emotion that causes the feeling, my judgement that spurs the adrenalin, not the chemistry that causes the emotion. I make myself angry, make myself depressed, make myself elated. It is not a simple relationship; I cannot readily and consciously create such effects but I can and do occasionally make myself angrier by reflecting upon a slight, constituting the offence as greater than I or others took it to be at the time.

In all of this talk about reflection, it is important to remember the capacity we each have to interact within our skulls. I argued in the previous chapter that I had the capacity to define my self-concept and to conduct an internal dialogue between the 'I' and the 'me'; the self being the capacity to hold the ring, as it were, for this process to occur. Given that perspective, it is possible to argue that emotions are not direct experiences, they are interpretations (the gist of the points I have been making in this chapter) and to claim that what we take to be the experience of passivity (of being seized by or overwhelmed by emotion) is not intrinsic to the response but is an interpretation. In the theatre of our heads, we disclaim reponsibility for our emotions. Such a view may be taken as more plausible if we consider the enormous investment we make in advising others how to control themselves; on the one hand we acknowledge the overwhelming force of passion and on the other we are convinced it is not beyond our control.

All emotions may be said to be judgements but, of course, not all judgements are emotions. You and I, Paul and George, can and do make decisions without arousing feelings, without becoming emotional. Most of the time they do. They do so 'rationally', 'calmly' and 'objectively' (or so they would claim). The judgements that constitute our emotions are especially important to us and concern matters in which we have invested ourselves. George, who identifies with his professional self – that of Finance Director – is more likely to experience intense feelings and emotions over financial matters than are his colleagues. On the other hand, he is less interested in maintaining close relationships with his peers and is thus less concerned than they about what they take to be matters of trust and equality in the debate around the revision of the figures sent to Manchester.

The notion of investment or involvement is an important one in understanding the development and invocation of particular patterns of emotional response. If I am not invested in a particular circumstance or relationship, my emotional role therein will be a matter of formality. Should I ask one of the members of the team, for example, how they are, it is likely to be taken as an expression of politeness, a desire to initiate conversation, rather than a serious inquiry about their health. Should they respond, 'Not too good, feeling a bit down', I would not be expected to say more than 'I am sorry to hear that'. To be sure, I should not laugh at the same time, but little more would be expected of me. Indeed, deep concern on my part for someone with whom I have but little contact would be deemed odd. It is unlikely in such circumstances that I will experience any physiological arousal.

With greater involvement comes greater arousal, such that I take the emotional role I am enacting to be ultimately a matter beyond my control. In becoming involved and behaving as I do, I am making a bid for others to judge me and respond to me as a person possessed. And your reaction to me in such circumstances must be guided by standards which are taken to apply to such performances rather than those that apply to deliberate ritual acts. In effect, I am warning you that my self is heavily committed in the particular circumstances and that I am to be treated with caution.

For me, much of the time, my emotions involve other people and my relations with them; I am concerned with their judgements of me and mine of them. I am also very much concerned with my judgement of myself. In a fundamental sense I am my emotions. I am proud, ashamed, guilty. I am in love, angry, jealous, full of bile. The ultimate object of my emotions as judgements is always my own sense of personal dignity and self-esteem. Eric Wragg resents the lack of concern for Parts and Service shown by his colleagues but, in essence, their behaviour is an affront to his status and self-esteem. Show respect to Parts and Service and you show respect to me; ignore it, devalue it, and you attack me. An emotion, any emotion is essentially and intimately concerned with personal power and status.

7　An End and a Beginning

For the past two or three chapters I have been presenting some ways of considering the executive process as a form of Commedia dell' Arte, a circumstance in which the social actors perform off the cuff (*a bracchia*) against relatively well-known canvasses (*canovacci*), realizing in the performance a form of ritual. Not an empty form, as so many of the usages of the term now imply; rather a celebration and a grounding of the relations which obtain between those concerned. Who each of the actors *is* is constituted out of their relations with each other; it is with other people that I am first provided with a self-concept of myself and it is to other people that I turn time and again for confirmation. Each of us in the Boardroom constitutes his self-concept intersubjectively, anchored, to be sure, in one's own subjectivity, but defined in terms of how we behave towards each other. Interpersonal behaviour, the patterns of self-presentation and altercasting that is observable throughout most of the exchanges I have depicted, is enacted to maintain or enhance each actor's relative comfort, security and freedom from anxiety. The manner of doing this is to induce from the other actors that behaviour which is complementary to that proffered by yourself. It can only be assumed that, bizarre though a particular piece of behaviour may be to an observer or another participant, it expresses something of importance to the performer.

　Foa wrote some twenty or so years ago that each 'interpersonal act is an attempt to establish the emotional relationship of the actor toward himself and toward the other . . . (and) each behaviour serves the purpose of giving or denying love *and* status to the Self and the Other.' My terminology and my basic metaphor differs, but I am fully in accord with his conclusions.[1] Interaction in which selves are committed, where there is a self-role merger, where the essence of the social actor is taken to be involved are matters of emotion, since the self is constructed out of emotion. Eric *is* churlish, aggressive, a terrier amongst the mastiffs. To maintain this identity, he must induce aggression from others and must not succeed in his avowed intent to persuade them of the importance of Parts and Service. His identity as the little man kicking against the pricks could not survive the warm embrace of his colleagues and their total capitulation to his complaints. His construction of his world requires opposition and unrewarded struggle; his performance induces such behaviour from his colleagues.

Eric, like most of the rest of his colleagues, has a limited repertoire. He acts hurt, suspicious and distrustful in virtually every circumstance and in most of them succeeds in provoking rejection. Neither he nor most of his colleagues has an extensive repertoire. Eric can and does modify the intensity of his behaviour – his realistic wariness and scepticism concerning the change of logo is of a different order and receives a different response to that which he offers elsewhere. For the most part, however, Paul, George, Eric, Alec and the rest express their relationships within the relatively narrow confines of a limited number of roles (emotional and cognitive).

To do so and to do so with the skill and regularity that these actors do is to persist in a form of maladjustment which ensures that the executive process – that reconciliation of interests which is arrived at through cooperative efforts – is unlikely to be particularly effective. The interaction of the group consists of a number of relatively rigid, inappropriate and inflexible behaviours produced with great skill and maintained with the appropriate display of emotion. There is not much managing, directing or leading (Paul occasionally resorts to a disguised form of 'bossing'), little guiding, advising or teaching, little help, little support or sympathy, little sensitivity, little frankness, few confidently independent stances. There is a heroic reliance upon distrust, attack, withholding and conforming behaviour.

I am content to conclude this book as I began it – with the good Chester Barnard: 'Cooperation and organization consist of concrete syntheses of opposed facts, and of opposed thoughts and emotions of human beings . . . it is precisely the function of the Executive to facilitate the synthesis in concrete action of contradictory forces, to reconcile conflicting forces, instincts, interests, conditions, positions and ideals.' Throughout these pages I have tried to keep elements of this quote in mind: it is now time to summarize and seek to generalize my position. In so doing I will, of course, draw heavily upon the preceding pages but will go beyond them in a number of respects.

The executives I depict are individuals with goals, values and interests which are not necessarily shared by their colleagues. Nonetheless, they may well aspire to the kind of association envisaged by Barnard. They are not simply individuals isolated in time, space and purpose any more than you or I are simply an individual independent of others. For all the appearance of selfish, egotistical behaviour the foregoing pages may have left you with, it would be folly to conclude that there is nothing more to social and organizational life than the struggle of the individual for power and status. The themes of interaction are indeed power and status but where one stands on these dimensions enables one to create, sustain, modify or transform particular scripts. It matters to George that the figures are 'bad', it matters desperately that his colleagues should share his view of them; that they don't, that they persist in what he takes to be an altogether wilful perspective upon them is a matter of consequence.

The problem for George, as for each one of us, lies in the fact that meaning is contained not in what we say but in the responses of others to what we say. Declaring the figures signifies nothing; meaning is not immanent. Declaring the figures and renting one's garments, tearing one's hair and gnashing one's dentures does not signify either. What matters is the response to such displays. One can either be believed, ignored or certified. It is, of course, quite likely that, in many situations, behaving like George does will lead others to accept your putative definition. Emotional display is a particularly powerful form of altercasting. In the particular circumstances of this group, however, with the exception of Paul most choose to designate the event as one in which no interest is to be shown, no contest is to be joined. The script – that figures are to be taken lightly – persists despite George's valiant efforts to challenge, or at least modify, the pattern.

The response is, of course, part individual; it may even be informed by an attempt on the part of one individual to modify the meaning of the figures himself; Paul wishes them to be seen in a positive light. For most, however, the response is determined by what they take to be appropriate behaviour; they know how to respond because they share a pattern of mutual expectation. Between them they have elaborated a series of scripts; they each know what to expect of each other when figures are discussed. By and large, discussion of figures will always produce a similar response within this group. Prior socialization and the tendency rapidly to categorize events into ones requiring simple responses severely constrain the range of possible behaviours. They do not determine the behaviour, otherwise there would be little point in the struggle nor could there be any explanation of Paul's response, but they do strongly influence it. Such is indeed the activity of such groups; they are about controlling the range of response, they are about shared meaning and mutual expectation; they are about rendering the world more stable and predictable. The social actors create and respond to scripts. In the accomplishment of such purposes, however temporarily and however imperfectly, they render the novel response difficult.

The Commedia dell' Arte troupe, as I indicated, realizes its performances through improvisation around a number of themes and characters and thus constitutes a good analogy for the issue I have been struggling with in these pages. In effect the performer in such an enterprise both constitutes and is constituted by the form. There is a subject-object unity which is the essence of social and organizational life. The actors on the stage improvise off the cuff against a canvas which both guides and is formed by their improvisations; they are what they create, just as Paul and his colleagues constitute and are constituted by their interactions. Let me push this a little further. The Commedia dell' Arte performance is always interaction within a context in the sense that elements of the story, setting and circumstances shape what will be transacted by the performers and in the sense that what a particular performer improvises provides the context for his co-performers. Now the same is true for Paul et al; they perform within a context set not only by themselves but by generations of previous performers, but what they do is contextualized for each of them by each of the others. Context from this perspective is not fixed but is the consequence of lines of activity, it is enacted and only enters into the field when it is enacted. Just as we can only understand the nature of the Commedia as and when it is enacted, so we can only recognize the structural context as it is manifest within a particular set of interactions. Until George raises the issue of cost, the pattern of interaction is not influenced by it; once mentioned, it constrains. Improvisation is the process through which human beings create significance and respond to that significance. Behaviour on the social stage is neither micro nor macro; what Paul and his executives do is dependent upon what larger features of the canvas enter into their consideration and are rendered meaningful through the very process of their interaction; context is enacted or ignored. The one – the process of improvisation – accompanies and is constituted out of the other – the canvas – whilst in its very enactment realizing it.

That being said, it should be clear that I neither agree with those who hold that structure is all and that human beings as reflective agents have no place in organization analysis, nor with early interactionists who claim that there is nothing to observe in the world but *individual* definition. From the perspective I have advanced in these pages it is clear that social performers, like stage performers, perform within the context of more or less powerful organizations or canvasses. The context can and often does channel *thinking* along particular lines; the canvas can and does influence the off-the-cuff interaction. Scripts enacted in the responses of the executives towards one another are indeed the product of their energies and their activities (and of those long departed who preceded them) but they appear to be beyond the control of those who create them. Scripts attain a kind of objectivity, a distance from their creators which confronts them as 'reality'. Somewhere long ago and far away, some group of executives elaborated and indeed celebrated a set of responses to the division of labour which accorded meaning to the role of 'gaffer' or 'boss'; 'he's the gaffer, he can do what he likes', 'it's up to the boss, he can decide'. Such meanings are rarely challenged, they appear to be part of the natural order of events and such meanings now enter into and shape the responses of those who interact with 'bosses' and 'gaffers'. In a similar fashion Paul and his executives share a community of meaning around the nature of their business which they take to be self evident and beyond question. They do not challenge that they should be in the Castings business; they accept that the Headquarters group in Manchester is, at best, to be tolerated; for the most part they believe that the best way to bring about change is to assemble a mass of figures, analyse them and devise a strategy and to do all of this slowly, carefully and cautiously. I am not claiming that any of these scripts is necessarily wrong, simply asserting that they are not questioned. To those seated around the table it is obvious that change can only be brought about incrementally after exhaustive analyses of considerable sets of data. Any other approach is, literally, unthinkable. What they fail to recognize is that they both create and are the products of such performances.

What I have attempted to depict is a pattern in which social actors constitute themselves out of interaction and then seek to maintain the resultant intersubjective being through routines and rituals. I have argued that the dimensions around which they construct themselves and around which they improvise are those of power and status, but in seeking to de-emphasize the cognitive (as I have been doing in the past few pages), I would suggest that much of the improvisation that occurs is a matter of intuitive behaviour rather than the product of conscious reflection. It appears 'natural' and 'normal' for George to perform as he does, as it appears natural and appropriate for Paul to do what he does.

There are two cues which cause performances to be enacted without reflection: setting and *dramatis personae*. The Boardroom signals a very different kind of interaction than does the executive toilet; the canteen sanctions some performances and rules out others. Paul's office and where he sits in it – behind his desk or at the coffee table – elicits a different performance than does the photocopying room. Most of the repetitive, ritual behaviour takes place in specific settings with specific others.[2]

Imagine if you will a scene in a play, say *Hamlet*. The Prince is berating his mother for having married his uncle and is working himself up into a fine lather about this when Osric (a minor character) enters and wanders across the set. Whatever performance is being realized between Hamlet and Gertrude is violated by this intrusion. As in the theatre, so in social life; the meeting of the Executive includes some actors and excludes others and the performances mounted are people specific. Characters are specific to scenes and structure emerges from which characters are present in which scenes. Paul performs in Manchester and in South London, none of his colleagues appears in both settings. Each of them, however, belongs in the Boardroom and each expresses his belonging, his right to be there, as it were, in his interaction. I do not belong, am there by exception and must not draw too much attention to myself lest I be reminded of my marginal status. The rest celebrate their power and status without such concern. They talk about things they would not discuss in another setting nor in this setting with other characters and they do so with a degree of commitment that they may not display elsewhere.

Let me push this just a little further. Particular scenes involve specific actors and exclude others (Eric, for example, has been excluded from strategy discussions and resents it) and, as in a play, what gets talked about depends upon the membership; Alec, Hugh and Paul talk about strategy together but do not include Eric in such conversations. The Strategy Development Group (for such is its name) is rather like a Cabinet Committee, it exists yet it does not. Who its members are and what they deliberate about is known only to the elect. Alec, Hugh and Paul accept each other as members and share a solidarity which they demonstrate not only in their meetings but in other settings (such as the one I am concerned with), when Eric's questioning of their collective competence, serves to unify them further.

The Executive also share a sense of membership, but one that creates and maintains a hierarchy. Paul's membership of other groups perceived to be more senior sets him apart from the others and, as I have shown, issues of power and status serve to delineate and maintain relations between them. At a minimal level, nonetheless, the group shows a level of 'groupness', of solidarity that distinguishes it from other similar collections of people. The same individuals even meeting in the same setting but talking about something else would not necessarily see itself as the Executive. The script, the apparent purpose, the intent of coming together, would differ. Making decisions about significant company-wide issues is accepted as the script of the Executive and this distinguishes it from the same people meeting in the same room and talking about Christmas festivities or location of offices.

The Executive is also distinguished from other groupings in that it has a particular emotional tone. It deals with issues that are likely to be of consequence to each of the actors (or fails to deal with them) and since it is an arena in which matters of power and status are likely to arise with a frequency and intensity not found elsewhere, it is likely to be experienced as different from other kinds of encounter. As I have shown, this particular set of actors, on the occasion I have chosen for illustration, do not depart radically from their ritual. Nonetheless, there is an emotional tone to their interactions that they acknowledge would not be present elsewhere (in the formal Board meetings, for example). Not only do they share a cognitive reality (what work is to be done in such a setting), they share an emotional reality (what kind of feelings can be displayed here and what cannot). Both are important constituents of a script. Without these elements of shared reality, the interaction would be confused and unfocused and destined to fall apart.

The play is the sum of all the parts; Friction Free Castings Ltd is a series of interlocking scenes, a chain of scripts and improvisations stretching physically across a series of settings and temporally back as far as memory serves and forward into the next several months. What Paul does in the scenes in which we encounter him relates not only to the setting and the others on stage with him but also to previous and potential interactions with these people and to the self-concept that he brings to the encounter. That self-concept, that particular constellation of opinions and emotions, is constructed out of experiences with this group and others (in Manchester, at home or wherever), and is reinforced or challenged in this setting. As for him, so for all the others to a greater or lesser extent. If Paul's interactions in other settings have damaged his self esteem and confidence, his behaviour in this setting will reflect it and will bring about a degree of realignment. If Alec is feeling particularly aggressive, his conduct will have implications, and so on. Whatever the manifest content of the conversation, each and every social actor, insofar as he is engaged at all (considering himself something more than a bit player or a member of the audience) will improvise around the twin themes of power and status.

The Executive of Friction Free Castings Ltd is not a group which shows a high degree of solidarity, it is not a body of social actors that demonstrates a high degree of skill in 'reconciling conflicting forces, intents, interests, conditions, postures and ideals'. It constitutes, however, a crucial setting for whatever other improvisations occur in the company. The conduct elsewhere of each and every member of the Executive is strongly influenced by the interactions which occur in this particular setting. What Alec does back in his part of the business is a consequence of who he is encouraged to be and how he expresses himself on this afternoon in this Boardroom with these people. As for Alec, so for each of the others. The Commedia is by no means over when they leave the room, nor does it begin when they enter.[3]

Again I do not wish to overplay my hand. I do not wish to claim that for this group, nor for most others, shared meaning is total. If this were to be the case there would be no struggle, no conflict. In some areas – those mentioned above – there is no struggle, but in others there are substantial and deliberate efforts to sustain or modify shared meanings. George is very unhappy with the circumstance in which his figures are not taken seriously and struggles manfully to change this perspective; Eric is not simply amused by the antics of 'Manchester', he succeeds in redefining their activities as a threat.

To establish and sustain scripts, the responses of all, must be constrained along particular paths. This constraining and shaping is effected through persuasion, the deployment of power and the display of emotion. Once attained, such meaning may persist for a reasonable length of time, but in a complex society such as that in which we live, it is always likely to break down.

The very process of improvisation leads to circumstances in which the prevailing order will be challenged. Occasionally, and I would argue unusually, George, Paul and the others (and, of course, any one of us) may become conscious of their behaviour and that of others and may reflect upon their actions. Such rehearsal like activity occurs infrequently, since most of us find such cognitive activity exhausting. Nonetheless, it does occur when one or more of a number of conditions obtain:[4]

(1) when encountering a relatively novel situation;
(2) when a performance becomes 'laboured' – a matter of effort;
(3) when a performance is interrupted by external factors;
(4) when performers experience a consequence (negative or positive) not in line with prior expectations;
(5) when the situation does not allow for sufficient involvement.

Thus in the scene where Alec challenges the figures sent to Manchester, there is sufficient novelty to cause a number of those concerned to reflect upon their performances and those of others. The second condition is likely to occur shortly for George: he is having to shout nowadays to make his point and may well begin to hear himself so doing. Once upon a time, in the now dim and distant past, he could generate a high degree of emotion within himself with much less effort. It is not beyond possibility that a physiological disorder will cause him to reconsider his performance; a heart attack may be nature's way of signalling one has gone over the top.

The third condition is realized when someone like me intervenes in the performance and, in so doing, deliberately foregrounds the nature of it. Part of my activity as a consultant is to alienate social actors from their performances and to cause them to reflect upon them. Odd though this activity may be, it is not entirely unknown in what is taken to be more normal social interaction. People who obviously do not listen, people who interrupt, people who acknowledge suggestions and then do something else may all give occasion to review performance.

In a similar fashion, the fourth condition may occur when George, for example, is greeted with enthusiasm when he castigates himself and his colleagues. Imagine if you will the consequences for George of the following response:

George: . . . some of you were reporting losses of two and three million against forecast losses of four and five million and expecting a round of applause. A bloody standing ovation!

Alec: Your are absolutely right, George. I hereby tender my resignation.

Paul: And me. I feel thoroughly ashamed of our performance.

Whether or not Alec or Paul is serious does not matter, the pattern is now discrepant and George must deal with a new situation.

The final condition occurs where selves cannot become involved. The formal meeting of the Board may be one such scene for my group wherein they go through a routine which they are all aware is a routine with each one of them consciously (and no doubt distantly) playing a part.

The process of improvising itself may promote inconsistency and conflict. There are, for example, the seeds of inconsistency present in the group I have been analysing throughout these pages. On the one hand they evidently defer to Paul as the 'gaffer' and on the other they claim (or some of them do) that it is 'up to the group to decide'. In this particular circumstance, the group suffers (admittedly to a limited extent since the urge to defer remains strong) a degree of ambiguity or – at best – a sense of conflicting direction as to what kind of improvisation is appropriate. If all the world were to agree that 'gaffers' decide and that there are no circumstances where this does not obtain, then there would be little risk of ambiguity. We would all know how to behave and would not think of challenging. Such a totalitarian universe, however, is not with us nor is it viable since a group or society founded upon completely agreed scripts would be unable to adapt. What we have and what this group manifests is some agreement (without which we could not talk of a group) and some areas of contention. Responsibility is clearly an area of contention and members receive conflicting and inconsistent messages about who is in charge; the result is a degree of confusion and an attempt to constrain responses – to develop a script – along lines which particular individuals believe they will find more satisfactory.

Inconsistency, therefore, promotes conflict, as does inadequacy. What follows is conjecture, I do not have the evidence to sustain this view (at least in the material presented) but nonetheless will put it forward as an illustration of the point I wish to make. Paul and his group have a script for effecting change within their organization; it is to be brought about by analysis and planning, which they term 'strategy' and deem to be the responsibility of the Strategy Development Group. No one in the group questions this – yet. Sooner or later (though perhaps too late) it will be recognized that either the approach does not work or that others achieve better results without recourse to such extensive analyses: that, in short, strategic planning fails to deliver the goods. When and if this occurs, the struggle to deal with this inadequacy will be resumed, alternatives will proliferate, inconsistencies will be multiplied and the adequacies of particular resolutions will be challenged – the more so since, in the example I have chosen, no one would be in a position to determine the adequacy of a particular way of effecting change until after the event.

Let me complicate the situation which obtains within my group (or any other) by returning again to the matter of power and status. Not only will inconsistency and inadequacy contribute to the breakdown of scripts, but struggles over power and status may also contribute. If it is accepted by Alec, George and the rest that position or status enables one to control scripts, then it is likely that each will be involved in the struggle to attain more of each in order to shape the responses of others. The signs are evident in the extracts: Eric challenges the power of the Strategic Development Group. He does not recognize their authority and makes his resentment clear. He may at one level be concerned about the content of their report but at another, at least Alec recognizes the challenge:

> 'I don't know why we bother to spend so much time deciding things, some clown always knows better.'

There is also the struggle over the group's right to decide the figures that will be sent to Manchester which George clearly resents and looks to Paul to refute. He expects Paul to cut off this exchange but, earlier, has attempted to appeal to his colleagues against Paul in his misrepresentation of the results. What is going on, indissolubly linked to the attempt to control response and therefore to sustain a particular interpretation of the circumstance, is a struggle over the resources necessary to have one's view of the appropriate script prevail. Each member of the team is seeking to enhance his authority, legitimacy and status *in order to* control the scripts that are up for discussion. In turn, control of scripts may enhance authority, legitimacy and status. George claims to speak with authority as the Finance Director, but his view of the figures is not accorded legitimacy by the others, particularly not by Paul. Nor is his status such that the rest of the group believe that his view is an appropriate one to follow in this instance. Paul's authority and legitimacy, on the other hand, appears relatively free from question although there are signs of challenge to it in the discussion around the right to decide forecasts. His status, however, the degree to which others follow him because of his personal qualities, is open to real question and if status is more important to him than the exercise of power (as at times it seems to be), then the potential for competition is greater. If he wishes to earn respect for his views rather than impose them (which others nonetheless see as legitimate), he opens up the group and himself to more contention than would otherwise be the case.[5]

Let me be clear about the last point. The group accepts Paul's rights as a 'gaffer'; there is, therefore, an established shared meaning which validates his actions and each knows how to respond. Once Paul moves away from behaving how a gaffer should behave, however, and inviting comment from others, the competition for what new meaning shall prevail is open. Some – such as George – prefer the previous arrangement where their own authority derived from association with the gaffer (although he, like the others, is ambivalent about this), others – such as Alec and Derek – want authority to lie with the group.

One further source of conflict needs to be mentioned, related to the foregoing but capable of standing on its own. Given that the members of a particular group compete about the propriety of particular scripts and may also disagree about the nature of authority and legitimacy, it is likely that they will also disagree about the manner of arriving at decisions. Again such disagreements are incipient in the group from Friction Free Castings Ltd; there is little sense that George is convinced by Paul's arguments or that Eric is satisfied by his interaction with Alec and Hugh, still less are most satisfied with the decision concerning the figures sent to Manchester. It is possible to conceive of a continuum of satisfaction, as it were; at one end everyone is happy with the *process*, if not necessarily with the outcome, and at the other a great number are dissatisfied with the process of decision making and the outcome. At the one extreme is *consensus*, with each member willing to give up his or her position in favour of the greater good. At the other end we have *alienation*, where few support that which is claimed to be decided and few value the group sufficiently to give up their individual preferences. Paul and his subordinates are neither in a state of consensus nor alienation but the more they approach the latter the greater the individual competition and, inevitably, the larger the prospect of the group breaking up in disarray.

One final twist: not only does an executive group have the problems of conflict arising from inconsistency, inadequacy, struggles for power and status and alienation, it also has the problems of individuality and the instability of individual response. An executive group consists of people who for the most part are relatively predictable, but occasionally, either by deliberate choice or as the result of stress of one kind or another, one or other member may behave inconsistently. George may begin to laugh uncontrollably during his presentation of the results, or Alec may break the coffee pot on Eric's head. Less wild but equally startling, Derek may support Alec, Hugh may initiate a discussion, Paul may be firm and decisive. Such behaviours throw well-practised responses into disorder, change the ground of meaning and render whatever follows less determinate than otherwise would have been the case.

The trick, of course, as Barnard knew well, is to manage an executive group so that it is at once both stable and innovative. Too great a sharing of scripts, too happy a consensus, ensures that smooth and relatively predictable interaction and action can occur, but forfeits the opportunity for innovation to arise. Too little is equally likely to threaten the survival of a particular group, since nothing can be jointly determined and order itself will collapse. As I have indicated throughout these pages, the trick is not an easy one to perform. Someone – the leader – has to promote both the sharing of scripts and the destruction of them when they are deemed inadequate and he or she has to do this without bringing the entire executive process into disrepute. It is the most difficult process in the entire organization and the most critical for its survival.

How is it done? Clearly I am going to have to go beyond Paul and his colleagues to suggest an answer to this, since neither he nor they embody all of the characteristics of a successful enterprise. Nor, however, are they without such attributes. I will comment first upon the skills of the leader in containing conflict and stabilizing meanings and later upon the skills of promoting an appropriate level of innovative thinking and enactment.[6]

The inculcation of loyalty to a cause over and beyond the individual is a well-attested way to contain conflict and prevent interaction from breaking down completely. Paul no less than other leaders cultivates and, indeed, is himself subject to a belief that Friction Free Castings should be placed before anything else. As Vaughan and Sjoberg note, in many circumstances the individual's sense of self becomes intertwined with the organization; he or she may or may not think of themselves as a Friction Free person, an ICL person, or an IBM soul, but a large part of their behaviour is coloured by their identification with their organization. That is why, of course, redundancy for such committed people is so devastating; a part of who they are is expelled when they are deprived of their association with the company. Interesting though this observation may be, it does not offer an insight into why people may wish to seek such identification and become loyal. For an understanding of this I need to return to an earlier discussion of the self.

It will be recalled that who I am, my sense of worth, is to a large extent dependent upon others' validation of who I present myself to be and what I enact. As with meaning, the true me is not immanent, nor does it lie in my intent but rather in the response of others. (It is somewhat more complex than that but, for the moment, this summary will suffice.) Like all forms of meaning, it (my self-concept) is unstable and can never be nailed down once and for all, however desperately I may seek such a fix. It follows that to a greater or lesser extent each one of us looks to others for validation, for responses which confirm our self-worth; as I suggested earlier, we are likely to be particularly exercised by notions of power and status since, in our society and, arguably, most others, these are taken to be important signifiers. So here am I – like you – in search of validation of who I am and what I am doing. Thus my behaviour is likely to be controllable since I am looking for some signal as to how appropriate it is; remember Alec edging his way into confrontation with George but keeping his eye upon Paul throughout the interaction? Alec, no less than you or I, wishes to be considered effective and since it is largely others (present or not) who make this judgement, we are likely to surrender to their control – and they to ours.

Plausible, but not quite the whole story. Many of us for much of the time may seek such validation but, as I noted in the previous chapter, the self-concept is not often as volatile as implied here. To revert once more to Riesman's terms, some of us are more 'other-directed' than others; some of us cast about in desperation, eager to conform to whatever pattern is expected of us. Others, the more 'inner-directed' or 'autonomous', are not so susceptible to the immediate surroundings; they can and do avoid the anxious search for confirmation evident in their less stable colleagues. It is likely, however, that there are few autonomous individuals – apart from you and me, that is. Many of us do not have a strong internalized sense of self-worth that is resistant to the slings and arrows of outrageous others; still fewer are able to resist the hugs and kisses (metaphorical of course) of others. Even you and I in extremis need the support of someone on occasion and may therefore be affected by their judgement of what is or is not appropriate behaviour. The good leaders know this and use it; they rely upon and occasionally play upon the desire of each of us to be considered competent and effective; in particular they emphasize that the ability to contribute to the whole, to be part of the group, is a major criterion in their judgement of an individual's competence. The effective leader (who is, of course, more strongly inner-directed than the norm) inculcates a belief that the worth of the individual is directly related to his or her ability to operate in a team; any breakdown in cooperation is to be regretted, not applauded. Each and every one around the table is responsible and, more importantly, subject to blame if war breaks out and the group dissolves.

Nonetheless, even given a group predisposed to seek approval from each other and a leader skilled enough to capitalize upon this attribute, it does not follow that differences will be 'reconciled' nor that opposed thoughts, emotion and facts will be 'synthesized'. It could be, for example, that Eric disagrees so strongly with Alec and Hugh because his reference group are those who work for him; he is arguing their case and his sense of who he is will be validated by them, not by Alec and Hugh, still less by Paul. The good leader recognizes and provides for circumstances (the majority, perhaps) where a case has to be argued. The less good – Paul, in some of these scenes – sees argument as a challenge to the Friction Free way of doing things: 'I trust you are not going to say that at the Board.' The better encourage *rational* discussion to arrive at the 'correct' decision. Discussion, however, that remains within the frame of the search for agreement. The emphasis upon *rational* is deliberate; appeals to emotion are frowned upon and great stress is laid upon explanation, expectation, argument and persuasion. The expression of emotion is regarded as likely to overwhelm the process of debate and is thus declared out of bounds.

Again all good, clean stuff, nothing exceptional here. Any fool knows that the way to succeed is to encourage the possibility of a rational consensus emerging by stressing the need to lay out arguments convincingly and persuasively and avoiding emotional interactions. The problem is that some – perhaps at senior level many – of the issues are either not simple and unambiguous nor are they matters which lend themselves easily to the principles of rational discussion. Some are questions of value which cannot be justified by an appeal to the 'facts' and the 'figures'. Whether or not human beings should be treated as 'labour', or as 'human resources', is, in the final analysis, a matter of a value judgement. To be sure, the adoption of a particular posture has specific and calculable consequences but the value cannot be derived from these facts. A company willy nilly must adopt *some* moral standards and the consequences of these – whatever they are – may spill into and influence every debate. Issues like this can be resolved by performance, by persuasion and emotional appeal, by constraining and structuring the response of others. In some cases they are so resolved, skill in argument defeats or, occasionally, convinces the opponent that his or her case is not worth defending. In other cases the leader must be able to recognize that there is not likely to be a 'synthesis' and that they must impose a procedure rather than continue the struggle to arrive at a consensus.

Here I return to the exercise of authority. Leaders must be prepared to acknowledge that there are differences which are not reconcilable, there are positions which are opposed and are likely to remain so. In so doing they declare that, notwithstanding the arguments one way or the other, a specific course of action is to be followed. They decide and instruct. Such events should not be common since it is clear that they do not resolve conflict, at best they simply defer it to another time and place. On the other hand, they should not be avoided. Occasionally, the leader must be prepared to determine a course of action notwithstanding widespread and strong disagreement. To do so, nonetheless requires an agreement; an agreement that such a course of action can, in the last analysis, be tolerated. The script that proper authority can so assert itself has to be accepted. Conflict over this destroys the group entirely; if the dispute is about leadership itself, of course, then resort to fiat will not be viable.

So stability is maintained by subtle appeals to identification with the group and the organization, by the encouragement of rational discussion and, on occasion, by an agreement to disagree but an acquiescence (however temporary) in the leader's right to determine direction. Some leaders are very successful at maintaining scripts; they bind members together, they promote discussion and on the rare occasion when it appears necessary, they arbitrate and direct. This last feature provides a clue to *the* critical function of leaders; they are not simply holders of the ring within which others contend; they are instrumental in containing and/or transforming the meanings and beliefs of their executive colleagues. They may do it with different styles but they are the focus and locus of meaning. A democratic leader may choose to summarize what appears to emerge as the agreed position, an autocratic one may declare the position that others must follow, a confused one may veer uneasily from one style to the other.[7] Whatever the style, the leader's position is used to constrain and structure response. Leaders may declare goals which have been consensually validated or determined by them alone and it is these goals which influence response (for or against, they are still strongly influenced by what the leader declares to be the intent). Having declared the goal and thus attempted to render the organization one of purpose, the leader communicates and mobilizes support for the achievement of the specified ends.

Here I must highlight the idea of leadership as a performing art; whatever the style, successful leaders, whether sustaining or transforming organizations, must have their acts together. There is clear evidence that those who present themselves well and are articulate about their aims and objectives are judged to be more successful by peers and subordinates. Good leaders are seen to *inspire* their followers; it may be tough now, folks, but keep at it and we will win through – *Boys Own Paper* material, the stuff of heroes. Those who wonder about this reference should read Michael Edwardes' book or Lee Iacocca's, where the sense of winning against the odds shouts out from every page but where also the inspirational quality of both men is also much in evidence. Like other heroes, both men had a vision and a more or less coherent set of beliefs and values about what needed to be done and how to do it. Again like many others, both men are almost messianic and certainly dogmatic about their calling. In putting across their ideas as forcefully as they do, they provide a framework within which that which has hitherto appeared unthinkable or impossible may now be thought and done. Not that such inspirational performances need always be associated with change; conservative ideology may be witnessed just as much as radical rhetoric. A leader may be extremely powerful in sustaining the status quo by articulating its nature, he or she does not have to become a focus for change. So I return to where I was a few pages back, scripts can be sustained or they can be challenged and changed. The leader can maintain stability or can encourage innovation. It is to the transforming characteristics of leadership that I now turn.

Not before noting, however, that effecting a change in responses is not the sole prerogative of the leader. If, as I have argued and others such as Donaldson and Lorsch have confirmed, corporate managers have deep emotional attachments to the system of beliefs that they mutually elaborate, it is likely that such convictions will be difficult to shake.[8] On the other hand, from the perspective advanced throughout this text, all order is fragile and some of very short duration. It must be remembered that executive action consists of the *reconciling* of opposing points of view, not a once for all *reconciliation*, but a process. Change, therefore, is endemic. Under normal circumstances it is, however, likely to be incremental rather than substantial change, reform rather than innovation. In the complex balance of improvized order that Paul and his group manifest, any shifts are likely to be relatively small and themselves subject to constant redress. For substantial change to occur, there has to be a challenge to existing meanings *and* a restructuring of them. Donaldson and Lorsch who, in a very interesting series of studies conclude that there are these two phases to the process of fundamental change, hold that they are brought about when what they term 'objective forces' impinge upon the organization. For them, these forces are the economic and financial environment, the balance of constituency changes and those that arise when goals that managers set are not realized. Naturally you will not expect me to go along with the notion of 'objective' forces. Economic and financial factors are indeed part of the pattern of responses elaborated and sustained by executives but, as I have shown, they enter into consideration through the interpretations of particular individuals. There is nothing 'objective' about the numbers George presents to the group; they do not speak for themselves, the meaning of them lies in the group's response to them. There are plenty of examples where executives have taken their companies to the brink and over through 'reading' the figures in a way which others may regard as wilful or wrong-headed. Financial and economic factors in and of themselves do not lead to change; they may be used as a catalyst for it (more of this in a moment) but they do not precipitate innovative thinking. Indeed the thinking has to be there to interpret the figures in a different manner.

The other factors are much closer to ideas advanced here (providing the term 'objective' is again eschewed). The constituency one I have touched upon in the process paragraph, noting that the balance of interests is in more or less constant flux. The failure to meet expectations I have not remarked upon and it is an important source of instability, providing that failing to meet expectations is deemed culpable by the group concerned. In my experience – and it ranges over a whole spectrum of organizations – monitoring of performance is not always a high priority and where it is, often a great deal of energy is devoted to restoring stability by explaining away shortfalls. Failure to meet precisely agreed goals and objectives does not automatically or even often result in a challenge to fundamental beliefs, let alone a restructuring of them.

This is so because for many of us much of the time a great deal of our energy is devoted to rendering the environment – notably that part of it represented by other people – predictable. We do that by seeking to constrain their responses within established and familiar patterns. With the exception of you and me (and I'm not sure about you), humanity craves convention and routine; manners maketh man and man maketh manners. As Donaldson and Lorsch note and these pages, I trust, have amply demonstrated, we cannot innovate without challenging that which currently obtains; only when we are estranged from the meanings which surround and define us can we begin to consider innovation. I need to add a prior term to the Donaldson and Lorsch model which would now read: estrangement, challenge, restructuring.

I have written elsewhere on the nature of estrangement but a brief word or two is necessary as a prelude to the further discussion of innovative behaviour. Estrangement, in the way that I choose to use the term, is the act of making the familiar strange by stepping outside it. It is the process of disrupting the taken-for-grantedness of everyday life. As Berthold Brecht puts it, 'We make something natural incomprehensible in a certain way, but only in order to make it more comprehensible afterwards. In order for something known to become perceived, it must cease to be ordinary; one must break with the habitual notion that the thing in question needs no elucidation.' A thing which has not been changed for a long time appears completely natural and unchallengeable; the meaning that sustains the pattern of interaction that exists between, say, George and his colleagues can only be 'frightened out of its naturalness by estrangement'. Putting the frighteners on established conventions and routines and thus on meanings and responses is at the heart of innovation. Estrangement creates a circumstance in which '*givenness* becomes *possibility*'.[9]

Again, as I have noted in a previous book and as should be evident from much of what has been outlined earlier in these pages, as human beings we each *have* the capacity to distance ourselves from our interactions. We do not simply learn from schedules of punishment and reinforcement; we have the capacity to simulate situations internally and to select a piece of behaviour in line with our interpretations. We have, that is, a kind of theatre-in-the-head upon which stage we can play out our dramas before enacting them in real life. Even allowing for the fact that this rehearsal process is itself informed by the meanings and responses we derive and anticipate from others, there remains the capacity to adopt as it were a metatheatrical perspective upon our prospective and actual interactions. The ground upon which we stand to make such an observation may be shaky from a philosophical point of view, but is undeniable from an experiential one. We can reflect about what we have done, are about to do and may well do in the future. We have the capacity to diverge as well as to converge; what we lack in much of our lives in organizations is the opportunity.

We do not often do it, but anyone can stand back and reflect upon what is going on, the more so if he or she is inner-rather than outer-directed and has a high degree of tolerance for ambiguity, but it is often the leader who has to promote such reflective and divergent thinking. Departures from scripts, particularly when these are concerned with issues such as overall direction of the organization, fundamental values, patterns of hierarchy and authority are not to be undertaken lightly. Imagine Alec reflecting and declaring to the group and to Paul in particular: 'I notice that whenever George speaks about the results, we all suddenly ignore him except for you, Paul, who appears to take it upon yourself to correct his view of them. This seems to lead to George becoming angrier, us becoming more and more distant from him and you eventually losing your rag.' Possible, of course, but risky in a setting where nothing of this kind has ever been attempted by the leader, let alone his subordinates.

Let me assume for the moment that the leader (or someone else) can distance himself or herself (I will return later to the qualities and characteristics of such a person); what then ensues? Well, something of the character sketched in above: a challenge to the conventions, patterns of response and routine that appear to prevail and that here have the effect of constraining everyone's behaviour. Breakout from the Crystal Palace; the sound of glass being smashed on all sides. Given that others recognize the patterns highlighted and that they consider them less than satisfactory (a condition easy to put down and very problematic to achieve), a search for alternatives may begin. Such alternatives may be flashed upon the collective theatre-in-the-head; they are potential rather than actual responses. What if we tried listening to what George has to say? What if he tried laying out the figures without laying into us? What if Paul were to put aside his optimism for a moment? The process of innovation is thus one of running things up provisionally, seeing how they look and either abandoning them or modifying them. The greater the range of response, the greater the possibility of a change in behaviour. The leader, having promoted the exploration, can protect those who are wildly deviant and can prevent others from seeking to force events back along more conventional lines. At some point 'reality' must be allowed to return to the forum but, if innovation is valued, 'reality' should be denied access in order to stimulate the search for alternatives, however unfruitful they may appear at first glance – *particularly* if they appear unfruitful. Emotion may be a good indicator of which areas to explore. Since emotions are judgements and matters of consequence, their presence in such explorations may signal the very areas which *should* be trampled upon. George may be emotional about his view of the figures,

Eric about his treatment by Alec and Hugh, each of them about their relation with Manchester. Radical and fundamental change can only come about by confronting those areas in which individuals or the group is heavily invested in maintaining the status quo. It is arguable, for example, that despite the gestures to the contrary, each member of Paul's team is more or less content with the practice whereby the Strategic Development Group makes plans and Eric criticizes; the SDG feel that they have consulted him and he feels he can attack them for not so doing. A resolution of this scenario which, at best, simply wastes everyone's time, is to dismantle the charade: to declare that Eric will be excluded from the process entirely or that he will contribute during the elaboration of the plan and will be denied comment upon it subsequently. Either way the meaning of the event will be changed and the parties to it will have to enact different behaviours and elaborate different rationalizations for them. Such may be difficult to bring about since, in a perverse kind of way, each of them party to the current pattern of interaction seems to wish to sustain the ability to feel 'pissed off' rather than risk the shifts in power and status involved in a transformation of the pattern.

A key role in any organization is that of the leader; he or she epitomizes the authority system – the process through which ideas are translated into action. Paul's role, like that of any leader, is hedged about with status, power, rules and systems which other social actors are aware of, but it is his enactment of it that makes the difference between Friction Free Castings Ltd and other organizations in a similar market. *The* skill of leadership (insofar as any one factor can be said to make a difference) is to promote a degree of challenge to received ways of doing things, whilst at the same time maintaining the capacity of the organization to act. To encourage, that is, a degree of reflection within the context of having to deliver the widgets or whatever. The problem lies in the nature of authority as it is often conceived of and made operational within enterprises; put somewhat starkly, the system of rules, regulations, hierarchies and privilege arenas often works to suppress reflective behaviour rather than to promote it. Similarly, the organizational scripts are often antithetical to challenge. A high premium is placed upon loyalty, and arguing against one's boss or, worse, against the company may be taken to be disloyal. A great deal of effort goes into promoting the IBM way, the ICL way, the Hewlett-Packard way, the Friction Free Castings way of doing things. Not only are Eric, George, Paul and the rest defined by their emotions and their language, they are defined in large measure by the company they have worked for over the past twenty years. The general thrust of authority systems within many organizations is to restrain reflection and challenge by causing those subject to them through socialization to accept the status quo. More importantly – as I have shown in the earlier chapters – subordinates depend upon the formal leader for promotion and for financial reward; Paul can force his subordinates to accept a particular line of action. They know it and accept it as part of his 'gaffer' role. Given forceful behaviour on his part or that of any Chief Executive, they and others like them are likely to acquiesce.

On the one hand, therefore, we have the authority structure which, whilst mediated by individuals, appears to have the property of being separate from them: the bloody bureaucracy, the Friction Free Castings way of doing things. On the other, there are the conflicting interests and objectives of the individuals and the organization constituents they represent around the decision making table. In some organizations these differences are minimal; beliefs are shared and questioned by no one. In others, such as the one with which I have been concerned in these pages, personal agendas appear to be stronger than those dealing with the future direction of the business (though the distinction is a difficult one to sustain, since it is a matter more of emphasis than of anything else). In still other organizations there are strong challenges to existing practices and patterns of interaction, so strong that the institution is unable to cope and collapses into disarray and confusion.

My conclusion is, of course, implicit in my analysis. Given that the authority system militates against challenge and exploration, given that interactions at senior levels are fraught with issues of self, power, status and emotion, the success of an enterprise is going to be spectacularly dependent upon the skills of its leader in optimizing the estrangement, challenge, restructuring, and enactment processes. It is perhaps true to say that too much democracy is as useless to the survival of the enterprise as too much autocracy. I could go on to labour this point for pages, but I prefer simply to highlight it from a book about the theatre, Anthony Sher's *Year of the King*:

Monday 28 May
Another bad day on the group scenes. We've all got different solutions to the problems in those scenes and no one can agree. Bill, the most democratic of directors, sits silently, looking miserable . . . Bill should decide this one, but he continues to sit obstinately on the fence so it is left unresolved.

Tuesday 5 June
Queen Margaret Scene. We still can't agree on certain aspects of the scene and are very much the 'wrangling pirates' Queen Margaret calls us. Bill suddenly says, 'Right. We're obviously not going to agree, so

you'll have to accept that I can see better from the outside than you can from in there. *This* is how it will be . . .'

I've never seen him do that before. The problems are sorted out within five minutes.

Just like that. Obviously it is a matter of the utmost complexity knowing how to promote challenge, when to sustain it and when to cut it off. It is much easier to assert one's viewpoint as the crisis approaches (opening night, in this case) than earlier. It is *relatively* easier to challenge beliefs, ways of doing things and basic purposes when one is brought in to rescue enterprises than it appears to be in other circumstances. It is made easier still when rescuers such as Iacocca, Edwardes or Wilmot dismiss entire management teams upon their accession; the Chrysler way, the BL way and the ICL way are rewritten almost at a stroke. In saying this, I in no way wish to diminish their achievement, simply to note that wholesale changes of cast are not options which can be exercised often. The Chief Executive Officer in an enterprise which wishes to proceed relatively smoothly from success to success must facilitate in his most senior arenas estrangement, challenge and restructuring of beliefs and the consequent appropriate enactment of the revised patterns of behaviour which flow from the new purposes and processes. He or she must know when to sit obstinately on the fence and when to assert that this is how it will be.[10]

My example from the theatre, although having the twin advantages of brevity and of being apposite, is in one sense unfortunate. Creating plays for the theatre operates on a timetable which is tight and relatively short. Decisions must be made by a curtain date in order to achieve the end result. Most enterprises lack such clear timetables and deadlines for change. Achieving the kind of non-crisis dominated change I sketched in above is exceedingly difficult; business history is littered with examples of companies who persist in ineffective behaviour well beyond the point of no return. It is clear that the executives I have been dealing with in these pages are not going to make it without help. In my view this is so for a couple of reasons. Individually and severally, their interpersonal competence is low. They operate within very limited repertoires and have evolved over the years ways of relating to each other which, however comfortable they have become to them, are destructive of cooperation. Most of them appear to be either unaware of their impact upon each other and/or unwilling to reflect upon it. Part of this script is intolerance of each other's viewpoint; George repeatedly makes the point about poor financial performance and is repeatedly ignored as, for the most part, is Eric when he makes or attempts to make his points about the Parts and

Service business. Finally, Paul's style of leadership is confused and confusing; he claims that he wishes to hear divergent opinions such as George's and then tells him he has it wrong. In some sense it is a unique group (it is comforting to think it so, although almost certainly inaccurate), in others all too typical. They, like others, will only change their patterns of behaviour *if* and *when* they incorporate different views of the canvas against which they are operating into their present preoccupations and improvisations. George tries valiantly to interest them in his interpretation of the figures, someone else on some other occasion may seek to assert that the market has changed, that the technology has developed beyond what they currently use, that factors in the labour market demand change. Nothing will happen to restructure fundamental ways of operating unless someone can focus a number of such events so clearly and persistently that the events impose themselves, as it were, upon management belief and bring about a fundamental restructuring. Such impositions are rare because of the nature of senior management interaction; changes do occur but they take a long time and a great deal of skill.

In circumstances such as I have described, it may need the assistance of an outsider to create a consensus amongst the management team that some fundamental change needs to occur. Not that an outsider supplies objectivity, rather that his or her subjectivity is likely to be of a different order to that of those who have for years, perhaps, been closely identified with the company and its (their) way of doing things. The outsider's emotional attachment to particular relations and patterns of interaction is not likely to be such that it inhibits action, nor has he or she a particular constituency within the organization to protect. Clearly, however, as I have indicated on several occasions throughout these pages, as an outsider to Friction Free Castings, I can and do have personal beliefs, emotions and a constituency of my own to satisfy in whatever action I encourage the members of the organization to undertake. What I do will be informed by my needs and my beliefs about what makes for a good company, just as what any consultant does will be so informed. What an outsider does is to provide an assessment of both where he or she takes the company to be and where it *could* be (perhaps *ought* to be – some of us are more prescriptive than others). The nature of the assessment will differ from outsider to outsider; some emphasize financial performance, some market share, some technological leadership, some vision. Not surprisingly, although interested in each and every one of these factors, given what I have outlined in the previous pages, I provide primarily an assessment of the scripts which hold the company in place: for good or ill, this is what you appear to be doing to it, and to each other, and it is a matter of consequence. No great change is likely to occur until you change the way that you address each other and the context within which you operate.

Such an assessment is an unusual and shocking event; executives do not like to be told that *in my view* they spend inordinate amounts of time in behaviour that is unlikely to contribute to the survival of their organization. They particularly do not welcome having patterns of interaction (such as those contained within these pages) pointed out to them and tend to display their not inconsiderable verbal skills to refute what is being raised. It is not unusual to find such assessments marked by a high degree of emotional behaviour. It is therefore not something which should be suggested or implemented without a great deal of thought, nor is it appropriate in all circumstances.

In effect, what I and others offer is an opportunity to look at the pattern of executive action and to reflect upon it. Is this us? If it is, what do we wish to do about it? What is offered epitomizes and embodies the very process that successful teams everywhere operate upon; an estrangement and a challenge. Faced with a different perspective on their existing practices, managers can either ignore it or re-examine their beliefs, practices and emotions. This is not done with ease or with comfort. The estrangement does not lead directly to clear or immediate answers; what Paul and his colleagues are about will take more than an afternoon to unravel; it's taken a lifetime to perfect. Eventually, a degree of re-structuring can occur and new patterns can be improvised against a revised and revisable canvas.

They can and must be institutionalized; the new responses must become as much taken-for-granted as the old if the organization is not to be paralysed by excessive concern for its processes. In time, however, and it may be months or years, there will be the need for further appraisal, another bout of reflection and, perhaps, revolution. Paul and his colleagues have been through this process. They have stood back and examined themselves, their roles and their performances. As a consequence and not without considerable difficulty, they have elaborated different routines and their interactions now emblematize a largely different set of relationships. Their ability to 'reconcile conflicting forces, instincts, interests, conditions, positions and ideals' has, in the opinion of themselves and others, been much enhanced. They now function as an Executive for the greater part of their interactions together. It has taken courage, determination and fortitude for them to change their behaviour. How they did it is, of course, another story.

Notes

Preface and Acknowledgements

1 It is, of course, entirely possible that, having given up reading texts which purport to address 'Organizational Behaviour' or 'Human Resource Management', I am now quite out of touch and unaware of new ideas and developments. If so, it is a small price to pay for not having to wade again and again through theories of motivation and descriptions of the Hawthorne experiments. For those less irritable, I can recommend *Understanding Organizations* by Charles Handy (1985), *Applying Psychology in Organizations* by Frank Blackler and Sylvia Shimmin (1984), and – one of those American texts which include absolutely everything, even the author's laundry lists – *Organizations and Organization Theory* by Jeffrey Pfeffer (1982). As I say, there are dozens of others but in my view one should not knowingly subject oneself to indigestion.

2 A word of caution is perhaps in order. In my role as both teacher and examiner (in my own institution and others), I find that neither I nor many of my colleagues are tolerant of different ideas. Since I am an interactionist (of sorts), I tend to like and reward the expression of similar ideas in the stuff I mark. Functionalists do the same, as do Marxists. There exists a group of teachers – possibly a large group – who claim that they are eclectic. It means that they purport 'to select such doctrines as please them in every school'; in practice, it often means that they have not thought through what they are about. Such men and women are dangerous, if only because they are difficult to please.

3 Funny thing, acknowledgements. There is a tradition of mentioning only those who helped, not those who hindered. Throughout the writing of this book, my energies have been frequently diverted by the antics of the Secretary of State for Education and Science, Sir Keith Joseph, and the attempts he and his colleagues have been making to reduce the British University system to penury. Given the need to write reports, furnish evidence, raise cash, teach more students with fewer

staff and generally justify my activities to all and sundry, it is a wonder
the book was completed. Writing is best accomplished in periods of
time free from distraction – the chaos in one's mind needs to be tackled
within an ordered and relatively predictable setting. Such opportunities
are becoming rare in the world at large and almost non-existent in
British institutions of higher education.

Introduction

1 Barnard, who was at one time a business man and, subsequently, an
academic, has some interesting ideas hidden away in the text but it
takes diligence and persistence to dig them out. The prose style he
adopts is standard academic, instantly recognizable as such, but
impenetrable without a pair of strong wire cutters. The following is a
reasonable example of the style:

> But as respects the individual the spatial aspects of the situation
> are of equal relevance and time-order in an aspect of spatial
> factors. In order to do something requiring change of position,
> time is necessary. In the cooperative situation, however, although
> of course the spatial dimensions are inherent in the physical
> conditions, time-order is predominant . . .

Keep that up for 322 pages, as he does, and you have the academic
equivalent of the Berlin Wall.
2 The question of why one should wish to change the nature of
cooperation is one which occupies me in chapter 6. Put briefly, my
argument is that in order for an institution or enterprise to persist, the
members of its directing body – the executive team – must move
between stability and innovation. They must be able so to behave as to
get the widgets out of the door whilst being able to spot and change the
behaviour which prevents them reaching beyond widgets; there may
come a time when prevailing ideas about what it is they are doing and
how they should do it do not match the needs of the brave new world
outside the executive suite. History is full of institutions whose
members cooperate to the point of their own extinction.
3 Berthold Brecht (1965), *The Messingkauf Dialogues*. I make no
apology for what others may deem my tiresome habit of quoting from
playwrights, novelists, musicians and those of a similar ilk. Not only do
I find them relatively free from jargon, I also find their perspectives on
social and organizational life more valuable than many who claim to be
specialists in the area. Brecht – a Marxist playwright – has a mixed press
(some consider him vastly overrated) but his thoughts and his theatrical
practices (see in particular Willett (1964), *Brecht on Theatre*, and if you
are a convert, Volker (1979), *Brecht*), are worth reading.

4 This perspective is, of course, not unusual and has been put forcefully
   by many of us. Rather than provide an exhaustive list of who said what,
   where and when, I will simply refer you to *Organizations and
   Organization Theory* by Pfeffer (1982), most particularly his early
   chapter, 'The Variety of Perspectives' and the subsequent one,
   'Microlevel Rational Action'. Pfeffer himself is not an interactionist,
   nor is he committed to an individualistic perspective on behaviour in
   organizations, but he does provide a reasonable summary (a little thin
   on the interactionist literature but I will suggest some of that material
   later) and is clear about his sources. Although replete with jargon,
   Randall Collins' (1981) paper, 'On the Microfoundations of Macrosociology' is worth ploughing through at least once, as is Weinstein's
   chapter on the 'Development of Interpersonal Competence' (1969).

5 How do I know the way of things?
   By what is within me.
   Lao-tzee, 'Tao-te-ching' (6th century BC)

   Obviously an early psychologist. *The* person to read, who takes as his
   starting point the ability of each of us to do psychology on ourselves and
   on fellow beings, is George Kelly. His book, *A Theory of Personality*
   (1963) is reasonably accessible but a good introduction to his ideas may
   be had in Bannister, D. (1970), *Perspectives in Personal Construct
   Theory* and in Bannister, D. and Fransella, F. (1971), *Inquiring Man.*
       There is also a text by John Lofland (1976), a sociologist, called
   Doing Social Life which, whilst neither adopting Kelly's position nor
   that outlined here, is complementary to both and well worth a glance.
   Both Kelly and Lofland have manageable jargon levels of explanation
   for much of the time. A very accessible text with a somewhat daunting
   title, *Consciousness Regained: Chapters in the Development of Mind*, by
   Nicholas Humphrey (1983), informed my writing of this section. The
   first fifty or so pages are worth the price of the book – the rest less so,
   but where else can you get fifty splendid pages for less than four pounds
   nowadays?

6 In another sense it is, of course, a work of fiction; it is a 'fashioning' of
   the material available to me. I have spent more hours of my life with
   these executives than I care to remember and recorded in one form or
   another thousands of lines of text. Out of this mass of material I have
   selected less than fifteen minutes and from these confused and
   confusing minutes I have shaped my presentation. A verbatim
   transcript of what was actually said – the entire repertoire of false
   starts, incomplete sentences, talkings over, and the like – together with
   a detailed description of their non-verbal behaviour – the scratching,
   the fidgetting, the movements of feet, the twitching of the brows, the
   coughs, stomach rumbles and so on – would fill several volumes and
   still be but a poor record of the actual scenes and exchanges. To be

sure, I have not made anything up, I am not putting forward a deceit or a piece of inventiveness, but I have selected, edited, and shaped the raw material and my subsequent comments are as informed by imagination as the work of any (minor) novelist.

7 All good reasons for not attempting *qualitative* research such as this. Broadly speaking, there can be said to be two traditions of research into behaviour in social/organizational settings, the positivist and the not-positivist. (Those of us who determine we are not positivist cannot agree as to what we should be called – phenomenologists, ethnomethodologists, symbolic interactionists – all mouthfuls and now embracing all perspectives. But we know what we ain't, as they say in Yorkshire.) The not-positivists will probably agree that they are less interested in fundamental causes and much more interested in understanding *behaviour* from the point of view of the behaver (or actor). Interactionists, at least, are more committed to striving for an understanding of the *experience* of social life and of the motives and beliefs that underpin behaviour.

The positivists and the not-positivists reflect in their work two separate approaches which are matters of consequence. Alan Dawe (1970), in his paper 'The Two Sociologies', sums it up well:

> They are grounded in dramatically opposed concerns with two central problems, those of order and control. And, at every level they are in conflict. They posit antithetical views of human nature, of society, and of the relationship between the social and the individual. The first asserts the paramount necessity for societal and individual well being of external constraint; hence the notion of a social system ontologically and methodologically prior to its participants. The key notion of the second is that of autonomous man, able to realize his full potential and to create a truly human social order only when freed from external constraint. Society is thus the creation of its members; the product of this construction of meaning, and of the action and relationship through which they attempt to impose that meaning on the historical circumstances.

The adoption of one perspective or the other (or the retreat into eclecticism) is not to be undertaken lightly. Taking a stance can damage your health or at least your career.

What is at stake is the way of arriving at valid knowledge; the positivist sees that adhering to *scientific* protocol, engaging in surveys, operationalizing and testing hypotheses, is the way to proceed. The not positivists do not agree; some of us hold that we need to spend time with people, see how they deal with the variety of situations they encounter, listen to them:

> the study of interaction should be made from the position of the actor. Since action is forged by the actor out of what he perceives,

interprets and judges, one would have to see the operating situation as the actor sees it, perceive objects as the actor perceives them, ascertain their meaning in terms of the meaning they have for the actor, and follow the actor's line of conduct as the actor organizes it – in short, one would have to take the role of the actor and see the world from his viewpoint (Blumer, 1966).

The best introduction to the nature of qualitative, not positivist research is Taylor and Bogdan (1984), which itself contains a splendid bibliography. For a thorough and deservedly well-praised account of the differences between positivist and not-positivist thought, see Burrell and Morgan (1979). Less weighty and possibly more readable is David Silverman's (1970) book, *The Theory of Organisations*.

8 Metaphor and articles upon its nature are almost as popular in the literature of organization theory nowadays as are tomes on *culture* and as were those purporting to deal with *system*. In such a welter of views, it is difficult to know what to recommend. By far the most readable and, although slender, one of the most comprehensive is *Metaphor* by Terence Hawkes (1970), to whom the present discussion owes much. Somewhat lengthier but no less readable is Lakoff and Johnson (1980), *Metaphors We Live By*.

An article in the *Administrative Science Quarterly* (1980) by Gareth Morgan is all that one subsequently needs to claim thorough knowledge of the area. The piece by Pepper comes from his *World Hypotheses* (1942) and that of John Morris and John Burgoyne from *Developing Resourceful Managers* (1973). The tests of a good metaphor are largely derived from G. Psathas' (1973) book, *Phenomenological Sociology*.

9 I like the notion of a 'reading' since it derives from literature and implies an in depth assessment of a particular piece of work. I am not attempting here to say anything about Friction Free Castings Ltd in general, nor about the particular executives beyond that which is on the page. Furthermore, I am attempting a complete interpretation of these episodes and, in particular, I am seeking to explicate the meaning of these interactions. I am not simply interested in counting the number of questions, the kind of eye contact or whatever, I want to know what is or may be going through the minds of those concerned. The notion of 'reading' and its strengths is derived from Richard Levin's (1979) book, *New Readings vs Old Plays*.

Chapter 2

1 Humans are not creatures that simply respond to particular stimuli. My favourite illustration of a response is the three-spined stickleback, also much beloved of Tinbergen. Figure 2, taken from his *Social Behavior In Animals* (1953), depicts the sequence in which the response of one becomes the stimulus for the response of the other.

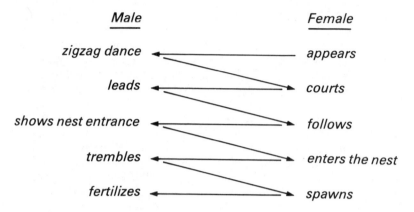

Figure 2   Reciprocal reactions of the three-spined stickleback (taken from N. Tinbergen (1953), Social Behavior in Animals *and reproduced with the permission of John Wiley and Sons).*

It is, of course, arguable that a great deal of human behaviour is of this kind: unthinking, unreflective, run off without consciousness. B. F. Skinner, in both *The Behavior of Organisms* (1938) and *Science and Human Behavior* (1953), holds that all behaviour can be subsumed under stimulus-response (S-R) models and more pertinent to the present discussion, so does George Homans. In his better known works, *The Human Group* (1950) and *Social Behaviour: Its Elementary Form* (1961), he struggles valiantly to render us all kin to the Three-Spined Stickleback. Skinner's approach, taken over lock, stock and most of the barrel by Homans, holds that human beings are *reactive* rather than calculative: 'We believe [Homans' editorial *we*, that is] that the propositions of behavioral psychology are the general explanatory propositions of all the social sciences.' As a consequence, his work reads like a parrotting of Skinner: 'If in the past the occurrence of a particular stimulus, or set of stimuli, has been the occasion on which a person's action has been rewarded, then the more similar the present stimuli are to the past ones, the more likely the person is to perform the action, or some similar action, now.'

Despite the weasel words such as 'likely' and 'similar', it can be objected that that which Homans and those of like mind proclaim ain't necessarily so. The same apparent stimulus, even under laboratory conditions, calls forth a range of responses. There is often a modal response but S-R (Stimulus-Response) theory cannot explain or account for the response. There are no such problems with stickle-backs: given the season, the appearance of the female always leads to a dance and to fertilization. Neither party refuses the invitation nor breaks it off complaining of 'feeling tired' or 'having a headache'. Responses in humans cannot be determined; human beings change their behaviour.

2 Since Mead himself committed little to paper, interactionists such as myself have to rely upon collections of his thoughts assembled by his students and colleagues: *The Philosophy of the Present* (1932) and *The Philosophy of the Act* (1938) and, in particular, *Mind, Self and Society* (1934). At a more accessible and introductory level, there is a good biography of the man and his work by David L. Miller (1973), *George Herbert Mead: Self, Language and the World*.

Blumer (1966) himself offers some insights in 'The Sociological Implications of the Thought of George Herbert Mead'. His own contribution to the perspective, which includes coining the phrase symbolic interactionism, has been crucial but is largely contained in 'Society as Symbolic Interaction' (1962) and *Symbolic Interactionism: Perspective and Method* (1969).

For those who wish to take the perspective further, I would strongly recommend for texts: *Social Psychology: The Theory and Application of Symbolic Interactionism* by Lauer and Handel (1977); *Social Psychology: A Sociological Approach* by McCall and Simmons (1982); *Self and Society: A Symbolic Interactionist Social Psychology*, 3rd edn, by Hewitt (1984); and *The Social Psychology of Interaction* by Heiss (1981).

3 The quotes come from Hewitt but the ideas are popular in many texts. Come to think of it, a good general introduction to this way of thinking, which is well written and full of quotable stuff, is Peter Berger's (1963) *An Introduction to Sociology* and, somewhat less accessible but valuable, his *Social Construction of Reality* with Thomas Luckmann (1967).

4 I am a sucker for a story I can't resist re-telling, the one reported in *Brief Lives* by Alan Watkins (1982) concerning Auberon Waugh.

> He did his national service in the Royal Horse Guards and was stationed in Cyprus. In an accident whilst inspecting a Browning machine gun, he was shot several times and lost a lung, his spleen, several ribs and a finger. As he awaited the ambulance stretched out upon the ground surrounded by his men, he said to his platoon sergeant: 'Kiss me, Chudleigh.' The good Chudleigh, however, did not spot the reference and afterwards treated his officer with considerable reserve and suspicion.

The point about the story for those who need it laboured is that meaning depends upon symbols reflecting *shared* meaning. Chudleigh did not know his Nelson but he did – no doubt – believe he knew a sexually ambiguous invitation when he heard one.

5 Another story, this time from a newspaper:

> He was wearing a stocking mask and appeared to have a gun under his jacket.

> But when he ordered Mr John Mackrill, 70, and his wife, Madge, 74, to lie down on the floor of their house in Pelican Lane, Newbury, Mr Mackrill told him, 'Don't be silly.'
> Mrs Mackrill then said: 'I am not going to lie down' and she walked out of the house.
> Tilley, of Newport Road, Cardiff, was so bemused by this reaction that he fled, but was later caught by police. (*Daily Telegraph*, London, September 6th, 1985)

Of course, the raider could have sought to assert his definition by producing the gun or, more directly, by hitting someone. Nonetheless the illustration seems to reinforce the point that the consequences of a definition are real: the couple define the situation as 'silly' rather than 'frightening' and behave accordingly.

The act of definition, the assignment of meaning, is pivotal in the thought of Mead and Blumer: 'To ignore the meaning of the things toward which people act is seen as falsifying the behaviour under study. To bypass the meaning in favour of factors alleged to produce the behaviour is seen as a grievous neglect of the role of meaning in the formulation of behavior' (Blumer, 1969). Interactionists are not primarily concerned with personality, attitudes, social class, values or whatever, but with meaning.

6 The quote is from my own work *Interactions and Interventions in Organizations* (1978) and I will do no more now than quibble with the word 'given' in it. Meaning may be influenced by the way that others respond but it is not given (that is to say *determined*) by the conduct of others. Blumer puts it, as always, better: 'meaning arises in the process of interaction between people' and '. . . grows out of the ways in which other persons act towards the person with regard to the thing'.

7 This assertion is also made by Berger and Luckmann (1967) in *The Social Construction of Reality* and is a fundamental tenet in interactionist thought (not that Berger and Luckmann are closet interactionists).

8 The literature on exchange theory is large, some of it technical and some abstruse. The present discussion is based upon the ideas of Thibaut and Kelley (1959). My presentation relies heavily upon Carson (1969), *Interaction Concepts of Personality* and in particular upon chapter 5. The preliminary chapters are a mixture of psychoanalytic and behaviourist material but his exposition of exchange theory is clear and free from jargon. Heavier in jargon but nonetheless a recommended read for those interested in exchange theory is Ekeh (1974), *Social Exchange Theory*, as is *Social Exchange Theory: Its Structure and Influence in Social Psychology* by Chadwick-Jones (1976). The quote is from Homans (1961).

9 This notion of 'imaginative participation' has a long and distinguished history in the literature. Weber (1947) was one of its clearest exponents with his notion of *Verstehen* but he, in turn, was influenced by scholars such as Rickert and Dilthey. According to the latter, knowledge of

human activity is best derived from re-experiencing the meanings deployed by specific actors in specific settings. In regard to human action we are not limited to counting the evidence of particular pieces of behaviour; Weber (1964) holds that sociology is 'that science which aims at the interpretive understanding (*Verstehen*) of social behaviour in order to gain an explanation of its causes, its course and its effects'. In his now classic definition of social action, Weber holds that the state of mind of the individual social actor is crucial. 'Action is social insofar as, by virtue of the subjective meaning attached to it by the individual (or individuals), it takes account of the behaviour of others and is thereby corrected in its course.' He goes on to argue that interpretation of events is rendered simpler if one is able 'to put one's self imaginatively in the place of the actor and then participate in his experiences'.

Another key figure in this context is W. I. Thomas (1923) who, quite independently of Weber, stressed the need for examining the structure of human action. He argued that 'one of the most important powers gained during the evolution of animal life is the ability to make decisions from within instead of having them imposed from without . . . Preliminary to any self-determined act of behaviour there is always a stage of examination and deliberation which we may call the definition of the situation. And actually not only are concrete acts dependent on the definition of the situation, but gradually a whole life policy and the personality of the individual himself follows from a series of such definitions.

I will not bore you by continuing; by far the best summary of these ideas is contained in *Imaginative Participation: The Career of an Organizing Concept in a Multidisciplinary Context* by Bedrich Baumann (1975).

10 McCall and Simmons, *Identities and Interactions* (1966 and 1978). Either of these editions is a must – they are both difficult to obtain but well worth the effort; first rate expositions of the dynamics of interaction, very low on jargon and very high on example and illustration.

11 Sooner or later I had to get to the big 'G': Erving Goffman, an extraordinary scholar who defies classification but most of whose work is concerned with the 'rules' which govern the ordinary, everyday, face-to-face interactions that occur between people like you and me. I will return to him in a later chapter but he is essential reading for any interactionist (although, again, he cannot easily be claimed to be one himself). His most accessible book is *The Presentation of Self in Everyday Life* (1959), but his other works may also be read with relative ease: *Asylums* (1961a), *Encounters* (1961b), *Behavior in Public Places* (1963a), *Stigma* (1963b), *Interaction Ritual* (1967) and *Frame Analysis* (1974).

The point being addressed here is that of performance. In any and, indeed, every situation individuals express themselves. I reveal who I am through my clothing, my posture, my facial expression, the length of my hair, the care I take with deodorants, my voice, my words; everything about me is considered to be representative of me by other people. What I 'give' is what I try to communicate directly to other people; what I 'give off' is what they infer both from what I say and how I say it but also through their response to gesture, smell, etc. In many cases, given a discrepancy between 'given' and 'given off', we resolve it in favour of believing the 'given off'. My colleagues and I were recently offered large sums of money for research by a character who said all of the appropriate things but said them in such a manner that we determined he could not deliver. When he failed to do so, we were disappointed with the outcome of our efforts but secretly pleased with our ability to see through such people. Nonetheless, up until the last moment, none of us was quite sure that he would not come up with the cash.

12 The notion of 'altercasting' comes from Weinstein and Deutschberger's (1963) article 'Tasks, Bargains and Identities in Social Interaction', and is discussed in Peter Hall's (1972) 'A Symbolic Interactionist Analysis of Politics'.

13 Underlying all of this, of course, is the notion of exchange. Interaction may be seen as a function of what each person gets out of a relationship. All behaviour is subject to the same bottom line: profit. You may well boggle at the thought that there is a price for everything and everyone of us has a price, just as you may remain unconvinced by a theory, behaviourist in essence, which places such a high reliance on *rational* behaviour. Watch this space; the criticism is reserved for a later chapter. What is pertinent is the mention of 'negotiating order' which surfaces in this section. It is an important idea which, for reasons of the flow of argument, I do not do justice to in the text itself. The key book and one which must be read is *Negotiations* by Anselm Strauss (1978). He holds that all social orders are in some respects negotiated orders and uses three concepts to outline his ideas: negotiation, negotiation context and structural context. The first refers to the strategies used by participants (something of the flavour is contained in the chapter to which these notes refer); the second concerns the relevant features of the setting which affect the course of the interaction (dimensions of power and status which are dealt with later); and the third concept deals with the larger circumstances (state, law, social class or whatever) within which the negotiation takes place. Strauss emphasizes that contexts affect negotiations and that negotiations affect contexts. Structural features condition the way people act *and* the way people act influences structures.

What I pick up in this section is the tentative and temporal aspects of interaction:

the shared agreements, the binding contracts which constitute the grounds for an expectable, non-surprising, taken-for-granted, even ruled orderliness are not binding and shared for all time. Contracts, understandings, agreements, rules – all have appended to them a temporal clause. (Blumer, 1962)

A good review of negotiated order theory and research is that provided by Day and Day (1977), 'A Review of the Current State of Negotiated Order Theory'.

14 The classification into 'routine' and 'problematic' comes from Heiss (1981), *The Social Psychology of Interaction*, as do some of the points made in the discussion. The idea of *performance* derives from Erving Goffman, but both this and the notion of *routine* have been written about extensively by myself and my colleague Michael Overington in *Organizations as Theatre: A Social Psychology of Dramatic Appearances* (1986) which has a variable amount of jargon, but is without doubt the most comprehensive attempt to apply a theatrical model to the conduct of people in organizations.

The idea of *scripts* which is introduced in this section comes from the work of Roger Schank, an expert in Artificial Intelligence, in *Scripts, Plans, Goals and Understanding* (1977), co-authored with Robert Abelson.

Chapter 3

1 They would not be likely to reject the idea of interaction as the working out of self-interests but they would tend to consider it – at best – a partial explanation. Most would tend to see the action of others to be matters of self-interest: 'He's so bloody ambitious it must hurt him', but would deny or simply fail to see their own actions in a similar light. Alec is seen as an arch politician by his colleagues, 'Out for all he can get', but believes himself to be acting primarily, if not exclusively, in the interests of Friction Free Castings Ltd. A perspective such as exchange theory, which highlights individual needs and goals, in his view 'trivializes' interaction; for him, the struggle is to secure a course of action which will enable the company to survive and prosper. I do not take this to be a mask or a rationalization. At this level of operation (and for reasons related to the self which I discuss in chapter 5), who I am, what I do and what I strive to bring about may be closely linked to the present and future of the organization for which I work.

2 Of course, in objecting to the notion of scripts and the theatrical metaphor which backs up the notion, they are joining the long line of souls who dislike such analogies. The idea of scripts *entails* notions such as *acting* which, for many, implies dissembling and deceit, play and pretence. I take such a response to be occasioned by ignorance of the nature and function of theatre (see Mangham and Overington, 1986), nonetheless I cannot deny that it will result from the talk of scripts and

settings. For evidence of prejudice against the theatre (and, by inference, models of behaviour based upon it), see Barish (1981).

3 The criticisms derive from many sources but are best summarized in Meltzer, Petras and Reynolds' (1975) book, *Symbolic Interactionism: Genesis, Varieties and Criticisms*, and in Manis and Meltzer (1978), *Symbolic Interaction*.

What is missing from this chapter is any criticism of social exchange theory. Granted the perspective would have surface validity for Paul and his colleagues and can be used to explain (or at least describe) some of my interactions with others. Nonetheless, to stick for the moment with the executive team, how can the theory be used to explain Derek's action in assisting Alec? Derek accepts that there is an element of exchange in it, but it is not difficult to imagine a circumstance in which someone like Derek sacrifices his own best interests for someone else. One cannot deny an incidence of altruism although it may occur very infrequently.

According to Homans, altruism can be dealt with in the framework; what people value determines their profit and it is possible (but in the present context unlikely) that Derek values the success of other people – seeing that *profits* him. It does seem a little far-fetched, however, when one is forced to argue that when someone deliberately takes another's place for execution (as apparently happened on occasion during the last war), that he or she is doing it for some form of personal profit. In any event, to understand such behaviour we would have to be able to see the event from the perspective of the actor which would take us beyond the simple S-R (Stimulus-Response) framework of exchange theory. Peter Ekeh's (1974) *Social Exchange Theory* offers some good criticisms of the theory.

4 The criticisms of Goffman's work are scattered about in various texts and are summarized in Meltzer, Petras and Reynolds (1975). Worth reading as well are the comments of Gouldner (1970), not only for his views on Goffman, but also for his very readable account of sociological ideas in general.

5 This account of the nature of 'self' in the works of Erving Goffman is derived largely from Jack Mitchell's excellent text, *Social Exchange, Dramaturgy and Ethnomethodology* (1978). Parts of 'Erving Goffman: His Presentation of Self' by Judith Posner (1978) also inform the comments.

6 I could not resist the line which is a paraphrase of the one offered by Wayne Wheeler (who he?), quoted in Biddle (1979), *Role Theory: Expectations, Identities and Behaviors*. The mention of role and the citing of this text is a forceful reminder that there is a framework or theory which is largely ignored in the main body of the text: role theory. It may appear odd that, given the explicitly theatrical nature of the framework, it receives such short shrift here:

> The word *role* is borrowed from the theatre, and there is little in its socio-psychological sense that is not prefigured in its theatrical

sense. A role in a play exists independently of any particular actor, and a social role has also a reality that transcends the individual performer. Shakespeare's Macbeth has lasted for about 350 years; very many actors have passed in and out of the role and have proved shorter lived than the role. Actors are human beings; a role is a scenario prescribing certain actions and a script prescribing the lines to be spoken. Roles in society, too, are prescribed actions and words rather than persons. (Brown, 1965)

Role theory has generated a great deal of research and speculation, but to quote its greatest proponents, Biddle and Thomas (1966): 'In essence, the role perspective assumes, as does the theater, that performance results from the social prescriptions and behavior of others, and that individual variations in performance, to the extent that they do occur, are expressed within the framework created by these factors.' It may be doing less than justice to role theorists to suggest that the notion of 'social prescription' is little more than another way of saying 'exchange'. What we observe when we witness role encounters is the playing out of a social contract whereby I normally behave in such and such a manner in order to derive a reward from so doing. Role theorists hold that role behaviour is determined by expectations and persist only to the extent that they appear to be efficacious. This sounds sufficiently close to exchange theory as to not warrant a great deal of separate attention in a text such as this.

Exchange theory is also at the heart of symbolic interactionist thought, as I have sought to demonstrate. Peter Singelmann (1972), in 'Exchange as Symbolic Interaction', notes the congruence of ideas and holds that exchange theory can be seen to be a process of symbolic interaction.

7 To the best of my knowledge, this criticism of Goffman is new. It derives from my own long association with the theatre and, in particular, from a period of research lasting several weeks following the rehearsal and performance of a play with a company of professional actors.

8 The problem of labelling once more is an issue. Norman K. Denzin has written extensively about emotion, most notably in *On Understanding Emotion* (1984) and he is clearly an unreconstructed interactionist. Arlie Hochschild is more of a closet interactionist and has produced a best seller, *The Managed Heart: Commercialization of Human Feeling* (1983), which is essential reading, if only for her excellent review of the literature in an appendix to her main text. The book is worth reading for much else beside and is very low on jargon. Thomas Scheff is not an interactionist, but his ideas are readily translatable, notably those outlined in *Catharsis in Healing, Ritual and Drama* (1979) and the article 'Towards Integration in the Social Psychology of Emotions' in *The Annual Review of Sociology* (1983). Randall Collins' paper (1981), 'On the Microfoundations of Macrosociology', with its emphasis upon

the tacit, emotional level of interaction, is also a significant contribution to interactionist thought. Shott (1979), 'Emotion and Life: A Symbolic Interactionist Analysis', is good value.

9 Sensitizing concepts are quite deliberately *not* rigid, operational definitions; the point of operationalization is delayed until the situated meanings of the concepts can be discovered. What those of us who subscribe to such method are interested in is *discovering*, not *verification*. The goal of all social science is, or should be, discovery followed – where possible – by verification. For many, the method (which is a tool for verification) *precedes* the effort to discover; if it cannot be reduced to numbers it is ignored. Measurement precedes existence. Having said this and having recommended a related text, Glaser and Strauss (1967) *The Discovery of Grounded Theory*, I have to admit that the amount of published, detailed analysis of qualitative material is slight and the number of sensitizing concepts few. For details of these precious few, see Taylor and Bogdan (1984), *Introduction to Qualitative Research Methods*.

Chapter 4

1 The books to read that take an explicitly dramaturgical perspective on social and organizational are Brissett and Edgley (1975), *Life as Theater: A Dramaturgical Sourcebook*; Burns (1972), *Theatricality: A Study of Convention in the Theatre and in Social Life*; Goffman, *The Presentation of Self in Everyday Life* (1959) and *Frame Analysis: An Essay on the Organization of Experience* (1974); Harré and Secord (1972) *The Explanation of Social Behaviour*; Lyman and Scott (1975), *The Drama of Social Reality*; Turner (1975), *Dramas, Fields and Metaphors: Symbolic Action in Human Society*; Wilshire (1982), *Role Playing and Identity: The Limits of Theatre as Metaphor*; Hare (1985), *Social Interaction as Drama*; Mangham and Overington (1986), *Organizations as Theatre: A Social Psychology of Dramatic Appearances*.

4 My comments upon the Commedia dell' Arte derive from Giacomo Oreglia's introduction to the subject, *The Commedia dell' Arte* (1968). The comments upon improvisation are informed by my own observation of actors in rehearsal for both theatre and television performances. The relevant books on improvisation are Hodgson and Richards (1974), *Improvisation*; and Johnstone (1979), *Impro: Improvisation and the Theatre*. Clements (1983), in *The Improvised Play: The Work of Mike Leigh*, also provides some useful insights into the notion of improvising around a theme.

4 The illustrations are drawn from my own researches, the description and analysis – at least in the first few pages – is heavily reliant upon T. D. Kemper (1978), notably upon chapter 2. In turn he derives his

ideas from Thibaut and Kelley (1959), Homans (1961) and Blau (1964). The two-dimensional model of behaviour has a long pedigree in the literature and has been derived in part from factor analysis of work groups, military combat teams, parent-child interaction, group therapy and the like. The factors are variously named: Assertiveness and Likeability (Borgatta, Cottrell and Mann, 1958); Control and Affection (Schutz, 1958). There are many more, but suffice it to say that, while the terminology may differ, there is agreement that there are a couple of fundamental dimensions to social life: 'Power as force, coercion, threat and the like is an incontrovertible reality of human afairs, and many have seen this. Equally, the award of status, as congeniality, respect, friendship, and love is also incontrovertibly a mode of human relationship. Many have seen this too.'

4 This is an attempt at an interactionist definition of power. Interactionists, as noted earlier, have not been very forthcoming in their references to power; theirs is a relatively cosy world with all of us – good souls that we are – working cooperatively to overcome problematic situations. The exceptions to this criticism are Peter Hall, 'A Symbolic Interactionist Analysis of Politics' (1972), and David Luckenbill, 'Power: A Conceptual Framework' (1979), upon whose analysis and definition this section of the book is dependent.

5 The case of the Emperor's Dog is another illustration of the nature of power (admittedly a rather bizarre one, but I rather like such examples).

> It was a small dog, a Japanese breed. His name was Lulu. He was allowed to sleep in the Emperor's great bed. During various ceremonies, he would run away from the Emperor's lap and pee on dignitaries' shoes. The august gentlemen were not allowed to flinch or make the slightest gesture when they felt their feet getting wet. I had to walk among the dignitaries and wipe the urine from their shoes with a satin cloth. This was my job for ten years. (From *The Emperor: Downfall of an Autocrat*, by Jay Kapuscinski)

Power is something that occurs between people; it is a relational concept. One individual – the source of control – announces his or her intent, demands support or compliance with it and manipulates or threatens to manipulate valued resources to secure such support or compliance. The other individual – the target of control – interprets the source's intent, assesses the consequence of non-support or non-compliance and constructs what he takes to be appropriate action. The behaviour of the Emperor's dog is a case in point, if a somewhat unusual one. The Emperor – the source – allows his dog to pee upon me and demands (in effect) that I do not notice it. Noticing it, reacting to it in a manner which may be taken as questioning the Emperor's rights (to be accurate, the rights devolved to the dog by the Emperor) is perceived to be hazardous in the extreme. The targets, therefore, do not flinch, do not make the slightest gesture. Clearly, the source and target are interdependent; the source requires a party from whom to extract compliance and the target requires a source with whom to comply for power to be said to exist. Haile Selassie's dog needs my feet as much as I need it.

As we mentioned earlier, power can be seen to be goal-orientated. Both Haile Selassie's dog and myself may be said to share a common objective: compliance. Compliance provides the Emperor with a show of complete deference and, presumably (my experience is imagined, not realized) provides me with the gratification of having avoided punishment. It is worth noting again that the source designs the gratifications I, as the target, am to receive – both what it is, and how much of it I am to have. Nonetheless it is still possible for me (or any target in any situation) to refuse to play the game; the consequences may be dire, but fundamentally Selassie's gratification depends upon my agreement to provide it for him. Power always and inevitably involves a common objective and is subject to negotiation and adjustment. This is not to say that power is symmetrical, but nor is it entirely asymmetrical either. Me and Haile Selassie's dog are in a power relationship only so long as I am willing to submit. It follows from all of this that a further distinctive feature of power is the element of conflict. Haile Selassie can have his dog pee on anyone present, despite potential objection.

Power also involves intention. The Emperor wishes to have my total deference and submission and wishes to have this position confirmed in every encounter. I comply because I imagine that failure to do so will have dire consequences. Nonetheless, it is just possible that I enjoy such self abasement, or I regard His Imperial Majesty as a deity and am honoured to receive the attentions of his familiar. Without the notion of intent and potential conflict, we cannot speak of a power relationship.

6 Peter Blau is not an interactionist by any stretch of the imagination but a scholar and theorist whose ideas have had a significant impact upon a number of fields. The key text to be read is *Exchange and Power in Social Life* (1964), but somewhat slighter and more readable is a collection of his essays, *On the Nature of Organizations* (1974), upon which much of the present discussion is based.

7 It is, in the final analysis, a matter of dependence. The relative power of one social actor over another is the result of the net dependence of one on the other. Richard Emerson is the key proponent of this view (see his 'Power-Dependence Relations', 1962).

8 Other writers. Once upon a time, not so far away and not so long ago, social science was short on the analysis of power. Would that it were still so; books and articles proliferate. By far the heaviest – useful for keeping doors open or trunks shut – is that of Mintzberg, *Power In and Around Organizations*, (1983) which, despite its length and breadth, is

somewhat disappointing. Much more readable is Jeffrey Pfeffer's *Power in Organizations* (1981), which covers the same ground as Mintzberg in a less self consciously academic manner. Much shorter but well worth a read is Steven Lukes' *Power: A Radical View* (1974).

9 The issue of leadership is taken up in chapter 7.

10 It is important to recognize the issue here. Beyond the gates of Friction Free Castings Ltd, the world may be changing. Someone may have invented a more sophisticated, effective and cheaper way of making castings, the market for garden machinery may have become saturated, the government may be about to ban certain types of machinery as dangerous, Islam may have placed an embargo on Western goods or whatever. Such may quite legitimately be regarded as 'reality' but if it has no correlate in the minds of Paul and his merry men, it cannot and does not determine their actions. If a tree falls undetected, not only does it not make a sound, it has no *meaning*; no event has a meaningful existence unless it is detected. Paul, George and the rest may go down with Friction Free Castings, but what matters to us in seeking to understand their behaviour is what they detect, what meanings they elaborate, not those we see. The tragedy (if one may be permitted such a high-flown term) of Friction Free Castings Ltd and many other firms like it is the relatively restricted view of 'reality' the members hold. They do not see the trees falling; failing to see them, they cannot take action to avoid them.

11 The quotation is from H. W. Simons 'The Carrot and Stick as Handmaidens of Persuasion in Conflict Situations' (1974).

Persuasion in many cases, of course, whilst not *directly* coercive, relies upon the credibility of threats offered or implied by the persuaders. Simons, in the piece cited, goes on to argue that in the real world such as the one inhabited by Paul and his subordinates, coercive potential, in fact, determines the relative impact of persuasive messages. Nonetheless, the point remains that naked coercion, brute force, conflicts with the way we are taught to believe persuasion ought to work in a democratic society and this awareness (which may and does change with time and circumstance) influences action.

12 I need to return to a line thrown in a number of pages back which the more astute among you will have underlined or marked off in the margin: 'Occasionally, one person appears to have the power to produce reality for others.' As you will have realized, these dozen or so words contribute a fundamental shift in the definition of power outlined in the first couple of pages. What I have outlined throughout this chapter are, as it were, the acceptable faces of power: those that can be observed and identified having the characteristics of conflict, intentionality and the like. There is a third face of power: the real power lies not in winning the game but in setting the rules of the game such that it is played consistently to your benefit. The social actor (or group) that can manipulate the values, beliefs and procedures is likely to be able to influence the kind of reality that is taken-for-granted. As Steven Lukes (1974) puts it:

A may exercise power over *B* by getting him to do what he does not want to do, he also exercises power over him by influencing, shaping or determining his very wants. Indeed, is it not the supreme exercise of power to get another or others to have the desires that you want them to have – that is to secure their compliance by controlling their thoughts and desires?

There is a great deal to be said for this approach, but since its focus is not upon explicit decision making nor upon actors with intent and in conflict, it is extraordinarily difficult to fill out by example. My contention is that a great deal of the behaviour I have subsumed under the general heading of persuasion is of this ilk: attempts to have others accept your definitions and your assumptions and insofar as one is successful, have them play to one's own rules. The art of coarse management thus lies in not having one's colleagues recognize that there is a conflict; if Paul and everyone else accepts that the purpose of Friction Free Castings Ltd is to make profit and if they never think to question this reality, then whoever persuaded them of it (and that might not have been a one-off overt act) effectively constrains their thoughts, words and deeds. For further discussion elsewhere, see, in particular, Bacharach and Lawler, *Power and Politics in Organizations* (1980) and Lukes, *Power: A Radical View* (1974).

13 'Sharing a language with other persons provides the subtlest and most powerful of all tools for controlling the behaviour of other persons to one's advantage.' So wrote C. W. Morris in *Signs, Language and Behavior* (1949). Louis Pondy's article, 'Leadership is a Language Game' (1978) is worth reading, as is Peter Gronn's (1983) paper, 'Talk as Work: The Accomplishment of School Administration'.

14 Jeffrey Pfeffer (1981), for example, is particularly keen on language as a tool of rationalization; he views organizations as systems of patterned activity in which the participants 'attempt to develop and convince others of rationalizations and expectations for these patterns of activity'. Much influenced by the ideas of Karl Weick (who has not been?), and in particular by his *The Social Psychology of Organizing* (1969), he is also clearly a disciple of Murray Edelman, *The Symbolic Uses of Politics* (1964) and *Political Language: Words that Succeed and Policies that Fail* (1977).

Chapter 5

1 It's reference to sources time again. The literature on self is vast so I will begin with the thinkers who inform this passage and pass on to the ranks of the honourable and less inspiring. The quotation is from Georg Simmel 'Zur Philosophie des Schauspieler' in his *Das Individuelle Gesetz* (1968). The extract from which the quote is taken appears in Elizabeth and Tom Burns' book, *Sociology of Literature and Drama*

(1973). The work of Aaron Cicourel is drawn from his discussion in *Cognitive Sociology* (1972).

A good introduction is to be had in Rosenberg and Turner's (1981) *Social Psychology: Sociological Perspectives*, notably in chapter 19, 'The Self-Concept: Social Product and Social Force' by Rosenberg himself. Louis A. Zurcher's *Social Roles* (1983) and *The Mutable Self* (1977) are also good value and contain extensive reference to the literature, as does the chapter on self-concept in Heiss (1981) *The Social Psychology of Interaction*. As always, Lauer and Handel (1977), and McCall and Simmons (1966, 1982) provide clear accounts. Much of what I have to say derives from R. C. Solomon's (1976) *The Passions*.

2 Not a text in social psychology or organizational behaviour, to be sure, but worth a barrow load of them in terms of the author's insight into social interaction. There are four books in the sequence: *Scenes from Married Life, Scenes from Metropolitan Life, Scenes from Provincial Life*, and *Scenes from Later Life*. The extract here is reproduced by kind permission of the author and Macmillan, London and Basingstoke. Kingsley Amis is another with great skill in revealing patterns of behaviour – the early work *Lucky Jim* (1954) has some splendid examples of role confusion, and the much more recent *Stanley and the Women* (1985) contains some excellent pieces of Goffmanesque observation.

3 To be fair, there is not *a* single interactionist perspective on the self. There are two. One focuses almost exclusively on the self-concept, 'the organized set of self-attitudes' (Heiss), and sees this as a stable entity. The other regards the self-concept as much less stable and sees it as varying from situation to situation. William James, in *The Principles of Psychology*, propounded this view almost a hundred years ago.

> The individual has as many different selves as there are distinct groups of persons about whose opinion he cares. He generally shows a different side of himself to each of these different groups. Many a youth who is demure enough before his parents and teachers, swears and swaggers like a pirate among his 'tough' young friends. We do not show ourselves to our children as to our club companions, to our customers as the labourers we employ, to our own masters and employers as to an intimate friend.

What I have attempted is a yoking together of some aspects of both approaches.

4 Taken from *Peer Gynt* by Henrik Ibsen. Gynt was obsessed with the question of selfhood. The play may be said to depict the idea of a self liberated, an 'I' on the rampage through life with but minimal constraint from the 'me'.

5 The basis for this distinction is to be found in Bolton, C. D. (1981), 'Some Consequences of the Meadian Self'.

6 This point about mirrors derives from Solomon, who points out that self-consciousness is not and cannot be as tangible a phenomenon as

looking in a mirror. In 'self consciousness the self is the subject, the consciousness, and what consciousness is about'. The self is not, as a reflection in the mirror is, the object of consciousness. It is consciousness itself.

7 We constitute the identity of the self (but not the *existence* of it) through this process. I can transcend those aspects of myself that I do not like, I can reject those qualities and weaknesses attributed to me by others (and up until the point of transcendence accepted by me as part of my self-concept); the process of acceptance, denial or transcendence is part of the self.

8 These ideas of 'autonomous self' and 'other-directed' self derive from the work of David Riesman (1950), *The Lonely Crowd*.

9 We all know of cases of low commitment to roles, indeed I experience every day lukewarm commitment to, say, my role as dog-lover. I know that the dogs need exercise and that I should take them for a long walk twice a day; it takes but the slightest change in the weather for me to abandon this role. I know that as an administrator I should monitor the regulations as to proper procedures within my department; not infrequently I find myself too busy to do so. High commitment to roles, however, is equally interesting; those who are not alienated are occasionally willing to follow the dictates of their chosen role to the grave. For example, the British in India found it extraordinarily difficult to prevent the wives of important Indians from throwing themselves upon their husband's funeral pyres. To be sure, suttee had religious overtones but a large part of the behaviour was determined by the wives' notions of duty or role.

10 The greater part of this discussion derives from ideas advanced by McCall and Simmons (1966).

11 This notion of 'possession' comes from my book with Michael Overington, *Organizations as Theatre: A Social Psychology of Dramatic Appearances* (1986). In that we cite one Ward Quaal, who is the epitome of possession, who *is* his work (or nearly so – he manages to recognize that holidays demand a different role of him even though he is unable to play it):

> My day starts between four-thirty and five in the morning, at home in Winnetka . . . I talk into a dictaphone. I will probably have as many as 150 letters dictated by seven-thirty in the morning. I have five full-time secretaries . . . This does not include my secretaries in New York, Los Angeles, Washington, and San Francisco. They get dicta-belts from me every day. . . . I get home around six-thirty, seven at night . . . I spend a minimum of two and a half hours each night going over the mail and dictating . . . Ours is a twenty-four-hour-a-day business. I dictate on Saturday and Sunday. When I do this on holidays, like Christmas, New Year's and Thanksgiving, I have to sneak a little bit, so the family doesn't know what I'm doing. (Terkel, 1972)

The basic idea derives from David Cole's splendid attempt to relate and derive theatre from ritual and ceremony: *Theatrical Event: A 'Mythos', a Vocabulary, a Perspective*, (1975).

Chapter 6

1 As indicated earlier, my views of emotion are informed by Denzin, Hochschild and Scheff, but most of what I have to say here comes directly from *The Passions*, by Robert C. Solomon (1976), and James Averill (1980), 'A Constructivist View of Emotion'. My position is also similar to that of Theodore R. Saskin, 'Role Transition as Social Drama', as presented in *Role Transitions: Exploration and Explanation* (1984); we seem to use similar sources but reach different conclusions. Paul Hare, in the introduction to his *Social Interaction as Drama* (1985), covers some of the same ground but draws very different conclusions and prosecutes a different kind of research.
2 The evidence for this assertion is complex. James and his followers hold that different emotions are associated with different physiological responses. Other later theorists and researchers hold – and can demonstrate – that a common set of physiological processes underlie all emotions; we experience different emotions because of what we take the situation to be. Rather than refer directly to the reference here, I suggest you read chapters 7 and 8 of Theodore D. Kemper's (1978) book, *A Social Interactional Theory of Emotion*. Unfortunately it is quite high on jargon, but an essential text for anyone wanting to understand this aspect of my argument and the subsequent passages on power, status and self. Schacter's (1971) *Emotion, Obesity and Crime* is also very useful background reading to both Kemper and Averill's work.
3 This is not the place to debate the differences between the approach outlined in these pages and that of Albert Ellis (1962) in *Reason and Emotion in Psycho-Therapy*. Certainly I would share much with Ellis's mentor, V. J. McGill (1954), who writes: 'It is as difficult to separate emotion and knowing as it would be to separate motivation and learning . . . Emotions . . . include a cognitive component, and an expectation or readiness to act.' Ellis, however, believes that emotions are 'largely the result of thinking illogically or irrationally' and, as a therapist, is naturally interested in disturbed behaviour. My focus is upon normal everyday interaction and I am a long way from believing that emotions (even 'disturbed' ones) result from illogical or distorted perception.
4 Back to Solomon (whom God preserve) and Denzin (1983), 'A Note of Emotionality, Self and Interaction'. An emotion that in some way does not have the self as its referent seems simply inconceivable. Try conceiving of one, if you doubt it.

5 The issue of third parties is one that I cannot handle well within the confines I have set myself for this chapter and for this book. As agents, it is possible to depict their influence upon events. Kemper (1978), for example, notes that when a third party intervenes to reduce the power of one member of a dyad vis-à-vis another, the 'anger' felt by the party thus cut down, whilst directed at the other member of the dyad, may be reduced if he or she is liked: after all, he or she is not responsible for my loss. The third party is responsible and can receive all of the displayed aggression (always providing, of course, that it is safe to unload it).

The problem of who gains and who loses, however, and who makes this judgement is avoided in Kemper, the assumption being that in any interaction, we are to be concerned with the values put upon it by the dyad directly concerned. The fact that my being downgraded by my boss may actually raise my status in the eyes of some of my colleagues (their appreciation of me is in an inverse relation to his) can only be accommodated by adopting the notion of my status as the sum of my relations with each person with whom I associate.

6 For this constraint to be effective, the excess of aggression must be felt by Paul. Dependent upon the degree to which he has internalized prohibitions against the excessive use of force will be the degree of guilt he experiences. In some societies the mildest affront to another person may evoke a very strong sense of guilt: some religious orders – the Quakers, for example – seek to inhibit the use of force to resolve issues,and there can be little doubt that resort to it is deeply disturbing to one committed to such a perspective. On the other hand, some people live in societies that justify the use of force; they have no notion of excess, especially when that force is directed against 'enemies'. Thus the slaughter of Jews in the Third Reich may have been experienced with pride rather than guilt by those party to such a set of norms and ideas. Cultural norms determine the modal response around which a range of behaviours and associated attributions of guilt, shame or whatever occur.

7 Again the extent to which I or anyone else feels shame at being awarded too much reward depends upon the culture within which we operate and the degree to which that culture has been internalized. Some cultural injunctions are clear but many are confused and ambiguous. The business culture, for example, may stress the notion of intense 'cut-throat' competition in which the weakest not only go to the wall but deserve to. It is clearly in conflict with the norm which urges each one of us to be responsible for each other, to strive for cooperation and the like. What Paul and his colleagues do to each other in the Boardroom and what they feel about that is related to the broader cultural environment they inhabit and those aspects of it that they (severally) take to be important. As a deeply committed Christian, Derek may have considerable problems in behaving in a punishing manner to one of his colleagues but as the 'businessman' he may feel that he has to 'for the good of the company'.

8 This entire discussion up to this point relies heavily upon the work of Theodore D. Kemper (1978) *A Social Interactional Theory of Emotion*, and is a much simplified and insufficiently qualified account of his ideas. The rest of the chapter relies variously upon the work of James R. Averill, 'A Constructivist View of Emotion' (1980) and *Anger and Aggression: An Essay in Emotion* (1982), that of Robert C. Solomon, *The Passions* (1976) and, to a lesser extent, upon the papers in Malatesta and Izard (1984). My section on 'rules' derives from the paper 'The Acquisition of Emotion During Adulthood' by James Averill in this collection and is by far the most accessible introduction to his ideas; Arlie Hochschild's interesting chapter 'The Sociology of Feeling and Emotion' in Millman and Kanter (1975) and a paper 'Emotion Work, Feeling Rules, and Social Structure' (1979). Jerrold Heiss also devotes a section to the notion of rules in *The Social Psychology of Interaction* (1981).

9 Again in writing this kind of statement I am in danger of denying any role to biology. If Darwin is to be accepted as a guide (and I am not smart enough to argue with the theory of evolution, although I remain deeply suspicious of it), then it is likely that our development as humans over the centuries has predisposed us to acquire some patterns rather than others. It could be, for example, that we are biologically programmed to be rule-generating and rule-following animals. It is manifestly the case that the human, faced with any situation (involving others or not), will seek to structure it and then react to the consequent structure as though it were not of his or her own making.

10 O, what a rogue and peasant slave am I!
Is it not monstrous that this player here,
But in a fiction, in a dream of passion
Could force his soul so to his own conceit
That from her working all his visage wann'd;
Tears in his eyes, distraction in's aspect.
A broken voice, and his whole function suiting
With forms to his conceit? And all for nothing!
For Hecuba!
What's Hecuba to him or he to Hecuba
That he should weep for her? What would he do,
Had he the motive and the cue for passion
That I have.
Hamlet, Act II, sc.ii

11 Given that the self is closely related to the passion, it would follow that emotional development must proceed more or less in line with ego development. It is unlikely that the young baby experiences anger, jealousy and the like. To be sure, a young child shows a variety of distress and pleasure reactions but, as Averill notes, the provocation to anger involves an intentional wrong done by another. Before a child can understand and experience this kind of anger (by no means the only kind), he or she must also understand the meaning of intent and wrongdoing.

Children play not only at fathers and mothers, cops and robbers, but also at being angry, being scared, being in love. During the course of development, therefore, we each learn how to experience and display emotional roles. Much of what we run off without reflection as adults is related to this period of our life.

Chapter 7

1 The relevant material from U. G. Foa is somewhat heavy going; 'Convergences in the Analysis of the Structure of Interpersonal Behavior' (1965); and 'Resource Exchange: Towards a Structural Theory of Interpersonal Communication' (with E. Foa), in A. W. Siegman and B. Pope (eds) *Studies in Dyadic Communication* (1972).

2 This passage does less than justice to the notion of setting which is more extensively treated in my book with Michael Overington (1986). Settings form the backdrop to interaction and may be created by particular actors who wish to create a particular image. My own office, for example, has modern prints on the wall, has shelves of books, deep carpets and subdued lighting. The image of up-to-date academic is heightened by the personal computer sitting on the desk and that aspect of me that signals informality is emphasized by the layout of the furniture – very different to that of one colleague whose desk forms a barrier to those whom he confronts, or that of another whose room resembles a junk shop: full of broken down furniture, bicycle parts, potted plants, bird cages, cushions, bottles, children's drawings, and the like. At one extreme, the tight, formal setting, at the other the informally chaotic with little me somewhere in the middle.

3 To put forward the case that scripts are elaborated and enacted with little or no question finds echoes in the wide literature of organization theory. Meyer and Rowan (1977), in 'Institutionalized Organizations: Formal Structure as Myth and Ceremony', are interested in the presentation and perpetuation of activity, the 'rule like status of social thought and action'. Zucker (1977) in 'The Role of Institutionalization in Cultural Persistence', and in particular in 'Organizations as Institutions'in Bacharach, S. B. (1981), develops similar ideas. Although using different language, these writers appear to be pointing in the same direction as I am: that some – perhaps many – patterns of behaviour or scripts are run off without reflection and that some – perhaps few – are the result of rational calculations or rehearsal.

4 This part of the discussion is taken from Langer (1976), 'Rethinking the Role of Thought in Social Interaction'.

5 Again there are echoes of this view elsewhere in the literature; more than echoes – deafening shouts. Put in other terms, what I choose to refer to as rehearsal or improvisation is seen as politics or micropolitics Wrong (1979), *Power – Its Force, Base and Uses*, has suggested that power is inherent in all social interaction and my own analysis to date has not disputed this – indeed it is central to my argment. Much of the

relevant literature has been cited earlier but Allison (1971), *Essence of Decision*, is essential reading for the general perspective and Dalton (1959), *Men Who Manage* (now sadly and inexplicably out of print) captures the essence of the perspective as it may be applied to organizations.

In his view of 'politics', Allison comes very close to (and has clearly strongly influenced) the perspective on non-scripted interaction advanced in these pages:

> no unitary actor but rather many actors as players – players who focus not on a single, strategic issue but on many diverse intra-national problems as well; players who act in terms of no consistent set of strategic objectives but rather according to various conceptions of national, organizational and personal goals; players who make government decisions not by a single, rational choice but by the pulling and hauling that is politics.

6 The literature of leadership is vast and I do not intend citing most of it. James McGregor Burns' (1978) *Leadership* is the definitive text for those with the stamina to carry it from the library. The other books which inform the comments made in this section are Schein (1985), *Organizational Culture and Leadership*; and *Leadership and Organizational Culture* (1984), edited by Sergiovanni and Corbally. The new book by Bennis and Nanus (1985) *Leaders*, is also constructive. Sir Michael Edwardes' book *Back from the Brink* (1983) and Lee Iacocca's *Iacocca* (1985) are essential reading.

7 This section can and should be related back to the discussion of language which occurred in chapter 4. Pondy (1978) in particular should be consulted, since he argues strongly that

> the effectiveness of a leader lies in his ability to make activity meaningful for those in his role set – not to change behaviour but to give a sense of understanding what they are doing and especially to articulate it so they can communicate about the meaning of their behaviour.

8 *Decision Making at the Top* by Donaldson and Lorsch (1983).

9 My early thoughts upon the effecting of change in organizations were outlined in two books, *Interactions and Interventions in Organizations* (1978), and *The Politics of Organizational Change* (1979). Neither is a satisfactory exposition of my present position and neither summarizes the literature upon change. Noel Tichy's book, *Managing Strategic Change* (1983), is comprehensive but not particularly well integrated. Andrew Pettigrew (1985), *The Awakening Giant: Continuity and Change in ICI*, has a good introduction and presents a thoroughly researched case example.

10 The book by Donaldson and Lorsch (1983) contains some interesting case material on how this is brought about.

References

Allison, G. T. (1971). *Essence of Decision*, Boston: Little, Brown.

Amis, K. (1954). *Lucky Jim*, London: Queens House.

Amis, K. (1985). *Stanley and the Women*, Harmondsworth: Penguin.

Averill, J. R. (1980). 'A Constructivist View of Emotion', in R. Plutchik and H. Kellerman (eds) *Theories of Emotions*, New York: Academic Press.

Averill, J. R. (1982). *Anger and Aggression: An Essay in Emotion*, New York: Springer-Verlag.

Averill, J. R. (1984). 'The Acquisition of Emotion During Adulthood', in C. Z. Malatesta and C.E. Izard (eds) *Emotion in Adult Development*, Beverly Hills: Sage.

Bacharach, S. B. and Lawler, E. J. (1980). *Power and Politics in Organizations*, San Francisco: Jossey Bass.

Bannister, D. (1970). *Perspectives in Personal Construct Theory*, New York: Academic Press.

Bannister, D. and Fransella, F. (1971). *Inquiring Man: Theory of Personal Constructs*, Harmondsworth: Penguin.

Barish, J. (1981). *The Anti-theatrical Prejudice*, Berkeley, University of California Press.

Barnard, C. (1938). *The Functions of the Executive*, Cambridge, Mass.: Harvard University Press.

Baumann, B. (1975). *Imaginative Participation: The Career of an Organizing Concept in a Multidisciplinary Context*, The Hague: Martinus Nijhoff.

Bennis, W. and Nanus, B. (1985). *Leaders*, New York: Harper & Row.

Berger, P. (1963). *An Introduction to Sociology*, Harmondsworth: Penguin.

Berger, P. and Luckmann, T. (1967). *The Social Construction of Reality*, New York: Doubleday Anchor.

Biddle, B. (1979). *Role Theory: Expectations, Identities and Behaviors*, New York: Academic Press.

Biddle, B. and Thomas, E. J. (1966). *Role Theory: Concepts and Research*, New York: John Wiley.

Blackler, F. and Shimmin, S. (1984). *Applying Psychology in Organizations*, London: Methuen.

Blau, P. (1964). *Exchange and Power in Social Life*, New York: John Wiley.

Blau, P. (1974). *On the Nature of Organizations*, New York: Wiley Interscience.

Blumer, H. (1962). 'Society as Symbolic Interaction', in A. Rose (ed.) *Human Behavior and Social Processes*, Boston: Houghton Mifflin.

Blumer, H. (1966). 'Sociological Implications of the Thought of George Herbert Mead', *American Journal of Sociology* 71, 534–44.

Blumer, H. (1969). *Symbolic Interactionism: Perspective and Method*, Englewood Cliffs, NJ: Prentice-Hall.

Bolton, C.D. (1981). 'Some Consequences of the Meadian Self', *Symbolic Interaction* 4(2), 245–61.

Borgatta, E., Cottrell, L. S. and Mann, J. H. (1958). 'The Spectrum of Individual Interaction Characteristics and Interdimensional Analysis', *Psychological Reports* 4, 279–319.

Brecht, B. (1965). *The Messingkauf Dialogues*, London: Eyre Methuen (translated by John Willett).

Brissett, D. and Edgley, C. (eds) (1975). *Life as Theater: A Dramaturgical Sourcebook*, Chicago: Aldine Publishing.

Brown, R. (1965). *Social Psychology*, New York: Free Press.

Burns, E. (1972). *Theatricality: A Study of Convention in the Theatre and in Social Life*, New York: Harper & Row.

Burns, E. and Burns, T. (1973). *Sociology of Literature and Drama*, Harmondsworth: Penguin.

Burns, J. M. (1978). *Leadership*, New York: Harper & Row.

Burrell, T. and Morgan, G. (1979). *Sociological Paradigms and Organizational Analysis*, London: Heinemann.

Carson, R. C. (1969). *Interaction Concepts of Personality*, London: Allen & Unwin.

Chadwick-Jones, J. K. (1976). *Social Exchange Theory: Its Structure and Influence in Social Psychology*, London: Academic Press.

Cicourel, A. (1972). *Cognitive Sociology*, Harmondsworth: Penguin.

Clements, P. (1983). *The Improvised Play: The Work of Mike Leigh*, London: Methuen.

Cole, D. (1975). *Theatrical Event: A 'Mythos', a Vocabulary, a Perspective*, Middletown: Wesleyan University Press.

Collins, R. (1981). 'On the Microfoundations of Macrosociology', *American Journal of Sociology* 86, 984–1014.

Cooley, C. H. (1964). *Human Nature and the Social Order*, Scribner: New York.

Cooper, W. (1982a). *Scenes from Married Life*, London: Macmillan.

Cooper, W. (1982b). *Scenes from Metropolitan Life*, London: Macmillan.

Cooper, W. (1982c). *Scenes from Provincial Life*, London: Macmillan.

Cooper, W. (1983). *Scenes from Later Life*, London: Macmillan.

Dalton, M. (1959). *Men Who Manage*, New York: John Wiley.

Dawe, A. (1970). 'The Two Sociologies', *British Journal of Sociology* **21**, 207–19.

Day, R. A. and Day, J. V. (1977). 'A Review of the Current State of Negotiated Order Theory', *Sociological Quarterly* **18**, 126–42.

Denzin, N. K. (1983). 'A Note of Emotionality, Self and Interaction', *American Journal of Sociology* **2**, 402–9.

Denzin, N. K. (1984). *On Understanding Emotion*, San Francisco: Jossey Bass.

Donaldson, G. and Lorsch, W. (1983). *Decision Making at the Top*, New York: Basic Books.

Edelman, M. (1964). *The Symbolic Uses of Politics*, Urbana: University of Illinois Press.

Edelman, M. (1977). *Political Language: Words that Succeed and Policies that Fail*, New York: Academic Press.

Edwardes, M. (1983). *Back from the Brink*, London: Collins.

Ekeh, P. (1974). *Social Exchange Theory*, London: Heinemann.

Ellis, A. (1962). *Reason and Emotion in Psycho-Therapy*, Secaucus, NJ: Citadel Press.

Emerson, R. (1962). 'Power-Dependence Relations', *American Sociological Review* **27**, 31–41.

Etzioni, A. (1960). 'Authority Structure and Organization Effectiveness', *Administrative Science Quarterly* **4**, 43–67.

Foa, U. G. (1965). 'Convergences in the Analysis of the Structure of Interpersonal Behavior', *Psychological Review* **68**, 341–53.

Foa, U. G. and Foa, E. (1972). 'Resource Exchange: Towards a Structural Theory of Interpersonal Communication', in A. W. Siegman and B. Pope (eds) *Studies in Dyadic Communication*, New York: Pergamon Press.

Glaser, B. and Strauss, A. (1967). *The Discovery of Grounded Theory*, Chicago: Aldine.

Goffman, E. (1959). *The Presentation of Self in Everyday Life*, Garden City, NJ: Anchor Books.

Goffman, E. (1961a). *Asylums*, Garden City, NJ: Anchor Books.

Goffman, E. (1961b). *Encounters*, Indianapolis: Bobbs-Merrill.

Goffman, E. (1963a). *Behavior in Public Places*, New York: Free Press.

Goffman, E. (1963b). *Stigma*, Englewood Cliffs, NJ: Prentice-Hall.

Goffman, E. (1967). *Interaction Ritual*, Garden City, NJ: Anchor Books.

Goffman, E. (1974). *Frame Analysis: An Essay on the Organization of Experience*, New York: Harper & Row.

Gouldner, A.W. (1970). *The Coming Crisis of Western Sociology*, London: Heinemann.

Gronn, P. (1983). 'Talk as Work: The Accomplishment of School Administration', *Administrative Science Quarterly* **28**, 1–21.

Hall, P. (1972). 'A Symbolic Interactionist Analysis of Politics', *Sociological Inquiry* **42**, 35–75.

Handy, C. (1985). *Understanding Organizations*, 3rd edn, Harmondsworth: Penguin.

Hare, P. (1985). *Social Interaction as Drama*, Beverly Hills: Sage.

Harré, R. and Secord, P. F. (1972). *The Explanation of Social Behaviour*, Oxford: Blackwell.

Hawkes, T. (1970). *Metaphor*, London: Methuen.

Heiss, J. (1981). *The Social Psychology of Interaction*, Englewood Cliffs, NJ: Prentice-Hall.

Hewitt, J. P. (1984). *Self and Society: A Symbolic Interactionist Social Psychology*, 3rd edn, Boston: Allyn and Bacon.

Hochschild, A. R. (1975). 'The Sociology of Feeling and Emotion', in M. Millman and R. M. Kanter (eds), *Another Voice*, New York: Anchor Books.

Hochschild, A. R. (1979). 'Emotion Work, Feeling Rules, and Social Structure', *American Journal of Sociology* **85**, 551–75.

Hochschild, A. R. (1983). *The Managed Heart: Commercialization of Human Feeling*, Berkeley: University of California Press.

Hodgson, J. and Richards, E. (1974). *Improvisation*, London: Eyre Methuen.

Homans, G. (1950). *The Human Group*, New York: Harcourt Brace.

Homans, G. (1961). *Social Behaviour: Its Elementary Form*, New York: Harcourt Brace.

Humphrey, N. (1983). *Consciousness Regained: Chapters in the Development of Mind*, Oxford: Oxford University Press.

Iacocca, L. (1985). *Iacocca*, London: Sidgwick and Jackson.

James, W. (1890). *The Principles of Psychology*, New York: Dover.

Johnstone, K. (1979). *Impro: Improvisation and the Theatre*, New York: Theatre Arts Books.

Kelly, G. (1963). *A Theory of Personality*, New York: W. W. Norton.

Kemper, T. D. (1978). *A Social Interactional Theory of Emotion*, New York: Wiley Interscience.

Lakoff, G. and Johnson, M. (1980). *Metaphors We Live By*, Chicago: University of Chicago Press.

Langer, E. V. (1976). 'Rethinking the Role of Thought in Social Interaction', in J. Harvey, W. Ickes and R. Kidd (eds) *New Direction in Attribution Research*, Hillsdale, NJ: Erlbaum.

Lauer, R.H. and Handel, W.H. (1977). *Social Psychology: The Theory and Application of Symbolic Interactionism*, Boston: Houghton Mifflin.

Levin, R. (1979). *New Readings vs Old Plays*, Chicago: University of Chicago Press.

Lofland, J. (1976). *Doing Social Life*, Chichester: John Wiley.

Luckenbill, D. F. (1979). 'A Symbolic Interactionist Analysis of Politics', *Symbolic Interaction* **2**(2), 97–114.

Lukes, S. (1974). *Power: A Radical View*, London: Macmillan.

Lyman, S. M. and Scott, M. B. (1975). *The Drama of Social Reality*, New York: Oxford University Press.

McCall, G. J. and Simmons, J. L. (1966 and 1978). *Identities and Interactions*, New York: Free Press.

McCall, G. J. and Simmons, J. L. (1982). *Social Psychology: A Sociological Approach*, New York: Free Press.

McGill, V. J. (1954). *Emotion and Reason*, Springfield, Ill.: Thomas.

Malatesta, C. Z. and Izard, C. E. (eds) (1984). *Emotion in Adult Development*, Beverly Hills: Sage.

Mangham, I. L. (1978). *Interactions and Interventions in Organizations*, Chichester: John Wiley.

Mangham, I. L. (1979). *The Politics of Organizational Change*, London: Associated Business Press.

Mangham, I. L. and Overington, M. A. (1986). *Organizations as Theatre: A Social Psychology of Dramatic Appearances*, Chichester: John Wiley.

Manis, J. G. and Meltzer, B. N. (1978). *Symbolic Interaction* 3rd edn, Boston: Allyn and Bacon.

Mead, G. H. (1932). *The Philosophy of the Present*, Illinois: Open Court Publishing.

Mead, G. H. (1934). *Mind, Self and Society*, Chicago: University of Chicago Press.

Mead, G. H. (1938). *The Philosophy of the Act*, Chicago: University of Chicago Press.

Meltzer, B. N., Petras, J. W. and Reynolds, L. T. (1975). *Symbolic Interactionism: Genesis, Varieties and Criticisms*, London: Routledge & Kegan Paul.

Meyer, J. and Rowan, B. (1977). 'Institutionalized Organizations: Formal Structure as Myth and Ceremony', *American Journal of Sociology* **83**, 340–63.

Miller, D. L. (1973). *George Herbert Mead: Self, Language and the World*, Austin: University of Texas Press.

Mintzberg, H. (1983). *Power In and Around Organizations*, Englewood Cliffs, NJ: Prentice-Hall.

Mitchell, J. (1978). *Social Exchange, Dramaturgy and Ethnomethodology*, New York: Elsevier.

Morgan, G. (1980). 'Paradigms, Metaphors and Puzzle Solving in Organization Theory', *Administrative Science Quarterly* **25**, 605–22.

Morris, C. W. (1949). *Signs, Language and Behavior*, Englewood Cliffs, NJ: Prentice-Hall.

Morris, J. and Burgoyne, J. (1973). *Developing Resourceful Managers*, London: Institute of Personnel Management.

Natchkirk, A. (1976). *My Years with Liquorice Allsorts*, Alice Springs: Limpley Stoke Press.

Oreglia, G. (1968). *The Commedia dell' Arte*, London: Methuen.

Pepper, S. C. (1942). *World Hypotheses*, Berkeley: University of California Press.

Pettigrew, A. (1985). *The Awakening Giant: Continuity and Change in ICI*, Oxford: Blackwell.

Pfeffer, J. (1981). *Power in Organizations*, Boston: Pitman.
Pfeffer, J. (1982). *Organizations and Organization Theory*, Boston: Pitman.
Pondy, L. (1978). 'Leadership is a Language Game', in M. W. McCall and M. M. Lombardo (eds) *Leadership: Where Else Can We Go?*, Durham: Duke University Press.
Posner, J. (1978). 'Erving Goffman: His Presentation of Self', *Philosophy of Social Science* **8**, 67–78.
Psathas, G. (1973). *Phenomenological Sociology: Issues and Applications*, New York: John Wiley.
Riesman, D. (1950). *The Lonely Crowd*, New Haven, Connecticut: New Haven Press.
Rosenberg, M. (1981). 'The Self-Concept: Social Product and Social Force', in M. Rosenberg and R. H. Turner (eds) *Social Psychology: Sociological Perspectives*, New York: Basic Books.
Rosenberg, M. and Turner, R. H. (eds) (1981). *Social Psychology: Sociological Perspectives*, New York: Basic Books.
Saskin, T. R. (1984). *Role Transitions: Exploration and Explanation*, New York: Plenum.
Schacter, S. (1971). *Emotion, Obesity and Crime*, New York: Academic Press.
Schank, R. and Abelson, R. (1977). *Scripts, Plans, Goals and Understanding*, Hillsdale, NJ: Lawrence Erlbaum Associates.
Scheff, T. (1979). *Catharsis in Healing, Ritual and Drama*, Berkeley: University of California Press.
Scheff, T. (1983). 'Towards Integration in the Social Psychology of Emotions', *Annual Review of Sociology* **9**, 333–54.
Schein, E. H. (1985). *Organizational Culture and Leadership*, San Francisco: Jossey Bass.
Schutz, W. C. (1958). *FIRO: A Three Dimensional Theory of Interpersonal Behaviour*, New York: Holt, Rinehart and Winston.
Sergiovanni, T. J. and Corbally, J. E. (eds) (1984). *Leadership and Organizational Culture*, Urbana: University of Illinois Press.
Sher, A. (1985). *The Year of the King*, London: Chatto and Windus.
Shibutani, T. (1961). *Society and Personality*, Englewood Cliffs, NJ: Prentice-Hall.
Shott, S. (1979). 'Emotion and Life: A Symbolic Interactionist Analysis', *American Journal of Sociology* **84**, 1317–34.
Siegman, A. W. and Pope, B. (1972). *Studies in Dyadic Communication*, New York: Pergamon.
Silverman, D. (1970). *The Theory of Organisations*, London: Heinemann.
Simmel, G. (1968). *Das Individuelle Gesetz*, Frankfurt: Suhrkamp.
Simons, H. W. (1974). 'The Carrot and Stick as Handmaidens of Persuasion in Conflict Situations', in G. Miller and H. W. Simons, (eds) *Perspectives on Communication in Social Conflict*, Englewood Cliffs, NJ: Prentice-Hall.

Singelmann, P. (1972). 'Exchange as Symbolic Interaction', *American Sociological Review* **37**, 414–24.

Skinner, B. F. (1938). *The Behavior of Organisms*, New York: Appleton-Century-Crofts.

Skinner, B. F. (1953). *Science and Human Behavior*, New York: Macmillan.

Solomon, R. C. (1976). *The Passions: The Myth and Nature of Human Emotion*, New York: Anchor Press.

Solomon, R. and Denzin, N. (1983). 'A Note on Emotionality, Self and Interaction', *American Journal of Sociology* **89**(2), 402–9.

Strauss, A. (1978). *Negotiations*, San Francisco: Jossey Bass.

Taylor, S. J. and Bogdan, R. (1984). *Introduction to Qualitative Research Methods*, 2nd edn, New York: John Wiley.

Terkel, S. (1972). *Working*, London: Wildwood House.

Thibaut, J. W. and Kelley, H. H. (1959). *The Social Psychology of Groups*, Chichester: John Wiley.

Thomas, W. I. (1923). *The Unadjusted Girl*, Boston: Little, Brown.

Tichy, N. (1983). *Managing Strategic Change*, New York: John Wiley.

Tinbergen, N. (1953). *Social Behavior in Animals*, New York: John Wiley.

Turner, V. (1975). *Dramas, Fields and Metaphors: Symbolic Action in Human Society*, Ithaca: Cornell University Press.

Vaughan, T. and Sjoberg, G. (1984). 'The Individual and Bureaucracy', *Journal of Applied Behavioural Science* **20**(1), 57–69.

Volker, K. (1979). *Brecht*, Davenport, Illinois: Marion Boyars.

Watkins, A. (1982). *Brief Lives*, London: Hamilton.

Weber, M. (1947). *The Theory of Social and Economic Organization*, New York: Oxford University Press.

Weber, M. (1964). *Basic Concepts in Sociology*, New York: Free Press.

Weick, K. (1969). *The Social Psychology of Organizing*, Reading, Mass.: Addison-Wesley.

Weinstein, E. A. (1969). 'Development of Interpersonal Competence', in P. Goslin (ed.) *Handbook of Socialization Theory and Research*, Chicago: Rand McNally.

Weinstein, E. A. and Deutschberger, P. (1963). 'Tasks, Bargains and Identities in Social Interaction', *Social Forces* **42**, 451–6.

Whitehead, A. N. quoted in Hawkes, T. (1970). *Metaphor*, London: Methuen.

Willett, J. (1964). *Brecht on Theatre*, London: Methuen.

Wilshire, B. (1982). *Role Playing and Identity: The Limits of Theatre as Metaphor*, Bloomington: University of Indiana Press.

Wrong, D. (1979). *Power – Its Forms, Base and Uses*, New York: Harper & Row.

Zurcher, L. A. (1983). *Social Roles: Conformity, Conflict and Deviance*, Beverly Hills: Sage.

Zucker, L. G. (1977). 'The Role of Institutionalization in Cultural Persistence', *American Sociological Review* **42**, 726–43.

Zucker, L. G. (1981). 'Organizations as Institutions', in S. B. Bacharach (ed.) *Perspectives in Organizational Sociology: Theory and Research*, Greenwich, Conn.: JAI Press.

Zurcher, L. A. (1977). *The Mutable Self: A Self Concept for Social Change*, Beverly Hills: Sage.

Index